SOCIAL EVOLUTION

BY

BENJAMIN KIDD

FOURTEENTH THOUSAND

London

MACMILLAN AND CO.

AND NEW YORK

1895

First Edition (Demy 8vo) printed January 1894
Reprinted March, May, June, July (twice), August (twice), October 1894
January 1895
Second Edition (Crown 8vo) May 1895. Reprinted June 1895

Printing Statement:

Due to the very old age and scarcity of this book,
many of the pages may be hard to read due to the
blurring of the original text, possible missing pages,
missing text, dark backgrounds and other issues
beyond our control.

Because this is such an important and rare work, we
believe it is best to reproduce this book regardless of
its original condition.

Thank you for your understanding.

PREFACE

ONE of the most remarkable epochs in the history of human thought is that through which we have passed during the latter half of the nineteenth century. The revolution which began with the application of the doctrines of evolutionary science, and which received its first great impetus with the publication of Darwin's *Origin of Species*, has gradually extended in scope until it has affected the entire intellectual life of our Western civilisation. One after the other we have seen the lower sciences revivified, reconstructed, transformed by the new knowledge. The sciences dealing with man in society have naturally been the last to be affected, but now that the movement has reached them the changes therein promise to be even more fundamental in character. History, economics, the science of politics, and, last, but not least important, the attitude of science to the religious life and to the religious phenomena of mankind, promise to be profoundly influenced. The whole plan of life is, in short, being slowly revealed to us in a new light, and we are beginning to perceive that it presents a single majestic unity, throughout every part of which the conditions of law and orderly progress reign supreme.

Nothing is more remarkable in this period of reconstruction than the change which is almost imperceptibly taking place in the minds of the rising generation respecting the great social and religious problems of our time. We have lived through a period when the very foundations of human thought have been rebuilt. To many, who in the first stage saw only the confusion occasioned by the moving of old landmarks, the time has been one of perplexity and changing hope. But those whose lot it has been to come later have already an inspiring and uplifting conception of the character of the work which the larger knowledge is destined eventually to accomplish. That the moral law is the unchanging law of progress in human society is the lesson which appears to be written over all things. No school of theology has ever sought to enforce this teaching with the directness and emphasis which it appears that evolutionary science will in the future be justified in doing. In the silent and strenuous rivalry in which every section of the race is of necessity continually engaged, permanent success appears to be invariably associated with certain ethical and moral conditions favourable to the maintenance of a high standard of social efficiency, and with those conditions only.

No one who engages in a serious study of the period of transition through which our Western civilisation is passing at the present time can resist the conclusion that we are rapidly approaching a time when we shall be face to face with social and political problems, graver in character and more far-reaching in extent than any which have been hitherto encountered. These problems are not peculiar to any nationality included in our civilisation. But in the method of their solution, the social efficiency of the various sections of the Western peoples will probably be put to a severer test than any which it has yet had to undergo. Those who realise, however dimly, the immense part which the English-speaking peoples are not improbably destined to play in the immediate future of the world, will feel how great a gain any advance may be which enables us through the methods of modern science to obtain a clearer perception of the stern, immutable conditions of fitness and uprightness through which alone a people can long continue to play a great part on the stage of the world. No race in the past has ever looked out upon such an opportunity as presents itself before these peoples in the twentieth century. Will they prove equal to it ? The world will be poorer indeed and the outlook for our civilisation gloomy if they fail. Those of us who believe that they will not fail, feel that anything which helps the world to a better understanding of the large permanent causes which make for the improvement or decay of peoples, must needs act as a strengthening and bracing influence in the work which is before us.

CONTENTS

CHAPTER I

CHAPTER II

CHAPTER III

CHAPTER IV

CHAPTER V

CHAPTER VI

CHAPTER VII

CHAPTER VIII

CHAPTER IX

CHAPTER X

CHAPTER I

THE OUTLOOK

To the thoughtful mind the outlook at the close of
the nineteenth century is profoundly interesting.
History can furnish no parallel to it. The problems
which loom across the threshold of the new century
surpass in magnitude any that civilisation has
hitherto had to encounter. We seem to have
reached a time in which there is abroad in men's
minds an instinctive feeling that a definite stage in
the evolution of Western civilisation is drawing to a
close, and that we are entering on a new era. Yet
one of the most curious features of the time is the
almost complete absence of any clear indication from
those who speak in the name of science and authority
as to the direction in which the path of future
progress lies. On every side in those departments
of knowledge which deal with social affairs change,
transition, and uncertainty are apparent. Despite
the great advances which science has made during
the past century in almost every other direction,
there is, it must be confessed, no science of human
society properly so called. What knowledge there
is exists in a more or less chaotic state scattered

B

under many heads; and it is not improbably true, however much we may hesitate to acknowledge it, that the generalisations which have recently tended most to foster a conception of the unity underlying the laws operating amid the complex social phenomena of our time, have not been those which have come from the orthodox scientific school. They have rather been those advanced by that school of social revolutionists of which Karl Marx is the most commanding figure. Judged by the utterances of her spokesmen, science, whose great triumph in the nineteenth century has been the tracing of the steps in the evolution of life up to human society, stands now dumb before the problems presented by society as it exists around us. As regards its further evolution she appears to have no clear message.

In England we have a most remarkable example of the attitude of science when she is appealed to for aid and enlightenment in those all-engrossing problems with which society is struggling. One of the monumental works of our time is the "Synthetic Philosophy" of Mr. Herbert Spencer, begun early in the second half of the century, and not yet completed. It is a stupendous attempt not only at the unification of knowledge, but at the explanation in terms of evolutionary science of the development which human society is undergoing, and towards the elucidation of which development it is rightly recognised that all the work of science in lower fields should be preliminary. Yet so little practical light has the author apparently succeeded in throwing on the nature of the social problems of our time, that his investigations and conclusions are, according as they are dealt with by one side or the other, held to lead up to the opinions of the two diametrically opposite camps of individualists and collectivists into which society is slowly becoming organised.

From Mr. Herbert Spencer in England, who himself regards the socialistic tendencies of the times with dislike if not with alarm, and whose views are thus shared by some, and opposed by others of his own followers, to Professor Schäffle in Germany, who regards the future as belonging to purified socialism, we have every possible and perplexing variety of opinion. The negative and helpless position of science is fairly exemplified in England by Professor Huxley, who in some of his recent writings has devoted himself to reducing the aims of the two conflicting parties of the day — individualists and socialists—to absurdity and impossibility respectively. These efforts are not, however, to be regarded as preliminary to an attempt to inspire us with any clear idea as to where our duty lies in the circumstances. After this onslaught his own faith in the future grows obscure, and he sends his readers on their way with, for guiding principle, no particular faith or hope in anything.[1]

Yet that the times are pregnant of great changes the least observant must be convinced. Even those who indulge in these destructive criticisms seem to be conscious of this. Professor Huxley himself, despite his negative conclusions, is almost as outspoken as a Nihilist in his dissatisfaction with the existing state of things. " Even the best of modern civilisations," said he recently, " appears to me to

---

[1] See his "Government : Anarchy or Regimentation," *Nineteenth Century*, May 1890. See also his *Social Diseases and Worse Remedies*, pp. 13-51, and *Evolution and Ethics* (the Romanes Lecture, 1893, delivered before the University of Oxford).

exhibit a condition of mankind which neither embodies any worthy ideal nor even possesses the merit of stability. I do not hesitate to express the opinion that if there is no hope of a large improvement of the condition of the greater part of the human family; if it is true that the increase of knowledge, the winning of a greater dominion over nature which is its consequence, and the wealth which follows upon that dominion, are to make no difference in the extent and the intensity of want with its concomitant physical and moral degradation amongst the masses of the people, I should hail the advent of some kindly comet which would sweep the whole affair away as a desirable consummation." [1] It is the large body of thought which this kind of feeling inspires which is now stirring European society to its depths, and nothing is more certain than that it will have to be reckoned with. M. de Laveleye, a few years ago, put the feeling into words. The message of the eighteenth century to man was, he said, " Thou shalt cease to be the slave of nobles and despots who oppress thee ; thou art free and sovereign." But the problem of our times is : " It is a grand thing to be free and sovereign, but how is it that the sovereign often starves? how is it that those who are held to be the source of power often cannot, even by hard work, provide themselves with the necessaries of life ? " [2] Mr. Henry George only fairly presses the matter home by asking whither in such circumstances our progress is leading; for, " to educate men who must be condemned to poverty is

[1] "Government : Anarchy or Regimentation," by Professor Huxley, *Nineteenth Century*, May 1890.
[2] "Communism," by Emile de Laveleye, *Contemporary Review*, March 1890.

but to make them restive ; to base on a state of most glaring social inequality political institutions under which men are theoretically equal is to stand a pyramid on its apex." [1]

Those who wish to see the end of the present condition of society have, so far, taken most part in the argument. Those who have no desire for change are of the class which always waits for action rather than argument. But a large section of the community, probably the largest section, while remaining unconvinced by the arguments used and more or less distrusting the methods proposed, feel that some change is inevitable. It is with these will probably rest the decisive part in shaping the course of future events. But at present they simply sit still and wait. They have no indication as to the direction in which the right path lies. They look in vain to science and authority for any hint as to duty. They are without a faith, for there is at the present time no science of human society. Many of the spokesmen of science who concern themselves with social problems continue to speak and act as if they conceived that their duty to society was to take away its religious beliefs. But it is not that they have any faith of their own to offer instead ; they apparently have themselves no grasp of the problems with which the world is struggling as best it can. Science has obviously herself no clear perception of the nature of the social evolution we are undergoing. She has made no serious attempt to explain the phenomenon of our Western civilisation. We are without any real knowledge of the laws of its life and development or of the principles which underlie

[1] *Progress and Poverty*, Introduction.

the process of social evolution which is proceeding around us.[1]

To many the spirit of the French Revolution which caused so universal a feeling of unrest at the end of the last century seems to be again unloosed, and after an epoch of progress unexampled in the history of the world we would appear to have returned to the discussion of the ideals of society which moved men's minds at that period of upheaval. Nothing can, however, be more out of place than comparisons which are instituted between society one hundred years ago and at the present time. We have little in common with this past. It may be searched in vain for any clue to the solution of the problems which confront us in the future. The great political revolution which began one hundred years ago, and which has been in progress in England and on the Continent throughout the nineteenth century, has well-nigh attained its ends. The middle classes having succeeded in enfranchising themselves have been in turn driven to enfranchise the lower classes ; and with the possession of universal education and universal suffrage, and the long list of measures tending the more fully to secure the political enfranchisement of the people which has accompanied them, this revolution is, to all intents, complete. We have in reality entered on a new stage of social evolution in which the minds of men are moving

[1] So far the larger part of the most useful work of the century in the department of sociology appears to have been merely destructive. "It may be stated," said Mr. Leslie Stephen recently, "that there is no science of sociology properly scientific—merely a heap of vague empirical observations, too flimsy to be useful in strict logical inference." —*Presidential Address, Annual Meeting of the Social and Political Education League*, March 1892.

towards other goals; and those political parties
which still stand confronting the people with rem-
nants of the political programme of political equality
are beginning to find that the world is rapidly
moving beyond their standpoint.

In other directions, too, the changes have been
vast. Since the beginning of the century applied
science has transformed the world. Amongst the
advanced nations, the great wave of industrial expansion which follows in its wake is slowly but
inevitably submerging the old landmarks of society,
and preparing for us a world where the old things,
material and social as well as political, have passed
away, and in which the experience of the past is no
longer a reliable guide. The marvellous development
of practical science, the revolution in industry which
it has effected, the application of steam and electricity
on an immense scale to machinery, the enormous
extension of railways, telegraphs, and other means of
rapid communication, the development of commerce
to a degree never before imagined, are amongst the
wonders of the present age. They are only the
earnest apparently of the future. Even a superficial
acquaintance with the means and methods of modern
science can hardly fail to leave the conviction that
no limit can be set to the possibilities of even the
near future, and that the achievements of the past,
extraordinary as they have been, are not improbably
destined to be eclipsed at no distant date.

But it is the more slowly ripening fruits of the
industrial revolution which arrest attention. Social
forces new, strange, and altogether immeasurable
have been released among us. Only one hundred
years ago, nations and communities were as distant

from each other in time as they were at the Christian
era.   Since then the ends of the world have been
drawn together, and civilised society is becoming one
vast highly organised and interdependent whole—
the wants and requirements of every part regulated
by economic laws bewildering in their intricacy—
with a nervous system of five million miles of telegraph wire, and an arterial system of railways and
ocean steamships, along which the currents of trade
and population flow with a rapidity and regularity
previously unimagined.   The old bonds of society
have been loosened ; old forces are becoming extinct ; whole classes have been swept away, and new
classes have arisen.   The great army of industrial
workers throughout the world is almost entirely a
growth of the past hundred years.   Vast displace-
ments of population have taken place, and are still
taking place.   The expansion of the towns, one of the
most remarkable features of the industrial revolution,
still continues unabated, no less in America and
Australia than in England, Germany, and France ;
and civilisation is everywhere massing together,
within limited areas, large populations extremely
sensitive to innumerable social stimuli which did not
exist at the beginning of the century.   The air is
full of new battle-cries, of the sound of the gathering
and marshalling of new forces and the reorganisation
of old ones.   Socialism seems to many minds to
have been born again, and to be entering on the
positive and practical stage.   It has ceased to be a
theory, it has begun to be a kind of religion.

Nor does the new faith appear to be without its
credentials and its aids to belief.   It has, in the
products of the times, a background as luridly

effective as any which stirred the imagination of the
early Christians in the days of degenerate Rome.
We are told that the immense progress of the century
and the splendid conquests of science have brought
no corresponding gain to the masses. That, on the
contrary, to the wage-earning class, which carries
society on its shoulders, the century has been in
many respects a period of progressive degeneration.
That the labourer has ceased to be a man as nature
made him ; and that, ignorant of all else, he is only
occupied with some small detail in the huge mill
of industry. That even the skilled worker holds
desperately to the small niche into which he has
been fitted, knowing that to lose his place is to
become part of the helpless flotsam and jetsam of
society, tossed to and fro on the tide of poverty
and misery. The adherents of the new faith ask,
What avails it that the waste places of the earth
have been turned into highways of commerce, if the
many still work and want, and only the few have
leisure and grow rich ? What does it profit the
worker that knowledge grows, if all the appliances
of science are not to lighten his labour ? Wealth
may accumulate, and public and private magnificence
may have reached a point never before attained in
the history of the world ; but wherein is society the
better, it is asked, if the Nemesis of poverty still sits
like a hollow-eyed spectre at the feast ? The wheels
of the world go round quicker, for science stokes the
furnace ; but men work sullenly. A new patrician
class, we are told, has arisen with all the power, but
none of the character or the responsibilities of the
old. We hear of the "robber knights of capital,"
and of the "unclean brigand aristocracy of the

Stock Exchange." We are told that they who profit are the organisers who set the machine to work, who pull the levers, study its pulses, and know its wants. They divide and govern, and the world works that they may grow rich.

What wonder that with such a creed the new battle-cries have an ominous sound. We hear no longer of the privileged and the people, but of the idlers and the workers, the usurpers and the disinherited, the robbers and the robbed. Many who think that we have heard all this before, and who are relieved to remember that socialism is as old as Fourier, Robert Owen, and Louis Blanc, leave out of consideration what is an all-important factor at the present time. In England, when early in the century Robert Owen's theories were discussed, and for long after, the working classes, it must be remembered, were almost without political rights of any kind. They lived like brutes, huddled together in wretched dwellings, without education and without any voice in politics or in the management of public affairs. Since then all this has gradually been changed. One of the most striking and significant signs of the times is the spectacle of Demos, with these new battle-cries ringing in his ears, gradually emerging from the long silence of social and political serfdom. Not now does he come with the violence of revolution foredoomed to failure, but with the slow and majestic progress which marks a natural evolution. He is no longer unwashed and illiterate, for we have universal education. He is no longer muzzled and without political power, for we have universal suffrage. With his advent, socialism has ceased to be a philanthropic sentiment merely. It still enlists the sympathies of

many of the best minds, but it has become at the
same time a direct appeal to the selfish instincts of
a considerable portion of the community wielding
political power.[1]   The advent of Demos is the
natural result of a long series of concessions, beginning in England with the passing of the Factory
Acts, and the legalisation of combination, and
leading gradually up to the avowedly socialistic
legislation for which the times appear to be ripening.

But so far all the changes are said to have only
increased the power without materially lessening the
misery of the working classes ; and the goal towards
which all efforts are directed seems still far off.
Science may be content to sit still and wait for the
arrival of the avenging comet to put an end to prevailing misery ; but it is not to be expected that
those who have to bear and suffer will, with the
power they at present possess, be content to be
equally patient should they discover themselves to
be equally hopeless.   Nay more, it is not even likely
that the average political mind, which is always in
favour of anything which it really believes to be for
the improvement and uplifting of society, will be
content to remain passive ; there are signs that it is
being deeply moved by what is taking place around
us.

We are told that society in its present state does
not possess the elements of stability.   Those who
are determined that something shall be done are not
without able leaders ; and, as has been well remarked,
misdirected genius in circumstances like the present

[1] Communism, as M. de Laveleye very truly points out, tends to
be specially attractive to two classes of men,—reformers and the
workers.   " The former are drawn to it by a sentiment of justice, the
latter by their own necessities."

beats gunpowder hollow as an explosive.[1] The new creed is indeed already forging its weapons. The worker is beginning to discover that what he has lost as an individual, he has gained as a class; and that by organisation he may obtain the power of meeting his masters on more equal terms. The shrinkage of space, the perfecting of the means of communication, the consolidation of society, the power of the press and public opinion are all, factors and forces as much on his side as on the other, and we are beginning to see the result. Even national lines of demarcation are disappearing. Society is being organised by classes into huge battalions, the avowed object of which is the making war on each other. We have syndicates, corporations, and federations of capital on one side, and societies, trades-unions, and federations of labour on the other.

But this has been already not only anticipated but described for us by Karl Marx and his disciples. We are told that it is but part of a great natural development which society is undergoing, the steps in which can be foreseen, and the end of which is inevitable. The growing enslavement and degradation of the workers, the development of a class feeling amongst them, accompanied by combinations and organisations against the common enemy, extending not only throughout the community, but across national boundaries, are amongst the phenomena which we have been led to expect. We are told that, on the other side, we must also expect to see the smaller capitalists continue to be extinguished by the larger, until, with the accumulation of wealth in the hands of a few colossal capitalists, society at

[1] Huxley, *Critiques and Addresses*—"Administrative Nihilism."

length will feel the anarchy of production intolerable, and the end of a natural process of transformation must come with the seizing of political control by the proletariat, and the turning by them of the means of production into state property. After which, we must look forward, we are told, to the abolition of all class distinctions and class antagonisms, the extinction of an exploiting class within the community, and the disappearance of the individual struggle for existence.

All this has been described with a knowledge of social phenomena and a grasp of principle to which many of its critics so far cannot lay claim. The larger portion of the community, however, admitting the evils although remaining unconvinced by the arguments, stand in helpless confusion of mind and watch the forces drawing together, and the battle being set in array between them. To give or withhold their support to one or other of the combatants, often means success or failure for the time being to that side, and their support is accordingly eagerly solicited by each in turn. But these who may have to determine the issue are without knowledge of the first principles of the struggle. They look in vain for any authoritative definition of the laws or principles which underlie it, for any clear indication as to which side is right and which is wrong, or for any definite teaching as to whither our Western civilisation as a whole is tending.

Amongst other noteworthy aspects of the time not the least remarkable is the revolution which is silently taking place in men's minds with regard to matters previously held to be more or less outside the sphere of political discussion. The alteration which is taking place in the standpoint from which religion is regarded is very remarkable. The change is not exclusively, nor perhaps even principally confined to those professing religion, and it affects men of different views in widely different ways. The outward indications might appear at first sight puzzling and conflicting in the extreme, and it is not until they are grouped and compared that they are seen to all belong to one wide and general movement of opinion. Within the Churches one of the signs of this change is visible in a growing tendency to assert that religion is concerned with man's actual state in this world as well as with his possible state in the next; in the desire to dwell upon the features which ecclesiastical organisations have in common rather than upon those features in which they differ from each other; and in the increasing tendency to assert that the Churches should be judged by their deeds rather than by their doctrines.

We are beginning to hear from many quarters that the social question is at bottom a religious question, and that to its solution it behoves the Churches in the interests of society to address themselves. The head of the Roman Catholic Church, no less than the head of the Salvation Army, seems to have felt the influence of the spirit which is abroad. Both in the public press and in the pulpit, from nonconformity and orthodoxy alike, we have the note sounded in varying keys, that, after all, Christianity was intended to save not only men but man, and that its mission should be to teach us not only how to die as individuals but how to live as

members of society.[1] So pronounced is the change,
that when from time to time a protest to the contrary
comes from within the Church itself, and we are told,
as we recently have been, by one of the dignitaries
of the Anglican Church that it is "a mistake to
attempt to turn Christ's kingdom into one of this
world,"[2] that the *Regnum Hominis* can never be the
Civitas Dei, and that the state does not and could
not exist on Christian principles, we are startled as
if we had caught an echo from the *Contrat Social*,
and heard again, and from the other side, Rousseau's
doctrine that the Christian cannot be a true citizen.

But it is not within the Churches but rather outside them that the symptoms of the change are most
noticeable. Many who have watched the course of
the struggle which has been waged between Religion
and Science within the century, and who have realised
to the full the force of the new weapons which the
latter has brought to bear against her old antagonist,
have cause for reflection at the present time. Some
amongst them have already begun to see that the
result is likely to be different from what either side
expected, and strangely different from that which
the more impulsive spokesmen of science anticipated.
It is not too much to assert that we are at the present
time entering on an era in which we are about to witness one of the most striking revolutions in the aspect
of the conflict which has taken place since it first began.

There are two movements of opinion which have
deeply affected the inner religious life of the present
century. The first has its cause in what may be called

[1] *Vide* Sermon preached before Oxford University, 11th December
1887, by Rev. Prebendary Eyton.
[2] Bishop of Peterborough, Address at the Diocesan Conference,
Leicester, 25th October 1889.

the new revelation of the doctrine of evolution ; the
other has received its impetus from the historic
criticism of the Bible by various workers from
Strauss to Renan. Whatever may be the opinion
of individuals there can be little doubt that the
tendency of both these movements has been generally
considered to be on the whole profoundly anti-re-
ligious. There have been indeed many enlightened
minds so far affected as to regard the new knowledge
as having definitely and finally closed the controversy
between Religion and Science by the annihilation of
one of the antagonists. Nevertheless, when all due
allowance is made for these movements of opinion,
there is a tendency of the time which ought not to
escape the notice of an observant mind. Some
conception of the direction in which we are travelling
begins to shape itself when the present is contrasted
with the past. Perhaps one of the first things which
arrest attention on a comparison of the condition of
thought outside the Churches on religious questions
at the present and at the beginning of the century is
the disappearance of that condition of mind represented at the period of the French Revolution by
the assured and aggressive objector to religion. It
is not that the dogmas of religion are more widely
adhered to, but that this state of mind has been to
a large extent superseded in America, Germany, and
England, but more particularly in the last-mentioned
country by a remarkable earnestness, a general deep-
lying religiousness—using the word in its broadest
sense, for the disposition is often not less marked
amongst those openly rejecting the dogmas of
religion—which is perhaps without a parallel in any
previous age.

It would be a mistake to view now as representative of the time the aggressive and merely destructive form of unbelief which finds expression in England in opinions like those of the late Mr. Charles Bradlaugh, and in America in the writings and addresses of Colonel Ingersoll. Even with regard to the views of the new party of Agnostics, representing what may be called unbelief in a passive state, a current of change may be discerned in progress. The militant onslaughts of so cultured a representative as Professor Huxley, the founder of the party, do not find the response in men's minds they would have found at a previous time. They are, almost unconsciously, recognised as belonging to a phase of thought beyond which the present generation feels itself, in some way, to have moved. The general mind, so often more scientific than our current science, seems to feel that there is something wrong in the attitude of science towards this subject of religion, that the most persistent and universal class of phenomena connected with human society cannot be thus lightly disposed of, and that our religious systems must have some unexplained function to perform in the evolution which society is undergoing, and on a scale to correspond with the magnitude of the phenomena.

This ill-defined general feeling has found more active expression in individuals. The movement of a certain class of minds towards the Church of Rome, the most conservative and uncompromising of all the Churches, which began in England in the middle of the century, and which has continued in some degree down to the present time, is not to be considered merely as a religious incident ; it is of

deep sociological import. Even the tendency, visible
at the present time amongst another class of minds,
to seek cover under the vague shadows of the super-
rational in Theosophy and kindred forms of belief,
has a certain significance which will not escape the
attention of the student of social phenomena. It
is but the outward expression in another form of the
same movement affecting a different type of mind.
It was, probably, an overstatement on the part of
one of the leaders of the Comtists in England to say
recently that "the net result of the whole negative
attack on the Gospel has perhaps been to deepen
the moral hold of Christianity on society."[1] The
opinion, nevertheless, represents the imperfect expression of a truth towards which the present
generation is slowly feeling its way.

We have, undoubtedly, during the century, made
progress in these matters. The direction may appear
as yet uncertain, but all the indications denote a
definite and unmistakable advance of some kind.
The condition which the social mind has reached
may be tentatively described as one of realisation,
more or less unconscious, that religion has a definite
function to perform in society, and that it is a factor
of some kind in the social evolution which is in
progress. But as to what that function is, where it
begins, where it ends, and what place religious beliefs
are destined to fill in the future, science has given us
no indication.

But it is now when we turn to the domain which
science has made her own that the outlines and
proportions of the coming change begin to be dis-

---

[1] "The Future of Agnosticism," by Mr. Frederic Harrison, *Fortnightly Review*, January 1889.

tinguished. The time is certainly not far distant when she must look back with surprise, if not, indeed, with some degree of shamefacedness, to the attitude in which she has for long addressed herself to one of the highest problems in the history of life. The definition of the laws which have shaped, and are still shaping, the course of progress in human society is the work of science, no less than it has been her work to discover the laws which have controlled the course of evolution throughout life in all the lower stages. But the spirit in which she has addressed herself to the one task is widely different from that in which she has undertaken the other. To her investigations in biology, science has brought a single-minded devotion to the truth, a clear judgment, and a mind absolutely unfettered by prejudice or bias. The splendid achievements of the century in this department of knowledge are the result. But when, in the ascending scale of life, she has reached man, the spirit in which her investigations have been continued is entirely different. She finds him emerging from the dim obscurity of a brute - like existence possessing two endowments which mark him out for a great future, namely his reason and his social capacities. Like all that have come before him he is engaged in a fierce and endless struggle for the means of existence ; and he now takes part in this struggle not only against his fellows but in company with them against other social groups. He grows ever more and more social, and forms himself into clans and organised tribal groups. From the beginning science finds him under the sway of forces new to her, and with one of the strongest of these forces she herself at a very early stage comes into conflict. He holds beliefs which she asserts have no foundation in reason ; and his actions are controlled by strange sanctions which she does not acknowledge. The incidents and events connected with these beliefs occupy, however, a great part of his life, and begin to influence his history in a marked manner. He develops into nations and attains to a certain degree of civilisation ; but these beliefs and religions appear to grow with his growth and to develop with his development. A great part of his history continues to be filled with the controversies, conflicts, social movements, and wars connected with them. Great social systems arise in which he reaches a high degree of civilisation, which come into conflict and competition with each other, and which develop and decline like organic growths. But with the life and development of these his religions are evidently still intimately connected ; individual character is deeply affected ; and the course of history and the whole character of social development continue to be profoundly influenced by these religious systems.

We live at a time when science counts nothing insignificant. She has recognised that every organ and every rudimentary organ has its utilitarian history. Every phase and attribute of life has its meaning in her eyes ; nothing has come into existence by chance. What then are these religious systems which fill such a commanding place in man's life and history ? What is their meaning and function in social development ? To ask these questions is to find that a strange silence has fallen upon science. She has no answer. Her attitude towards them has been curious in the extreme, and

widely different from that in which she has regarded
any other of the phenomena of life.   From an early
stage in her career we find that she has been engaged
in a personal quarrel with these religions, which has
developed into a bitter feud.   In any other circumstances it would probably have occurred to science
at the outset to ask whether this feud had not itself
some meaning, and whether it was not connected
with some deep-seated law of social development
which it would be her duty to investigate.   But this
aspect of the position seems, hitherto, to have
received scarcely any attention.   These religions of
man form one of the most striking and persistent
of the phenomena of life when encountered under
its highest forms, namely, in human society.   Yet,
strange to say, science seems to have taken up, and
to have maintained, down to the present time, the
extraordinary position that her only concern with
them is to declare (often, it must be confessed, with
the heat and bitterness of a partisan) that they are
without any foundation in reason.

Now, to any one who has caught the spirit of
Darwinian science, it is evident that this is not the
question at issue at all.   The question of real importance is not whether any section of persons,
however learned, is of opinion that these beliefs are
without any foundation in reason, but whether
religious systems have a function to perform in the
evolution of society.   If they have, and one which
at all corresponds in magnitude to the scale on which
we find the phenomena existing, then nothing can
be more certain than that evolution will follow its
course independent of our opinions, and that these
systems will continue to the end, and must be

expected to play as great a part in the future as they have done in the past.

In such circumstances it is evident that the assault which science has conducted against religion in the past would have to be considered simply an attack on an empty fort. Not only has the real position not been assailed, but when we are confronted with it, it would seem to be impregnable. Many like the late Mr. Cotter Morison may have been so far impressed with the course of events in the past as to think that religious beliefs are so far shaken that their future survival "is rather an object of pious hope than of reasoned judgment;"[1] or to assume, like M. Renan, that they "will die slowly out, undermined by primary instruction, and by the predominance of scientific over literary education."[2] But no greater mistake can be made than to imagine that there is anything in evolutionary science at the end of the nineteenth century to justify such conclusions. On the contrary, if these beliefs are a factor in the development which society is undergoing, then the most notable result of the scientific revolution begun by Darwin must be to establish them on a foundation as broad, deep, and lasting as any that the theologians have dreamt of. According to the laws which science has herself enunciated these beliefs must then be expected to remain to the end a characteristic feature of our social evolution.

The more we regard the religious phenomena of mankind as a whole, the more the conviction grows upon us that here, as in other departments of social affairs, science has yet obtained no real grasp of the

[1] *The Service of Man*, p. 6.
[2] *Studies in Religious History*, p. 14.

laws underlying the development which is proceeding
in society.   These religious phenomena are certainly
among the most persistent and characteristic features
of the development which we find man undergoing
in society.   No one who approaches the subject
with an unbiassed mind in the spirit of modern
evolutionary science can, for a moment, doubt that
the beliefs represented must have some immense
utilitariaɴ function to perform in the evolution
which is proceedɪng.   Yet contemporary literature
may be searched almost in vain for evidence of any
true realisation of ɪhis fact.   Even the attempt mᴀde
by Mr. Herbert Spencer in his *Sociology* to deal
with the phenomena of religions can scarcely be
said to be conceived in the spirit of evolutionary
science as now understood.   It is hard to follow
the author in his theories of the development of
religious beliefs from ghosts and ancestor worship,
without a continual feeling of disappointment, and
even of impatience at the triviality and comparative
insignificance of the explanations offered to account
for the development of such an imposing class of
social phenomena.   His disciples have only followed
in the same path.   We find Mr. Grant Allen, one of
the most devoted of them, recently, in explaining the
principles of his master, going so far as to speak of
a characteristic feature of the higher forms of religion
as so much "grotesque fungoid growth," which has
clustered round the primeval thread of Ancestor
Worship.[1]   Neither Mr. Grant Allen nor any other
evolutionist would dream of describing the mam-
malian brain as a grotesque fungoid growth which

[1] "The Gospel according to Herbert Spencer," *Pall Mall Gazette*,
28th April 1890.

had clustered round the primitive dorsal nerve ; yet such language would not be more short-sighted than that which is here used in discussing a feature of the most distinctive class of phenomena which the evolution of society presents.

In whatever direction we look, the attitude presented by science towards the social phenomena of the day can hardly be regarded as satisfactory. She stands confronting the problems of our time without any clear faith of her own. That illustrious school of political philosophy which arose in England with Hobbes and Locke, and which eventually attained to such wide influence in the writings of Hume, Adam Smith, Bentham, Ricardo, and Mill, has towards our own time become unduly narrowed and egotistical largely through its own success. Although it has in the past profoundly influenced the higher thought of Europe and America in nearly all its branches, and has been in its turn enriched thereby, the departments into which it has become subdivided have shown a tendency to remain reserved and exclusive, and to a large extent unaffected by the progressive tendencies and wider knowledge of our time.

In this connection one of the remarkable signs of the time in England of late has been the gradually spreading revolt against many of the conclusions of the school of political economy represented by Adam Smith, Ricardo, and Mill, which has been in the ascendant throughout the greater part of the nineteenth century. The earlier and vigorous, though unofficial protests of Mr. Ruskin and others against the narrow reasoning which regarded man in general simply as a type of the " city man," or, in Mr. Ruskin's more forcible

phraseology, as a mere covetous machine,[1] have long
since in Germany and America found a voice amongst
the official exponents of the science.   Even in England, writers like Jevons and Cliffe Leslie have not
hesitated to condemn many of its dogmatic tendencies,
and conclusions arrived at from narrow and insufficient
premises, in terms almost as emphatic.   " Adhering
to lines of thought that had been started chiefly by
mediæval traders, and continued by French and English philosophers in the latter half of the eighteenth
century, Ricardo and his followers," says Professor
Marshall, " developed a theory of the action of free
enterprise (or as they said free competition), which
contained many truths that will be of high importance so long as the world exists.   Their work
was wonderfully complete within the area which
it covered : but that area was very narrow.   Much
of the best of it consists of problems relating to rent
and the value of corn ; problems on the solution
of which the fate of England just then seemed to
depend, but which in the particular form in which
they were worked up by Ricardo have very little
direct bearing on the present state of things."[2]

The school found its highest expression in John
Stuart Mill's *Principles of Political Economy*, a book
which has deeply influenced recent thought in England.
Mill, it has been truly pointed out,[3] has gone far
towards forming the thoughts of nearly all the older
political economists, and in determining their attitude
to social questions.   It is true that we have evidences
of a wide-reaching change which is now in progress

[1] *Vide* his *Unto this Last.*
[2] *Principles of Economics*, by Professor Alfred Marshall, vol. i.
pp. 92, 93.
[3] *Ibid.*, *vide* vol. i. p. 65.

in England; and Professor Marshall's book, *Principles
of Economics*, published in 1890, marks a worthy
attempt to place the science on a firmer foundation
by bringing it into more vitalising contact with
history, politics, ethics, and even religion.   The
departure, it must be confessed, is, nevertheless, but
the effort of a department of science to recover
ground which it has lost largely through its own
faults.   It marks a somewhat belated attempt to
explain social phenomena which political economists
at first ignored, and evidently did not understand,
rather than the development of a science with a firm
grasp of the laws and causes which are producing
these phenomena.   Judged by a simple scientific
principle, recently laid down by Mr. Leslie Stephen,
our political economy must certainly be found
wanting.   " A genuine scientific theory implies a
true estimate of the great forces which mould institutions, and, therefore, a true appreciation of the
limits within which they might be modified by any
proposed change."   But it can hardly be claimed
for economics in general that it has reached this
stage.   Our social phenomena seem to be continually
moving beyond its theories into unknown territory,
and we see the economists following after as best
they can, and, with some loss of respect from the
onlookers, slowly and painfully adjusting the old
arguments and conclusions to the new phenomena.[1]

It is almost the same with the other sciences

[1] The development which has been taking place in the views of
political economists during the century, mainly through pressure from
without, is very fairly described by Professor Marshall.   At the beginning of the nineteenth century the economists paid little attention to
the deeper problems of human nature which will always underlie the
science.   " Flushed with their victories over a set of much more solid

which deal with our social affairs. The comparative barrenness which appears to distinguish them, when we regard the work done during the century in the lower branches of science, is striking, and it is doubtless largely due to the point of view from which they have been approached. In nothing does Professor Marshall show truer philosophical insight than in remarking how deeply economics now tends to be affected by the developments which the biological sciences have undergone during the century, and in noting its relationship to these sciences rather than to the mathematico-physical group upon which it leant at the beginning of the century.[1] By those sciences which deal with human society it seems to have been for long ignored or forgotten that in that society we are merely regarding the highest

thinkers they did not trouble themselves to examine any of the doctrines of the socialists, and least of all their speculations as to human nature. But the socialists were men who had felt intensely, and who knew something about the hidden springs of human action of which the economists took no account. Buried among their wild rhapsodies there were shrewd observations and pregnant suggestions from which philosophers and economists had much to learn. And gradually their influence began to tell. Comte's debts to them were very great; and the crisis of John Stuart Mill's life, as he tells us in his autobiography, came to him from reading them."

" When we come later on to compare the modern view of the vital problem of distribution with that which prevailed at the beginning of the century, we shall find that over and above all changes in detail, and all improvements in scientific accuracy of reasoning, there is a fundamental change in treatment; for while the earlier economists argued as though man's character and efficiency were to be regarded as a fixed quantity, modern economists keep carefully in mind the fact that it is a product of the circumstances under which he has lived. This change in the point of view of economics is partly due to the fact that the changes in human nature during the last fifty years have been so rapid as to force themselves on the attention; partly it has been due to the influence of individual writers, socialists, and others; and it has been produced by a parallel change in other sciences." Vol. i. pp. 63-4.

[1] *Principles of Economics*, vol. i. pp. 64, 65.

phenomena in the history of life, and that consequently all departments of knowledge which deal with social phenomena have their true foundation in the biological sciences.

Even in economics, despite recent advances, it does not yet seem to be recognised that a knowledge of the fundamental principles of biology, and of the laws which have controlled the development of life up to human society, is any necessary part of the outfit with which to approach the study of this science. In history the divorce is even more complete. We have the historian dealing with the record of life in its highest forms, and recognised as the interpreter of the rich and varied record of man's social phenomena in the past; yet, strange to say, feeling it scarcely necessary to take any interest in those sciences which in the truest sense lead up to his subject. It is hardly to be wondered at if he has so far scarcely succeeded in raising history, even in name, to the dignity of a science. Despite the advances which have recently been made in Germany and England, historical science is still a department of knowledge almost without generalisations of the nature of laws. The historian takes us through events of the past, through the rise and decline of great civilisations where we seem to recognise many of the well-known phenomena of life, through the development of social systems which are even spoken of as organic growths, through a social development which is evidently progressing in some definite direction, and sets us down at last with our faces to the future with scarcely a hint as to any law underlying it all, or indication as to where our own civilisation is tending. Those who remember the impression not so long ago created in England by the modest attempt of Professor Freeman to bring us merely to see that history was past politics, and politics but present history, will feel how far off indeed historical science still is from the goal at which it aims.

Yet the social phenomena which are treated of under the heads of politics, history, ethics, economics, and religion must all be regarded as but the intimately related phenomena of the science of life under its most complex aspect. The biologist whose crowning work in the century has been the establishment of order and law in the lower branches of his subject has carried us up to human society and there left us without a guide. It is true that at an earlier stage he has been warned off the ground at the other side and treated with bitterness and intolerance. But there is no reason why the remembrance of such treatment should cause him still to so far forget himself and his duty to science, that we should find him in a state of mind capable of speaking of any class of social phenomena as grotesque fungoid growths. In the meantime, each of the departments of knowledge which has dealt with man in society has regarded him almost exclusively from its own standpoint. To the politician he has been the mere opportunist ; to the historian he has been the unit which is the sport of blind forces apparently subject to no law ; to the exponent of religion he has been the creature of another world ; to the political economist he has been little more than the covetous machine. The time has come, it would appear, for a better understanding and for a more radical method ; for the social sciences to strengthen themselves by sending their roots deep into the soil underneath from which they spring; and for the biologist to advance over the frontier and carry the methods of his science boldly into human society where he has but to deal with the phenomena of life where he encounters life at last under its highest and most complex aspect.

CHAPTER II

CONDITIONS OF HUMAN PROGRESS

LET us, as far as possible, unbiassed by preconceived ideas, endeavour, before we proceed further, to obtain some clear conception of what human society really is, and of the nature of the conditions which have been attendant on the progress we have made so far.

There is no phenomenon so stupendous, so bewildering, and withal so interesting to man as that of his own evolution in society. The period it has occupied in his history is short compared with the whole span of that history; yet the results obtained are striking beyond comparison. Looking back through the glasses of modern science we behold him at first outwardly a brute, feebly holding his own against many fierce competitors. He has no wants above those of the beast; he lives in holes and dens in the rocks; he is a brute, even more feeble in body than many of the animals with which he struggles for a brute's portion. Tens of thousands of years pass over him, and his progress is slow and painful to a degree. The dim light which inwardly illumines him has grown brighter; the rude weapons which aid his natural helplessness are better shaped ; the cunning with which he circumvents his prey, and which helps him against his enemies, is of a higher order. But he continues to leave little impress on nature or his surroundings ; he is still in wants and instincts merely as his fellow denizens of the wilderness.

We look again, after a comparatively short interval, and a marvellous transformation has taken place—a transformation which is without any parallel in the previous history of life. This brute-like creature, which for long ages lurked in the woods and amongst the rocks, scarcely to all appearances of so much account as the higher carnivora with which he competed for a scanty subsistence, has obtained mastery over the whole earth. He has organised himself into great societies. The brutes are no longer his companions and competitors. He has changed the face of continents. The earth produces at his will ; all its resources are his. The secrets of the universe have been plumbed, and with the knowledge obtained he has turned the world into a vast workshop where all the powers of nature work submissively in bondage to supply his wants. His power at length appears illimitable ; for the source of it is the boundless wealth of knowledge stored up in the great civilisations he has developed, every addition to this knowledge but offering new opportunities for further expansion.

But when we come to examine the causes of this remarkable development we find the greatest obscurity prevailing. Man himself has hitherto viewed his progress with a species of awe ; so much so that he often seems to hesitate to regard it as a natural phenomenon, and therefore under the control of

natural laws.   To all of us it is from its very nature
bewildering ; to many it is in addition mysterious,
marvellous, supernatural.

In proceeding to discuss in what manner natural
laws have operated in producing the advance man
has made in society we must endeavour to approach
the subject without bias or prejudice ; if possible in
the same spirit in which the historian feels it to be
his duty to deal with human history so far as it
extends before his more limited view, or in which
the biologist has dealt with the phenomena of the
development of life elsewhere.   Man, since we first
encounter him, has made ceaseless progress upwards,
and this progress continues before our eyes.   But
it has never been, nor is it now, an equal advance of
the whole of the race.   Looking back we see that
the road by which he has come is strewn with the
wrecks of nations, races, and civilisations, that have
fallen by the way, pushed aside by the operation of
laws which it takes no eye of faith to distinguish at
work amongst us at the present time as surely and
as effectively as at any past period.   Social systems
and civilisations resemble individuals in one respect ;
they are organic growths, apparently possessing
definite laws of health and development.   Such
laws science has already defined for the individual :
it should also be her duty to endeavour to define
them for society.

It is desirable at the outset to be able to realise
the importance of a preliminary study of the laws
which have operated in shaping the development of
life elsewhere.   These laws, the observer soon con-
vinces himself, have not been suspended in human
society.   On the contrary, he sees that they must

have their most important seat of action there. To recognise this truth one has only to remember that the discovery which in our time has raised biology from a mere record of isolated facts to a majestic story of orderly progress was not suggested by the study of life amongst the lower animals. The law, by the enunciation of which Darwin most advanced the science of the nineteenth century, took shape in the mind of the great biologist after observation of human society, and that society, in particular, which we see around us at the present day.[1] All the work, so far, of evolutionary science, should be preliminary to a higher end ; enriched with the harvest of information gathered in other fields, and equipped with a knowledge of principles, it should now return to human society and endeavour to trace the workings of its own laws under the complex conditions there prevailing.

Putting aside then, at first, all question of the future, let us see if we can say, from the point of view of evolutionary science, what have been the conditions of human progress in the past.

Looking round to-day at the lowest existing types of humanity and comparing them with the highest, one feels immediately constrained to ask—Do we

---

[1] Speaking of the workings of his mind before the *Origin of Species* was begun, Darwin says, "In October 1838, that is, fifteen months after I had begun my systematic inquiry, I happened to read for amusement Malthus on population ; and being well prepared to appreciate the struggle for existence which everywhere goes on, from long continued observation of the habits of animals and plants, it at once struck me that, under these circumstances, favourable variations would tend to be preserved and unfavourable ones to be destroyed. The result of this would be the foundation of a new species. Here, then, I had at last got a theory by which to work."—*The Life and Letters of Darwin*, by his son F. Darwin : Autobiographical chapter, vol. i.

ever fully realise how this advance of which we are so proud, and which is represented by the intellectual and social distance between these two extremes, has been brought about ? We talk vaguely about it, and take for granted many things in connection with it ; but the number of those who have grasped certain elementary biological laws of which it is the result, and which have controlled and directed it as rigidly as the law of gravity controls and directs a body falling to the earth, is surprisingly small.

In attempting to explain what these biological laws are it will be necessary, in order to clear the ground, to leave for later consideration the more special and peculiar features which man's evolution in society presents, and to confine ourselves in this chapter to the task of bringing into due prominence certain fundamental principles of development which are profoundly affecting him, in common with all other forms of life ; but which are, as a general rule, ignored or overlooked in the greater part of the literature on social questions and social progress which is the product of our time. It is of no little importance to begin at the beginning in these matters. We find man in everyday life continually subject to laws and conditions which have been imposed upon him in common with all the rest of creation, and we accept these conditions and make it our business to learn all we can of them. If in following his evolution in society, we find him in like manner subject to laws which have governed the development of the lower forms of life, and which are merely operating in society under more complex conditions, it is also our duty, if we would comprehend our own history, to take these laws as we find them, and to endeavour, at the very earliest stage, to understand them as far as possible.

Now, at the outset, we find man to be in one respect exactly like all the creatures which have come before him. He reproduces his kind from generation to generation. In doing so he is subject to a law which must never be lost sight of. Left to himself, this high-born creature, whose progress we seem to take for granted, has not the slightest innate tendency to make any progress whatever. It may appear strange, but it is strictly true, that if each of us were allowed by the conditions of life to follow his own inclinations, the average of one generation would have no tendency whatever to rise beyond the average of the preceding one, but distinctly the reverse. This is not a peculiarity of man; it has been a law of life from the beginning, and it continues to be a universal law which we have no power to alter. How then is progress possible? The answer to this question is the starting-point of all the science of human society.

Progress everywhere from the beginning of life has been effected in the same way, and it is possible in no other way. It is the result of selection and rejection. In the human species, as in every other species which has ever existed, no two individuals of a generation are alike in all respects; there is infinite variation within certain narrow limits. Some are slightly above the average in a particular direction as others are below it; and it is only when conditions prevail which are favourable to a preponderating reproduction of the former that advance in any direction becomes possible. To formulate this as the immutable law of progress since the beginning of life has been one of the principal results of the biological science of the nineteenth century ; and recent work, including the remarkable contributions of Professor Weismann in Germany, has all tended to establish it on foundations which are not now likely to be shaken. To put it in words used by Professor Flower in speaking of human society, " Progress has been due to the opportunity of those individuals who are a little superior in some respects to their fellows, of asserting their superiority and of continuing to live and of promulgating as an inheritance that superiority."[1] The recognition of this law must be the first step towards any true science of society ; and it is only right that we should find Professor Flower insisting, although such a spectacle is somewhat unusual at present amongst exponents of biological science, that it is " the message which pure and abstract biological research has sent to help us on with some of the commonest problems of human life."[2] Where there is progress there must inevitably be selection, and selection must in its turn involve competition of some kind.

But let us deal first with the necessity for progress. From time to time we find the question discussed by many who only imperfectly understand the conditions to which life is subject, as to whether progress is worth the price paid for it. But we have really no choice in the matter. Progress is a necessity from which there is simply no escape, and from which there has never been any escape since the beginning of life. Looking back through the history

[1] Reply to an Address by the Trades Council, Newcastle, September 1889.
[2] *Ibid.*

of life anterior to man, we find it to be a record of
ceaseless progress on the one hand, and ceaseless
stress and competition on the other. This orderly
and beautiful world which we see around us is now,
and always has been, the scene of incessant rivalry
between all the forms of life inhabiting it—rivalry,
too, not chiefly conducted between different species
but between members of the same species. The
plants in the green - sward beneath our feet are
engaged in silent rivalry with each other, a rivalry
which if allowed to proceed without outside interference would know no pause until the weaker were
exterminated. Every part, organ, or quality of these
plants which calls forth admiration for its beauty or
perfection, has its place and meaning in this struggle,
and has been acquired to ensure success therein.
The trees of the forest which clothe and beautify
the landscape are in a state of nature engaged in
the same rivalry with each other. Left to themselves they fight out, as unmistakable records have
shown, a stubborn struggle extending over centuries
in which at last only those forms most suitable to
the conditions of the locality retain their places.
But so far we view the rivalry under simple conditions; it is amongst the forms of animal life as
we begin to watch the gradual progress upwards to
higher types that it becomes many-sided and complex.

It is at this point that we encounter a feature
of the struggle which recent developments of biological science tend to bring into ever-increasing
prominence. The first necessity for every successful
form engaged in this struggle is the capacity for
reproduction beyond the limits which the conditions
of life for the time being comfortably provide for.

The capacity for multiplying in this way is at first one of the principal resources in the development upwards, and in the lower forms of life it is still almost the sole equipment. But as progress begins to be made, a deeper cause, the almost illimitable significance of which science is beginning to appreciate, requires that all the successful forms must multiply beyond the limits of comfortable existence.

Recent biological researches, and more particularly the investigations and conclusions of Professor Weismann, have tended to greatly develop Darwin's original hypothesis as to the conditions under which progress has been made in the various forms of life. It is now coming to be recognised as a necessarily inherent part of the doctrine of evolution that, if the continual selection which is always going on amongst the higher forms of life were to be suspended, these forms would not only possess no tendency to make progress : they must actually go backwards. *That is to say, if all the individuals of every generation in any species were allowed to equally propagate their kind, the average of each generation would continually tend to fall below the average of the generation which preceded it, and a process of slow but steady degeneration would ensue.*

The significance of this recent development of biological science is scarcely as yet realised outside the department of knowledge which it more immediately concerns. But that the higher branches of thought must in time be profoundly affected by it, is certain. What we are coming to see is, that, as the higher forms of life have behind them an immense line of ancestry of lower development, the maintenance of the position they have attained to represents a kind of never relaxed effort ; and that the tendency of every organ or quality, which they have acquired, to fail to reach its maximum development, is a constant quantity which outweighs in the average, where it is allowed to act, all other developmental tendencies whatever. It is only by continual selection that this tendency can be kept in check. In order that any part, organ, or quality may be kept at the maximum degree of development, it is necessary that individuals possessing it in a less perfect degree must be prevented from propagation. If in any species all the individuals are allowed to equally propagate their kind, there follows a mixture of all possible degrees of perfection, resulting, in course of time—as where an organ is no longer useful, and where selection in respect of it has, therefore, ceased—in a steady deterioration of average development. This conclusion, which biology is now approaching, greatly enlarges the Darwinian hypothesis. The selection of the fittest acquires an immensely widened significance, if we realise it to be an inherent principle of life, that, by the simple process of the individuals of each generation propagating their kind without selection, the higher forms of life would tend to gradually sink back again by a degenerative process through those stages of development by which they reached their present position.

The point which claims attention in connection with this theory of life is that it offers the explanation of much that we previously felt to be true while only dimly understanding why it should come to be. We see, in brief, why it has necessarily been that the history of the evolution of life presents a record of continuous rivalry and effort. Amongst the higher forms it is an inevitable law not only that competition and selection must always accompany progress, but that they must prevail amongst every form of life which is not actually retrograding. Every successful form must, *of necessity*, multiply beyond the limits which the average conditions of life comfortably provide for. Other things being equal, indeed, the wider the limits of selection the keener the rivalry, and the more rigid the selection the greater will be the progress; but rivalry and selection in some degree there must inevitably be.

The first condition of existence with a progressive form is, therefore, one of continual strain and stress, and along its upward path this condition is always maintained. Once begun, too, there can be no pause in the advance; for if by any combination of circumstances the rivalry and selection cease, then progress ceases with them, and the species or group cannot maintain its place; it has taken the first retrograde step, and it is immediately placed at a disadvantage with other species, or with those groups of its own kind where the rivalry still goes on, and where selection, adaptation, and progress continue unchecked. So keen is the rivalry through-out, that the number of successful forms is small in comparison with the number which have failed. Looking round us at the forms of life in the world at the present day, we see, as it were, only the isolated peaks of the great range of life, the gaps and valleys between representing the number of possible forms which have disappeared in the wear and stress of evolution.

It would be a mistake to regard this rivalry from

a very common point of view, and to think that the extinction of less efficient forms has been the same thing as the extermination of the individuals comprising them. This is not so. Nor would it be strictly correct to regard it as entailing the measure of suffering which our imagination sometimes reads into it.[1] With whatever feelings we may regard the conflict it is, however, necessary to remember that it is the first condition of progress. It leads continually onwards and upwards. From this stress of nature has followed the highest result we are capable of conceiving, namely, continual advance towards higher and more perfect forms of life. Out of it has arisen every attribute of form, colour, instinct, strength, courage, nobility, and beauty in the teeming and wonderful world of life around us. To it we owe all that is best and most perfect in life at the present day, as well as all its highest promise for the future. The law of life has been always the same from the beginning,—ceaseless and inevitable struggle and competition. ceaseless and inevitable selection and rejection, ceaseless and inevitable progress.

When at last we reach man, the stage enlarges. We find him born into the world with two new forces destined eventually to revolutionise it ; namely, his reason and his capacity for acting, under its influence, in concert with his fellows in organised societies. The conditions and limitations of exist-

[1] See, for instance, in this connection Mr. Alfred Russel Wallace's remarks on the ethical aspect of the struggle for existence (*Darwinism*, chap. ii.) He gives examples in support of the opinion that the supposed sufferings caused to animals by the struggle for life have little real existence ; they are rather the reflections of the imagined sensations of cultivated men and women in similar circumstances.

ence have been altered, new and complex conditions
have arisen, and the great drama slowly unfolds
itself. We shall presently have to deal with those
special aspects which man's evolution in society
presents ; but in this chapter it is necessary to keep
the mind fixed upon one fundamental feature of the
development which we see in progress.

As we watch man's advance in society, the conviction slowly forces itself upon us that the conflict
which has been waged from the beginning of life has
not been suspended in his case, but that it has
projected itself into the new era. Nay, more, all the
evidence would seem to suggest that he remains as
powerless to escape from it as the lowliest organism
in the scale , of life. When we look back over
history, and regard it with those feelings of humanity
which have been developed to such an extraordinary
degree by the process of evolution which is in
progress in our Western civilisation, it appears
without doubt an unparalleled record of rivalry and
stress. When man first gathered himself into
societies, and for long ages before we have any
definite information about him, his history must
have been one of endless conflict. Some faint conception of it may be obtained from the study of
the history of savage tribes of the present day. The
wars constantly waged between societies—those ceaseless armed struggles carried on by group against
group, and apparently continued purely from a
fighting instinct—must have formed one of his most
persistent characteristics. The strife can have
known no pause save that enforced from time to
time by exhaustion. That whole sections of the
race must in this manner have repeatedly dis-

appeared before stronger and more efficient peoples, science leaves us in little doubt. How the conflict must have gone on during all that immense period when man was slowly toiling up the long slope which brings him within the purview of history, the imagination can only feebly picture.

At last when history takes account of him, his onward path appears to be pursued under the same conditions, namely, continual rivalry and conflict with his fellows. The first prominent feature which we have everywhere to notice in groups and associations of primitive men is their military character. In whatever part of the world savage man has been met with, he is engaged in continuous warfare. The great business in the life of the society to which he belongs is always war with other societies of the same kind. To ensure success in this direction, every aspiration of the individual and the community seems to be directed. Savage societies rise, flourish, and disappear with marvellous rapidity, but the secret of their progress or decadence is always the same—they have grown strong or weak as fighting organisations. In the individual, every attribute and quality which tends to military success is prized; every other is despised, or held in less respect; and all the ability which the society produces must find an outlet in this direction. The past and present of uncivilised man may be summed up in a single pregnant sentence once used by one of our military commanders[1] in recounting the history of the tribes with which he came into conflict in different parts of Africa. " In whatever negro people a great law-

[1] Lord Wolseley, "The Negro as a Soldier," *Fortnightly Review*, December 1888.

giver has appeared, there a powerful army and a
military spirit has been called into existence, and
the nation has prospered until its national existence has been destroyed by a still stronger people."
This is the brief history of savage man from the
beginning.

In all this we have to notice a feature of importance. The progress of savage man, such as it
is, is born strictly of the conditions in which he lives.
Aimless as his history might seem when viewed from
the level on which it is enacted, there can be no
doubt of the progress made. But as to the nature
of the progress there can also be no mistake. It is
at once both inevitable and involuntary, the product
of the strenuous conditions under which he lives.
One of the commonest ideas surviving from a pre-
evolutionary period is that which represents the
stages of man's social progress as being steps consciously and voluntarily taken. Rousseau's picture
of him leaving " the state of nature " to put " his
person and his power under the superior direction of
the general will " with certain imaginary reservations,[1]
survives even in Mr. Herbert Spencer, who sees him
leaving this state and submitting to political subordination " through experience of the increased satisfaction derived under it." [2] But man in making the
momentous advance from a more primitive state to
the first beginnings of organised society must have
acted without any conscious regard, either to ex-
pediency or increased satisfactions, or any other of
the considerations which philosophical writers have
so often attributed to him. His progress was beyond
doubt the result of the conditions of his life, and

[1] *Vide* his *Contrat Social.*   [2] *Data of Ethics.*

was made under force of circumstances over which
he had no control. His first organised societies
must have been developed like any other advantage,
under the sternest conditions of natural selection.
In the flux and change of life the members of those
groups of men which in favourable conditions first
showed any tendency to social organisation, became
possessed of a great advantage over their fellows,
and these societies grew up simply because they
possessed elements of strength which led to the
disappearance before them of other groups of men
with which they came into competition. Such
societies continued to flourish until they in their
turn had to give way before other associations of
men of higher social efficiency. This, we may
venture to assert, is the simple history of a stage
in human development over which much controversy
has taken place.

As we watch the growth of the great powers of
antiquity, the Babylonian, Assyrian, and Persian
empires, and the Greek states, we find that it is
made under the same conditions of stress and conflict. States are cradled and nurtured in continuous
war, and grow up by a kind of natural selection,
having worsted and subordinated their competitors
in the long-drawn-out rivalry through which they
survive. In the Roman Empire we reach at length
the culminating point in an immensely long stage
of human history, during the whole of which the
struggle for existence is waged mainly under military
forms between societies organised for war against
each other. Ancient Rome was a small city state
which grew to be mistress of the world by a process
of natural selection, its career from the beginning

being a record of incessant fighting. From the
outset the Roman people devoted all their best
energies to the furtherance of schemes of conquest.
The state was organised to ensure military success ;
the highest ambition amongst the leading citizens
was to serve it in a military capacity and to bring
about the subjugation of other states and peoples.
The natural and unquestioned ambition of all such
organisations was universal conquest, and during
that long period in the world's history which inter-
vened between the year 675 B.C., when Esar-haddon,
king of Assyria, by the conquest of Egypt, brought
the whole of the ancient world for a short space
under his rule, and the final break-up of the Roman
Empire, this ideal of state policy was ever practically
before men's minds.

With the enormous significance of the change in
the base from which this struggle takes place in our
Western civilisation we are not now closely concerned ; it will be dealt with under its fuller and
wider aspect at a later stage. At present it is
necessary to keep the mind fixed on a single feature
of man's history, namely, the stress and strain under
which his development proceeds. His societies, like
the individuals comprising them, are to be regarded
as the product of the circumstances in which they
exist,—the survivals of the fittest in the rivalry
which is constantly in progress. Only an infinitesimal number of them have become known to us even
in name, and these have come to occupy a dispro-
portionate space in our imagination, because of the
little corner of the great stage of the world's history
of which alone we are able, even with the aid of
science, to obtain a view.

We watch universal paralysis and slow decay following universal dominion; and even before the downfall of the Western Empire in 476 we see the greater part of Europe being once more slowly submerged under successive waves of more vigorous humanity. From the invasion of the Roman Empire by the Visigoths in 376, onwards for nearly seven centuries, the tide of conquest which flowed from the East and North surges backwards and forwards over Europe, making its influence felt to almost the extreme Western and Southern limits, and leaving at last, when it subsides, a new deposit of humanity overlying the peoples the invaders found in possession, who had in prehistoric times similarly superimposed themselves on still earlier peoples.

In the meantime, in the World wherein the foundations of our Western civilisation have been laid, unmeasured forces, destined to play a great part in the future, have begun slowly to gather. We descend into the great plain of the Middle Ages, and history takes its course through this extraordinary period—the seed-time of the modern world. The conditions of the rivalry slowly change, even though the direction of the movement is not at the time perceptible; but the ideas and ideals of the past continue to retain their influence over men's minds. The ages of faith prove to be the ages of fighting no less than those which preceded them, and the progress of the world still continues amid the sound of battle and conflict. The Western powers gradually rise into prominence, the vigorous life which they represent making itself felt in ever-widening circles. Out of the more local rivalries the great struggle for the possession of the New

World, and for room for the expanding peoples to develop, begins slowly to take shape. The seventeenth and the eighteenth centuries are filled with events marking the progress of a great ethical and political revolution destined, as we shall see, to affect in the most marked manner the future development of the world. But these events in no way stay the course of the rivalry which is proceeding; the conflict of nations continues, and the eighteenth century draws to a close leaving still undecided that stupendous duel for an influential place in the future in which the two leading peoples of Western Europe, facing each other in nearly every part of the world, have closed.

We watch the Anglo - Saxon overflowing his boundaries, going forth to take possession of new territories, and establishing himself like his ancestors in many lands. A peculiar interest attaches to the sight. He has been deeply affected, more deeply than many others, by the altruistic influences of the ethical system upon which our Western civilisation is founded. He had seen races like the ancient Peruvians, the Aztecs, and the Caribs, in large part exterminated by others, ruthlessly driven out of existence by the more vigorous invader, and he has at least the wish to do better. In the North American Continent, in the plains of Australia, in New Zealand, and South Africa, the representatives of this vigorous and virile race are at last in full possession,—that same race which, with all its faults, has for the most part honestly endeavoured to carry humanitarian principles into its dealings with inferior peoples, and which not improbably deserves the tribute paid to it on this account by Mr. Lecky who

E

counts its " unwearied, unostentatious, and inglorious crusade against slavery " amongst " the three or four perfectly virtuous acts recorded in the history of nations." [1]

Yet neither wish nor intention has power apparently to arrest a destiny which works itself out irresistibly. The Anglo-Saxon has exterminated the less developed peoples with which he has come into competition even, more effectively than other races have done in like case ; not necessarily indeed by fierce and cruel wars of extermination, but through the operation of laws 'not less deadly and even more certain in their result. The weaker races disappear before the stronger through the effects of mere contact. The Australian Aboriginal retires before the invader, his tribes dispersed, his hunting-grounds taken from him to be utilised for other purposes. In New Zealand a similar fate is over-taking the Maoris. This people were estimated to number in 1820, 100,000 ; in 1840 they were 80,000 ; they are now estimated at 40,000.[2] The Anglo-Saxon, driven by forces inherent in his own civilisation, comes to develop the natural resources of the land, and the consequences appear to be inevitable. The same history is repeating itself in South Africa. In the words used recently by a leading colonist of that country, " the natives must go ; or they must work as laboriously to develop the land as we are prepared to do ; " the issue in such a case being already determined. In North

---

[1] *History of European Morals*, vol. i. p. 160.

[2] *Vide* Report by Registrar-General of New Zealand on the condition of that country in 1889, quoted in *Nature*, 24th October 1889. *Vide* also paper by F. W. Pennefather in *Journal of Anthropological Institute*, 1887.

America we have but a later stage of a similar history.   Here two centuries of conflict have left the red men worsted at every point, rapidly dwindling in numbers, the surviving tribes hemmed in and surrounded by forces which they have no power to resist, standing like the isolated patches of grass which have not yet fallen before the knives of the machine-mower in the harvest field.

No motives appear to be able to stay the progress of such movements, humanise them how we may. We often in a self-accusing spirit attribute the gradual disappearance of aboriginal peoples to the effects of our vices upon them ; but the truth is that what may be called the virtues of our civilisation are scarcely less fatal than its vices.   Those features of Western civilisation which are most distinctive and characteristic, and of which we are most proud, are almost as disastrous in their effects as the evils of which complaint is so often made.   There is a certain grim pathos in the remark of the author of a paper on the New Zealand natives, which appeared in the *Journal of the Anthropological Institute* a few years ago,[1] who, amongst the causes to which the decay of the natives might be attributed, mentioned, indiscriminately, drink, disease, European clothing, peace, and wealth.   In whatever part of the world we look, amongst civilised or uncivilised peoples, history seems to have taken the same course. Of the Australian natives " only a few remanents of the powerful tribes linger on. . . . All the Tasmanians are gone, and the Maoris will soon be following.   The Pacific Islanders are departing childless.   The Australian natives as surely are

[1] 1887, F. W. Pennefather.

descending to the grave. Old races everywhere
give place to the new."[1] There are probably, says
Mr. F. Galton, " hardly any spots on the earth that
have not within the last few thousand years been
tenanted by very different races." [2]   Wherever a
superior race comes into close contact and competition with an inferior race, the result seems to be
much the same, whether it is arrived at by the
rude method of wars, of conquest, or by the silent
process which we see at work in Australia, New
Zealand, and the North American Continent, or by the
subtle, though no less efficient, method with which
science makes us acquainted, and which is in operation in many parts of our civilisation, where extinction works slowly and unnoticed through the earlier
marriages, the greater vitality, and the better chance
of livelihood of the members of the superior race.[3]

Yet we have not perhaps in all this the most
striking example of the powerlessness of man to
escape from one of the fundamental conditions under
which his evolution in society is proceeding. There
is scarcely any more remarkable situation in the
history of our Western civilisation than that which
has been created in the United States of America
by the emancipation of the negro as the result of
the War of Secession. The meaning of this extraordinary chapter in our social history has as yet
scarcely been grasped. As the result primarily of
an ethical movement having its roots far back in the
past, the United States abolished slavery with the
conclusion of the Civil War in 1865. The negro

[1] J. Bonwick, *Journal of the Anthropological Institute*, 1887.
[2] *Inquiries into Human Faculty*.
[3] Vide *Inquiries into Human Faculty*, by F. Galton.

was raised to a position of equality with his late
masters in the sight of the law, and admitted to full
political rights.   According to the census of 1890
the negroes and persons of African descent in the
United States numbered 7,470,040, principally distributed in some fifteen of the Southern States
known as the " Black Belt."   In some of these
states the black population outnumbers the white.

Any one who thinks that the emancipation of the
negro has stayed or altered the inexorable law which
we find working itself out through human history
elsewhere, has only to look to the remarkable literature which this question is producing in the United
States at the present day, and judge for himself.
The negro has been emancipated and admitted to
full voting citizenship ; he has grown wealthy, and
has raised himself by education.   But to his fellow-
men of a different colour he remains the inferior
still.   His position in the United States to-day is
one of absolute subordination, under all the forms
of freedom, to the race amongst whom he lives.   To
intermarry with him the white absolutely refuses ; he
will not admit him to social equality on any terms ;
he will not even allow him to exercise the political
power which is his right in theory where he possesses
a voting majority.   Mr. Laird Clowes, whose careful
and detailed investigation of this remarkable question
has recently attracted attention in England, says that
the impartial observer might expect to find in some
of the coloured states of the Union the government
almost, if not entirely, in the hands of the negro and
coloured majority ; but he finds no trace of anything
of the kind.   " He finds, on the contrary, that the
white man rules as supremely as he did in the days

of slavery. The black man is permitted to have
little or nothing to say upon the point ; he is simply
thrust on one side. At every political, crisis the
cry of the minority is, ' This is a white man's question,' and the cry is generally uttered in such a tone as
to effectually warn off the black man from meddling
with the matter."[1] In the midst of democratic
civilisation, and under its forms and cover, the war
of races is waged as effectively and with practically
the same results as in any other state of society.
Says Mr. Clowes : " Throughout the South the social
position of the man in whose veins negro blood
courses is unalterably fixed at birth. The child may
grow to be wise, to be wealthy, to be entrusted even
with the responsibilities of office, but he always bears
with him the visible marks of his origin, and those
marks condemn him to remain for ever at the bottom
of the social ladder. To incur this condemnation
he need not be by any means black. A quarter, an
eighth, nay, a sixteenth of African blood is sufficient
to deprive him of all chances of social equality with
the white man. For the being with the hated taint
there is positively no social mercy. A white man
may be ignorant, vicious, and poor. For him, in
spite of all, the door is ever kept open. But the
black, or coloured man, no matter what his personal
merits may be, is ruthlessly shut out. The white
absolutely declines to associate with him on equal
terms. A line has been drawn ; and he who, from
either side, crosses that line has to pay the penalty.
If it be the negro who dares to cross, cruelty and
violence chase him promptly back again, or kill him
for his temerity. If it be the white, ostracism is the

[1] *Black America* (1891), by W. Laird Clowes, p. 8.

recognised penalty.   And it is not only the uneducated and the easily prejudiced who have drawn the
line thus sharply." [1]   Many thoughtful and earnest
persons are so impressed with the gravity of the
problem, that they recommend and seriously advocate the deportation of the seven millions of the
coloured race back to their original home in Africa
as the only effective solution.   The whites find it
simply intolerable and impossible to live under the
rule of the blacks, and they are determined, come
what may, to prevent that rule.   The present state
of things is not maintained simply by the ignorant
whites.   The intelligent, the educated, and the
respected give it their countenance and support.
Power is maintained by the whites when they are
in the minority by fraud, violence, and intimidation
in default of other means ; yet, says Mr. Clowes,
" strange to say, even the most respected and (in
ordinary dealings) upright white people of the South
excuse and defend this course of procedure, and,
stranger still, very many honourable citizens of the
North, Republicans as well as Democrats, do not
hesitate to declare, ' If I were a Southern white man
I should act as the Southern white men do.'   The
cardinal principle of the political creed of 99 per
cent of the Southern whites is that the white man
must rule at all costs and at all hazards.   In comparison with this principle every other article of
political faith dwindles into ridiculous insignificance.
White domination dwarfs tariff reform, protection,
free trade, and the very pales of party.   The white
who does not believe in it above all else is regarded
as a traitor and as an outcast.   The race question is,

[1] *Black America* (1891), by W. Laird Clowes, p. 87.

in the South, the sole question of burning interest.
If you are sound on that question you are one of
the elect ; if you are unsound, you take rank as a
pariah or as a lunatic." [1]

All this, the conflict of races before referred to,
the worsting of the weaker, none the less effective
even when it is silent and painless, the subordination
or else the slow extinction of the inferior, is not a
page from the past or the distant ; it is all, taking
place to-day beneath our eyes in different parts of the
world, and more particularly and characteristically
within the pale of that vigorous Anglo-Saxon civilisation of which we are so proud, and which to many
of us is associated with all the most worthy ideals
of liberty, religion, and government that the race
has evolved.

But it is not until we come to draw aside the veil
from our civilisation, and watch what is taking place
within our borders between the individuals and
classes comprising it, that we begin to realise, with
some degree of clearness, the nature of this rivalry
which compels us to make progress whether we will
or not, its tendency to develop in intensity rather
than to disappear, and our own powerlessness either

---

[1] *Black America* (1891), by W. Laird Clowes, p. 15.
It would appear from the last census of the United States that,
despite recent opinions to the contrary, the coloured population is not
holding its own against the white races even in numbers in the states
best suited to its development. In the region known as the Black
Belt there were, in 1890, 6,996,166 coloured inhabitants, and in 1880,
6,142,360. The coloured element increased during the decade at the
rate of 13.90 per cent. The white population of these states in 1890
numbered 16,868,205, and in 1880, 13,530,408. They increased
during the decade at the rate of 24.67 per cent, or nearly twice as
rapidly as the coloured element. The interesting report on the subject by the Superintendent of Census will be found printed in full in
the Appendix.

to stay its course or to escape its influence. We had, in the conception of the ancient state, as a condition of society in which the struggle for existence was waged, mainly between organised groups rather than between the individuals comprising them, the key to history before the modern period. In the later type of civilisation, the conditions of the rivalry have greatly changed ; but if we look closely at what is taking, place, we may see that there has been no cessation or diminution of the rivalry itself. On the contrary, the significance of the change has consisted in the tendency to raise it to a higher level, to greatly enlarge its scope and its efficiency as a cause of progress, by bringing all the members of the community into it on more equal terms, and to render it freer and fairer, but, therefore, none the less strenuous.

The movement of progressive societies, remarks Sir Henry Maine, has been uniform in one respect ; throughout its course we have everywhere to trace the growth of individual obligation, and the substitution of the individual for the group as the unit of which the civil laws take account.[1] In this profoundly significant transition which has taken place in our legal codes, we have the outward expression of the great process of development which has worked itself out through our Western civilisation.

We have only to look round us in the world in which we live to see that this rivalry which man maintains with his fellows has become the leading and dominant feature of our civilisation. It makes itself felt now throughout the whole fabric of society. If we examine the motives of our daily life, and of

[1] *Ancient Law*, p. 168.

the lives of those with whom we come in contact, we shall have to recognise that the first and principal thought in the minds of the vast majority of us is how to hold our own therein.   The influence of the rivalry extends even to the innermost recesses of our private lives.   In our families, our homes, our pleasures, in the supreme moments of our lives, how to obtain success or to avoid failure for ourselves, or for those nearest to us, is a question of the first importance.   Nearly all the best ability which society produces finds employment in this manner.   It is no noisy struggle ; it is the silent determined striving of vigorous men in earnest, who are trying their powers to the utmost.   It leaves its mark everywhere in the world around us.   Some of the most striking literature modern civilisation has produced has taken the form of realistic pictures of phases of the struggle which are always with us.

In our modern industrial societies nearly all classes are involved.   The springs of action lie very deep. The love of action, the insatiable desire for strenuous energetic labour is everywhere characteristic of the peoples who have come to occupy the foremost places in the world.   Amongst the many failings which have been attributed to the English character, by a class of foreign writers who have not clearly understood the causes contributing to the extraordinary expansion which the English-speaking peoples have undergone in modern times, has been the supposed national love for huckstering and trafficking in all its forms.   But, as Professor Marshall has recently correctly pointed out, the English " had not originally, and they have not now, that special liking for dealing and bargaining, nor for the more abstract side of financial business, which is found amongst the Jews, the Italians, the Greeks, and the Armenians ; trade with them has always taken the form of action rather than of manœuvring and speculative combination. Even now the subtlest financial speculation on the London Stock Exchange is done chiefly by those races which have inherited the same aptitude for trading which the English have for action."[1] Our vital statistics show that the severest stress, the hardest work, and the shortest lives are not so much the lot of the poor as of the business and professional classes. The appetite for success is really never satisfied, and a deeper insight into the conditions of the rivalry reveals that it is necessarily so ; it grows with eating, but it remains insatiable.

We shall perceive, when we understand the nature of the forces at work beneath the social phenomena of our time, that in whatever direction we may cast our eyes, there is no evidence that the rivalry and competition of life, which has projected itself into human society, has tended to disappear in the past, or that it is less severe amongst the most advanced peoples of the present, or that the tendency of the progress we are making is to extinguish it in the future. On the contrary, all the evidence points in the opposite direction. The enormous expansion of the past century has been accompanied by two well-marked features in all lands affected by it. The advance towards more equal conditions of life has been so great, that amongst the more progressive nations such terms as lower orders, common people, and working classes are losing much of their old meaning, the masses of the people are being slowly

[1] *Principles of Economics*, vol. i. pp. 32, 33.

raised, and the barriers of birth, class, and privilege
are everywhere being broken through.   But, on the
other hand, the pulses of life have not slackened
amongst us ; the rivalry is keener, the stress severer,
the pace quicker than ever before.

Looking round at the nations of to-day and
noticing the direction in which they are travelling, it
seems impossible to escape the conclusion that the
progressive peoples have everywhere the same distinctive features.   Energetic, vigorous, virile life
amongst them is maintained at the highest pitch of
which nature is capable.   They offer the highest
motives to emulation ; amongst them the individual
is freest, the selection fullest, the rivalry fairest.   But
so also is the conflict sternest, the nervous friction
greatest, and the stress severest.   Looking back by
the way these nations have come, we find an equally
unmistakable absence of these qualities and conditions amongst the competitors they have left behind.
From the nations who have dropped out of the race
within recent times backwards through history, we
follow a gradually descending series.   The contrast
already to be distinguished between the advancing
and the unprogressive peoples of European race is
more noticeable when the former are compared with
non-European peoples.   The difference becomes still
more marked when the existence of the careless,
shiftless, easily satisfied negro of the United States
or West Indies is contrasted with that of the dominant race amongst whom he lives, whose restless,
aggressive, high-pitched life he has neither the desire
to live nor the capacity to endure.

We follow the path of Empire from the stagnant
and unchanging East, westward through peoples

whose pulses beat quicker, and whose energy and activity become more marked as we advance. Professor Marshall, who notices the prevailing energy and activity of the British people, and who has recently roundly asserted that men of the Anglo-Saxon races in all parts of the world not only work hard while about it, but do more work in the year than any other,[1] only brings into prominence the one dominant feature of all successful peoples. It is the same characteristic which distinguishes the people of the great Anglo-Saxon republic of the West, whose writers continually remind us that the peculiar endowment which its people have received from nature is an additional allowance of nervous energy.

A similar lesson is emphasised in the northward movement of rule and empire throughout historic times. The successful peoples have moved westwards for physical reasons ; the seat of power has moved continually northwards for reasons connected with the evolution in character which the race is undergoing. Man, originally a creature of a warm climate and still multiplying most easily and rapidly there, has not attained his highest development where the conditions of existence have been easiest. Throughout history the centre of power has moved gradually but surely to the north into those stern regions where men have been trained for the rivalry of life in the strenuous conflict with nature in which they have acquired energy, courage, integrity, and those characteristic qualities which contribute to raise them to a high state of social efficiency. The shifting of the centre of power northwards has been a feature alike of modern and of ancient history.

[1] *Principles of Economics*, vol. i. p. 730.

The peoples whose influence to-day reaches over the greater part of the world, both temperate and tropical, belong almost exclusively to races whose geographical home is north of the 40th parallel of latitude. The two groups of peoples, the English-speaking races and the Russians whose rule actually extends over some 46 per cent of the entire surface of the earth, have their geographical home north of the 50th parallel.

Nor can there be any doubt that from these strenuous conditions of rivalry the race as a whole is powerless to escape. The conditions of progress may be interrupted amongst the peoples who have long held their place in the front. These peoples may fail and fall behind, but progress continues nevertheless. For although the growth of the leading shoot may be for the time arrested, farther back on the branch other shoots are always ready to take the place of that which has ceased to advance. The races who maintain their places in the van do so on the sternest conditions. We may regulate and humanise those conditions, but we have no power to fundamentally alter them; the conflict is severest of all when it is carried on under the forms of the highest civilisation. The Anglo-Saxon looks forward, not without reason, to the day when wars will cease; but, without war, he is involuntarily exterminating the Maori, the Australian, and the Red Indian, and he has within his borders the emancipated but ostracised Negro, the English Poor Law, and the Social Question; he may beat his swords into ploughshares, but in his hands the implements of industry prove even more effective and deadly weapons than the swords.

These are the first stern facts of human life and progress which we have to take into account. They have their origin not in any accidental feature of our history, nor in any innate depravity existing in man. They result, as we have seen, from deep-seated physiological causes, the operation of which we must always remain powerless to escape. It is worse than useless to obscure them or to ignore them, as is done in a great part of the social literature of the time. The first step towards obtaining any true grasp of the social problems of our day must be to look fairly and bravely in the face these facts which lie behind them.

CHAPTER III

THERE IS NO RATIONAL SANCTION FOR THE CONDITIONS OF PROGRESS

HAVING endeavoured to place thus prominently before our minds the conditions under which human progress has been made throughout the past, and under which it, so far, continues to be made in the midst of the highest civilisation which surrounds us at the present, we must now direct our attention to another striking and equally important feature of this progress. The two new forces which made their advent with man were his reason, and the capacity for acting, under its influence, in concert with his fellows in society. It becomes necessary, therefore, to notice for the first time a fact which, later, as we proceed, will be brought into increasing prominence. As man can only reach his highest development and employ his powers to the fullest extent in society, it follows that in the evolution which we witness him undergoing throughout history, his development as an individual is necessarily of less importance than his development as a social creature. In other words, although his interests as an individual may remain all-important to himself, it has become inevitable that they must henceforward be subordinated—whether he be conscious of it or not—to those larger social interests with which the forces that are shaping his development have now begun to operate.

The evolutionist who endeavours to obtain a fundamental grasp of the problems which human society presents, will find, therefore, that there is one point, above all others, at which his attention tends to become concentrated—the point where he stands, as it were, between man as a member of society endowed with reason on the one side, and all the brute creation that has gone before him on the other. The problem which presents itself here is of unusual interest.

Looking back to the beginning of life, we observe that the progress made up to this point has been very great, so great indeed that it is almost beyond the power of the imagination to grasp its full meaning and extent. We see at one end of the scale the lowest forms of life, simple, unicellular, almost structureless and without sense of any kind ; and at the other we have, in the highest forms below man, a complexity of structure and co-ordination of function which, to the ordinary mind, appears marvellous in the extreme. The advance so far has been vast and imposing ; but looking at the results, it is now necessary to call particularly to mind the teaching of evolutionary science as to the manner in which these results have been obtained.

Our admiration is excited by the wonderful attributes of life amongst the higher animals, but it must be remembered that the teaching of science is, that natural selection produced these results only by weeding out, during an immense series of genera-

F

tions, the unsuitable forms, and by the gradual development of the successful types through the slow accumulation of useful variations in the others. The conditions of progress must, therefore, from the very beginning, have involved failure to reach the ordinary possibilities of life for large numbers. We admire the wonderful adaptation of many of the ruminants to their mode of life, the keen scent by which they distinguish an enemy at a distance which seems remarkable to us, their wonderful power of vision, their exceeding fleetness of foot, and their graceful and beautiful forms. But the evolutionist has always before him the cost at which these qualities have been obtained. He has in mind the countless host of individuals which have fallen a prey to their enemies, or failed in other ways in the rivalry of life in the immense period during which natural selection was at work, slowly accumulating the small successful variations, out of which these qualities have been evolved. It is the same with other forms of life ; progress everywhere is evident, but the way is strewn with the unsuccessfuls which have fallen in the advance. The first condition of this progress has been, that all the individuals cannot succeed ; for, as we have already seen, no form can make any advance, or even retain its place, without deterioration, except by carrying on the species to a greater extent from individuals above the average than from those below it, and consequently by multiplying beyond the limits which the conditions of existence comfortably allow for.

There is, therefore, one feature of the situation which cannot be gainsaid. If it had been possible at any time for all the individuals of any form of

life to have secured themselves against the competition of other forms, it would, beyond doubt, have
been their interest to have suspended amongst
themselves those onerous conditions which thus,
by sacrificing the present welfare of individuals to
the larger interests of their kind in the future, continually prevented large numbers from reaching the
fullest possibilities of life. The conditions of progress,
it is true, might have been suspended, but this could
not have caused the present individuals any concern.
The results would, in any case, only have been visible
after a prolonged period, and they could not therefore be expected to have appeared to the existing
members as of any importance when weighed against
their own interests in the present.

But now at last, science stands confronted with
a creature differing in one most important respect
from all that have gone before him. He is endowed
with reason ; a faculty which is eventually destined
to gain for him, *inter alia*, the mastery of the whole
earth, and to place an impassable barrier between
him and all the other forms of life. As we regard
the problem which here begins to unfold itself, it
is seen to possess features of unusual interest. It
would seem that a conclusion, strange and unex-
pected, but apparently unavoidable, must present
itself. If the theories of evolutionary science have
been, so far, correct, then this new factor which has
been born into the world must, it would appear,
have the effect of ultimately staying all further
progress. Naturally recoiling from so extraordinary
a conclusion, we return and examine again the steps
by which it has been reached, but there seems, at
first sight, to be no flaw in the process of reasoning.

The facts present themselves in this wise.
Throughout the whole period of development
hitherto the conditions of progress have necessarily
been incompatible with the welfare of a large proportion of the individuals comprising any species.
Yet it is evident that to these, if they had been
able to think and to have any voice in the matter,
their own welfare must have appeared immeasurably
more important than the future of the species, or
than any progress, however great, that their kind
might make which thus demanded that they should
be sacrificed to it.   If it had been possible for them
to have reasoned about the matter, it must, beyond
doubt, have appeared to them that their interests
lay in putting an immediate stop to those onerous
conditions from which progress resulted, and which
pressed so severely upon them.   The advance which
the species might be making was, indeed, nothing
whatever to them ; their own immediate condition
was everything.   An indefinitely remote future, in
which they could have no possible interest, must
undoubtedly have been left to take care of itself,
even though it might involve the suspension of the
conditions of progress, the deterioration of their kind,
and the eventual extinction of the whole species.

Yet here at last was a creature who could reason
about these things and who, when his conduct is
observed, it may be noticed, actually does reason
about them in this way.   He is subject to the same
natural conditions of existence as all the forms of
life that have come before him ; he reproduces
his kind as they do ; he lives and dies subject to
the same physiological laws.   To him, as to the
others, the inexorable conditions of life render pro-

gress impossible in any other way than by carrying on his kind from successful variations to the exclusion of others ; by being, therefore, subject to selection ; by consequently reproducing in numbers beyond those which the conditions of life for the time being comfortably allow for ; and by living a life of constant rivalry and competition with his fellows with all the attendant results of stress and suffering to some, and failure to reach the full possibilities of life to large numbers. Nay, more, it is evident that his progress has become subject to these conditions in a more stringent and onerous form than has ever before prevailed in the world. For as he can reach his highest development only in society, the forces which are concerned in working out his evolution no longer operate upon him primarily as an individual but as a member of society. His interests as an individual have, in fact, become further subordinated to those of a social organism, with interests immensely wider, and a life indefinitely longer than his own. How is the possession of reason ever to be rendered compatible with the will to submit to conditions of existence so onerous, requiring the effective and continual subordination of the individual's welfare to the progress of a development in which he can have no personal interest whatever ?

The evolutionist looks with great interest for the answer which is to be given to a question of such unusual importance. The new era opens, and he sees man following his upward path apparently on exactly the same conditions as have prevailed in the past. Progress has not been suspended, nor have the conditions which produced it been in any

way altered. Man gathers himself into primitive
societies ; for, his reason producing its highest results
when he acts in co-operation with his fellows, he
of necessity becomes social in his habits through
the greater efficiency of his social groups in the
rivalry of existence. His societies in like manner
continue in a state of rivalry with each other, the
less efficient gradually disappearing before the more
vigorous types. The strife is incessant ; the military
type becomes established, and attains at length a
great development. All the old conditions appear
to have survived into the new era. The resources
of the individual are drawn upon to the fullest
extent to keep the rivalry at the highest pitch ; the
winning societies gradually extinguish their competitors, the weaker peoples disappear before the
stronger, and the subordination and exclusion of the
least efficient is still the prevailing feature of advancing humanity. Slowly, too, as we have seen, the
rivalry within those societies becomes two-sided.
Other things being equal, the most vigorous social
systems are those in which are combined the most
effective subordination of the individual to the
interests of the social organism with the highest
development of his own personality. A marked
feature, therefore, of all the most advanced and
progressive societies is the high pitch at which the
rivalry of life is maintained within the community,
the freedom of the conditions of this rivalry, and the
display of energy and the constant stress and strain
which accompany it. Look where he will, the
evolutionist finds no cessation of the strenuous conditions which have prevailed from the beginning of
life ; the tendency, on the contrary, seems to be to

render them more severe. Progress continues to be everywhere marked with the same inevitable consequences of failure and exclusion from the highest possibilities of life, for a large proportion of the individuals concerned.

The possession of reason must, it would seem, involve the opportunity of escape from the conditions mentioned. The evidence would, however, appear to point indubitably to the conclusion that these conditions can have had no sanction from reason for the mass of the individuals subjected to them. It may be held that they are conditions essential to progress, and that the future interests of the society to which we belong, and even of the race, would inevitably suffer if they were suspended. But this is not an argument to weigh with the individual who is concerned with his own interests in the present and not with the possible interests in the future of society or the race. It seems impossible to conceive how the conditions of progress could have had any rational sanction for the host of exterminated peoples of whom a vision rises before us when we compare the average European brain of to-day with that of the lowest savages, and consider the steps by which alone the advance can have been made. The conditions of progress may be viewed complacently by science, but it can hardly be said that they can have any rational sanction for the Red Indian in process of extermination in the United States, for the degraded negro in the same country, for the Maori in New Zealand, or for the Aboriginal in Australia.

The same conclusion is not less certain, although it may be less obvious elsewhere. The conditions of existence cannot really have had any rational

sanction for the great mass of the people during that
prolonged period when societies were developed
under stress of circumstances on a military footing.
An inevitable feature of all such societies was the
growth of powerful aristocratic corporations, and
autocratic classes living in wealth and power and
keeping the people in subjection while despising and
oppressing them. It is no answer, it must be
observed, to say that these societies were a. natural
product of the time, and that if any social group had
not been so organised, it must ultimately have disappeared before stronger rivals. We can scarcely
shut our eyes to the fact that the future did not
concern the existing members, and that to the great
mass of the people in these societies, who lived and
suffered in subjection to the dominant class which a
military organisation produced, the future of society,
or even of the race, was a matter of perfect indifference, compared with the actual and obvious hardships
of their own oppressed condition in the present.

When we come to deal with society as it exists
in the highest and most advanced civilisations of our
time, and put the same question to ourselves as regards the conditions of existence for the masses of
the people there, it is startling to find that we are
compelled to come to a like conclusion. The conditions of existence even in such communities can
apparently have no rational sanction for a large
proportion of the individuals comprising them.
When the convenient fictions of society are removed,
and examination lays bare the essential conditions
of life in the civilisation in which we are living, the
truth stands out in its naked significance. We are
speaking, it must be remembered, of a rational

sanction, and reason has, in an examination of this kind, nothing to do with any existence but the present, which it insists it is our duty to ourselves to make the most of.[1] The prevailing conditions of existence can, therefore, have no such sanction for large masses of the people in societies where life is a long onerous rivalry, where in the nature of things it is impossible for all to attain to success, and where the many work and suffer, and only the few have leisure and ease. Regard it how we may, the conclusion appears inevitable, that, to the great masses of the people, the so-called lower classes, in the advanced civilisations of to-day, the conditions under which they live and work are still without any rational sanction.

That this is no strained and exaggerated view, but the sober truth, a little reflection must convince any conscientious observer. If we look round and endeavour to regard sympathetically, and yet as far as possible without bias, the remarkable social

---

[1] The terms *reason* and *rational* are here, as everywhere throughout this book, used in their ordinary or natural sense, and not in that transcendent sense in which metaphysicians towards the end of the eighteenth century set the fashion of using them. It can hardly be that any justification will be found in evolutionary science for continuing to use the terms in this latter and certainly inaccurate sense. An imperfect understanding of the nature of the task which Kant set before himself in the *Critique of Pure Reason* is responsible for much subsequent confusion of mind concerning these terms. Some conception of what that task really was may be obtained by keeping clearly in view three points emphasised by Kant in his Introduction to the *Critique*. (1) That Pure Reason is defined by him as that faculty which supplies the principles of knowing anything entirely *à priori*. (2) That *à priori* knowledge is defined as that of general truths which bear the character of an inward necessity, entirely independent of experience. (3) That the inevitable problems with which Pure Reason is concerned are defined as God, Freedom, and Immortality. Vide *Immanuel Kant's Critique of Pure Reason*, vol. ii. ; translated by F. Max Müller.

phenomena of our time in Germany, France, America, and England, we shall find in the utterances of those who speak in the name of the masses of the people a meaning which cannot be mistaken. Whatever may be said of that class of literature represented in Germany by Karl Marx's *Kapital*, in America by Mr. Henry George's *Progress and Poverty* and Mr. Bellamy's *Looking Backward*, and in England by the *Fabian Essays*, it is deserving of the most. careful study by the student of social phenomena; for it is here, and here only, that he is enabled to see with the eyes, and to think through the minds of those who see and reason for that large class of the population who are confronted with the sterner realities of our civilisation. Whatever else may be the effect of a close study of this literature, it must leave the impression on the mind of an unprejudiced observer, that in our present-day societies, where we base on the fabric of political equality the most obvious social and material inequality, the lower classes of our population have no sanction from their reason for maintaining existing conditions. When all due allowance is made for the misstatements and exaggerations with which much of this kind of literature abounds, the evolutionist who understands his subject sees clearly enough that the main facts of the fundamental constitution of society are therein represented with sufficient approximation to truthfulness to quite justify this conclusion.

No greater mistake can be made than to suppose that the arguments of these writers have been effectively answered in that class of literature which is usually to be met with on the other side. What science has for the most part attempted to do—and

what, as we shall see when we come to deal with
socialism, she has not the least difficulty in succeeding in doing—is to prove that the constitution of
society proposed by socialist writers could not be
permanently successful, and that it must result in
the *ultimate* ruin of any people adopting it.   But
this is not a practical argument against socialism.
No lesson of the past or of the present can be more
obvious.than that men never have been, and are not
now, influenced in the least by the opinions of
scientists or any other class of persons, however
wise, as to what the result of present conduct,
apparently calculated to benefit themselves, may be
on generations yet unborn.   "How many workmen
of the present day," pertinently asks a recent writer,
"would refuse an annuity of two hundred pounds a
year, on the chance that by doing so they might
raise the rate of wages 1 per cent in the course of
three thousand years?"   But why talk of three
thousand years? he says.   "Our care as a matter of
fact does not extend three hundred.   Do any of us
deny ourselves a single scuttle of coals so as to make
our coal-fields last for one more generation?"   And
he answers truly that it is perfectly plain we do not.
The future is left to take care of itself.[1]   The
evolutionist may be convinced that what is called
the exploitation of the masses is but the present-day
form of the rivalry of life which he has watched from
the beginning, and that the sacrifice of some in the
cause of the future interests of the whole social
organism is a necessary feature of our progress.   But
this is no real argument addressed to those who most

[1] "The Scientific Basis of Optimism," W. H. Mallock, *Fortnightly Review*, January 1889.

naturally object to be exploited and sacrificed, and who in our modern societies are entrusted with power to give political effect to their objections. Science may be painfully convinced that the realisation of the hopes of socialism is quite incompatible with the ultimate interests of a progressive society ; but it would still be irrational to expect even this consideration to generally affect the conduct of those who are concerned not with the problematic .interests of others in the distant future, but with their own interests in the actual present.

It may be objected that the standpoint from which we have viewed existing society is not a fair one, and that we should not take the utterances of fanatical social reformers [1] as representative of the reasoning to which the lower classes at the present day find themselves driven when they consider their position. We have, however, only to look round us to find that striking confirmation comes from many other quarters of the view that the prevailing conditions of existence have no rational sanction for the masses of the population who submit to them. We have but to observe closely the literature of our time to notice that there appears to be an inherent tendency for a like conclusion to come to the surface in the utterances of many of the philosophical and

---

[1] Mr. Henry George does not mince matters. He says : "It is my deliberate opinion that if, standing on the threshold of being, one were given the choice of entering life as a Terra del Fuegan, a Black Fellow of Australia, an Esquimaux in the Arctic circle, or among the lowest classes in such a highly civilised country as Great Britain, he would make infinitely the better choice in selecting the lot of the savage" (*Progress and Poverty*, chap. ii. book v.) As Mr. George sees practically the same social conditions throughout the greater part of our Western civilisation, including the United States, we must take it that this condemnation applies to all our advanced societies.

scientific writers who discuss social questions. The
voice of reason could hardly find fitter utterance than
in the words of Professor Huxley already quoted, in
which, while telling us that at best our civilisation
does not embody any worthy ideal, or possess the
merit of stability, he does not hesitate to further
express the opinion that "if there is no hope of a
large improvement of the condition of the greater
part of the human family"—mark the uncompromising sweep of the words—he would hail the advent
of some kindly comet to sweep it all away.   "What
profits it," he asks pertinently, "to the human Pro-
metheus that he has stolen the fire of heaven to be
his servant, and that the spirits of the earth and the
air obey him, if the vulture of Pauperism is eternally
to tear his very vitals and keep him on the brink of
destruction?"

But it is not that Professor Huxley, and those
who feel with him, hold any large hope of improvement.   He has told us elsewhere, and more recently,
that the observer "must shut his eyes if he would
not see that more or less enduring suffering is the
meed of both vanquished and victor"[1] in our society,
and that nature therein "wants nothing but a fair
field and free play for her darling the strongest."[2]
The condition of life which the French emphatically
call *la misère*, that in which the prospect of even,
steady, and honest industry is a life of unsuccessful
battling with hunger, rounded by a pauper's grave,
he holds to be the permanent condition of a large
proportion of the masses of the people in our civilisation.   He says: "Any one who is acquainted with

---

[1] *Social Diseases and Worse Remedies,* 1891, p. 18.
[2] *Ibid.* p. 24.

the state of the population of all great industrial centres, whether in this or other countries, is aware that, amidst a large and increasing body of that population, *la misère* reigns supreme. I have no pretensions to the character of a philanthropist, and I have a special horror of all sorts of sentimental rhetoric ; I am merely trying to deal with facts, to some extent within my own knowledge, and further evidenced by abundant testimony, as a naturalist ; and I take it to be a mere plain truth that, throughout industrial Europe, there is not a single large manufacturing city which is free from a vast mass of people whose condition is exactly that described, and from a still greater mass who, living just on the edge of the social swamp, are liable to be precipitated into it by any lack of demand for their produce. And, with every addition to the population, the multitude already sunk in the pit and the number of the host sliding towards it continually increase." [1]

Here we have not the utterance of a fanatic, but the matured deliberate opinion of that leader of science in England, who, perhaps more than any of his contemporaries, has insisted that he has made it the highest aim and the consistent endeavour of a lifetime to bring us to look at things from the point of view of reason alone. It is an opinion as to the constitution of society, not, be it remembered, in some past and distant epoch, but of society in the midst of the highest civilisation of the present day, and at the highest point which human progress has reached. Nothing can be clearer than the meaning of that opinion ; it is a deliberate verdict that the conditions of life in the advanced societies of to-day are without

[1] *Social Diseases and Worse Remedies,* 1891, pp. 32, 33.

any sanction from reason for the masses of the people.

Nor if we turn to the facts upon which such a judgment may be founded do we find any reason for supposing that it is not justifiable. The remarkable series of statistical inquiries into the condition of the people in London, recently undertaken by Mr. Charles Booth and his assistants, has brought out in a far more impressive manner than any other kind of literature ever could, what is perhaps the most noteworthy aspect of the life of the masses in such a centre of our civilisation, namely, the enormous proportion of the population which exists in a state of chronic poverty. The total percentage of the population found to be "in poverty," as the result of these inquiries, is stated to be 30.7 per cent for all London. This very large percentage does not, it must be understood, include any of the "regularly employed and fairly paid working class." Despite the enormous accumulation of wealth in the richest city in the world, the entire middle and upper classes number only 17.8 per cent of the whole population. In estimating the total percentage of the population of London "in poverty," the rich districts are of course taken with the poor, but in 37 districts, each with a total population of over 30,000, and containing altogether 1,179,000 persons, the proportion in poverty in no case falls below 40 per cent, and in some of them it reaches 60 per cent.[1] It is impossible to rise from the study of the bulky volumes containing the enormous quantity of detail which lies behind these bare figures without feeling that, while

[1] *Labour and Life of the People:* London. Edited by Charles Booth, 1891, vol. ii. part I, chapter ii.

making all possible reservations and allowances, the evidence goes far to justify even the strongest words of Professor Huxley.

Nor must these features of our civilisation be held to be peculiar to London. Other European cities have a like tale to tell. Even when we turn to the great centres of population in the New World. we find the same conditions of life reproduced; the same ceaseless competition, the same keen struggle for employment and for the means of existence; the same want, failure, and misery meet us on every side. And we find these conditions denounced by a great body of social writers and social revolutionists, from Mr. Henry George and Mr. Bellamy onwards, in just the same unmeasured terms as in the Old World, and with perhaps even more bitterness and severity.

If we ask ourselves, therefore, what course it is the interests of the masses holding political power in our advanced societies to pursue from the standpoint of reason, it seems hardly possible to escape the conclusion that they should in self-interest put an immediate end to existing social conditions. Man in these societies has placed an impassable barrier between him and the brutes, and even between him and his less developed fellow-creatures. He no longer fears the rivalry or competition of either. The interest of the masses in such societies appears, therefore, clearly to be to draw a ring fence round their borders; to abolish competition within the community; to suspend the onerous rivalry of individuals which presses so severely on all; to organise, on socialistic principles, the means of production; and lastly, and above all, to regulate the population so as to keep it always proportional to the means of comfortable existence for all.   In a word, to put an end to those conditions which the evolutionist perceives to be inevitably and necessarily associated with progress now, and to have been so associated with it, not only from the beginning of human society, but from the beginning of life.

With whatever intention the evolutionist may set out, he will speedily discover, if he carries his analysis far enough, that so far from society existing firmly based on universal logic and reason, for large masses of the population, alike in past stages of our history and in the midst of the highest civilisations of the present day, reason has been, and continues to be, unable to offer any sanction for the prevailing conditions of life.   The conclusion which gradually forces itself upon his mind appears surprising at first sight, but there, nevertheless, seems to be no escape from it.   It is, that the only social doctrines current in the advanced societies of to-day which have the assent of reason for the masses are the doctrines of socialism.   These doctrines may be, he may be convinced, utterly destructive to the prospects of further progress, and to the future interests of society ; but he is compelled to admit that this is no concern of the individual whose interest it is not to speculate about a problematical future for unborn generations, but to make the best of the present for himself according to his lights.   Undoubtedly, as John Stuart Mill was clear-sighted enough to observe, if, apart from all speculations as to the regeneration of society in the future, the choice were to be " between communism with all its chances and the present state of society with all its sufferings and injustices . . .

all the difficulties great or small of communism
would be but as dust in the balance." [1]

It is necessary, if we would understand the nature
of the problem with which we have to deal, to dis-
abuse our minds of the very prevalent idea that the
doctrines of socialism are the heated imaginings of
unbalanced brains.   They are nothing of the kind ;
they are the truthful unexaggerated teaching of sober
reason.   Nor can we stop here.   It is evident that
any organisation of society with a system of rewards
according to natural ability can have no ultimate
sanction in reason for all the individuals.   For the
teaching of reason undoubtedly is that as we are all
the creatures of inheritance and environment, none
of us being responsible for his abilities or for the
want of them, so, their welfare in the present existence being just as important to the ungifted as to
the gifted, any regulation that the former should
fare any worse than the latter must be ultimately,
however we may obscure it, a rule of brute force
pure and simple.[2]   It would be an extremely diffi-

[1] *Principles of Political Economy*, p. 128.

[2] As the implications involved in the acceptance of the doctrines of
evolutionary science are better understood, it will probably be seen
that it is too readily assumed from the rationalistic standpoint that
there is in the nature of things a sanction for our conduct in society
other than that which a rule of force (maintained by the will of the
majority or of a ruling class) provides.   To commit a fraud on a railway company is an act which would probably be condemned by many
socialists from other motives than mere regard for its inexpediency.
But there are other socialists who do not hesitate to carry the logical
process out to the end.   Mr. Belfort Bax, for instance, in his *Religion
of Socialism*, justifies the defrauding of a railway company in an argument which may be applied equally effectively by the individual to
free himself from most of the obligations which society in any state
would recognise.   Addressing the railway company he says : " Business is business ; let us have no sentimentality.   We are on a footing
of competition, only that it is not ' free,' seeing that you have the law
on your side.   However, let that bide.   Your ' business ' is to get as

cult if not an impossible task to find any halting-
place for reason before the doctrines of anarchy, the
advocates of which, in the words of the anarchist
Michael Bakunin, " object to all authority and all
influence, privileged, patented, official, and legal, even
when it proceeds from universal suffrage, convinced
that it must always turn to the profit of a domineer-
ing and exploiting minority against the interest of
the immense majority enslaved." Reason may moderate the terms in which this conception is expressed,
and it might, and probably would, transpose the
terms majority and minority as used therein, but it
would find it difficult to show any convincing cause
to an absolutely unbiassed mind for otherwise with-
holding its assent to even this extreme view of
society.

The extraordinary character of the problem presented by human society begins thus slowly to come
into view.   We find man making continual progress
upwards, progress which it is almost beyond the

much money-value as possible out of me the passenger on your line
(' conveyance' being the specific form of social utility your capital
works in, in order to realise itself as surplus value), and to give as
little as possible in return, only in fact so much as will make your line
pay.   My ' business,' as an individual passenger, on the contrary, is
to get as much *use*-value, to derive as much advantage from the social
function which you casually perform in pursuance of your profit, as I
possibly can, and to give you as little as possible in return.   You seek
under the protection of the law to guard yourself from ' fraud,' as you
term it.   Good.   If I can evade the law passed in your interest and
elude your vigilance, I have a perfect right to do so, and my success
in doing so will be the reward of my ingenuity.   If I fail I am only
an unfortunate man.   The talk of ' dishonesty' or ' dishonour' where
no moral obligation or ' duty' can possibly exist is absurd.   You choose
to make certain arbitrary rules to regulate the commercial game.   I
decline to pledge myself to be bound by them, and in so doing I am
clearly within my moral right.   We each try to get as much out of
the other as we can, you in your way, I in mine.   Only, I repeat, you
are backed by the law, I am not.   That is all the difference."

power of the imagination to grasp. From being a competitor of the brutes he has reached a point of development at which he cannot himself set any limits to the possibilities of further progress, and at which he is evidently marching onwards to a high destiny. He has made this advance under the sternest conditions, involving in the average—as the price of continued resistance to the law of retrogression—a constant state of rivalry, effort, and self-sacrifice, and the failure and suffering of great numbers. His reason has been, and necessarily continues to be, a leading factor in this development ; yet, granting, as we apparently must grant, the possibility of the reversal of the conditions from which his progress results, these conditions can never have any universal sanction from his reason. They have had no such sanction at any stage of his history, and they continue to be as much without such sanction in the highest civilisations of the present day as at any past period.

There emerges now clearly into sight a fundamental principle that underlies that social development which has been in progress throughout history, and which is proceeding with accelerated pace in our modern civilisation. It is that in this development the interests of the individual and those of the social organism to which he belongs are not identical. The teaching of reason to the individual must always be that the present time and his own interests therein are all-important to him. Yet the forces which are working out our development are primarily concerned not with these interests of the individual, but with those of the race, and more immediately with the widely different interests of a social organism subject to quite other conditions and possessed of an indefinitely longer life. These latter interests are at any time not only greater than those of any class of individuals : they are greater than those of all the individuals of any single generation. Nay, more, as we shall see, they are at times greater than those of all the individuals of a whole series of generations. And in the development which is in progress it is a first principle of evolutionary science that it is these greater interests that must be always paramount. The central fact with which we are confronted in our progressive societies is, therefore, that :—

The interests of the social organism and those of the individuals comprising it at any particular time are actually antagonistic; they can never be reconciled; they are inherently and essentially irreconcilable.

The far-reaching consequences which flow from the recognition of this single fact, brought out when we come to apply the teaching of evolutionary science to society, will become evident as we proceed. Its revolutionary significance is, however, immediately apparent. If the interests of the progressive society as a whole, and those of the individuals at any time comprising it, are innately irreconcilable, it is evident that there can never be, for the individuals in those societies, any universal rational sanction for the conditions of existence necessarily prevailing. We look at the entire question of social development from a new standpoint. We stand, as it were, at the centre of the great maelström of human history, and see why all those systems of moral philosophy, which have sought to find in the nature of things a rational sanction for human conduct in society, must sweep round and round in futile circles. They attempt an inherently impossible task. The first great social lesson of those evolutionary doctrines which have transformed the science of the nineteenth century is, that there cannot be such a sanction.

From the first awakening of the Greek mind with Thales, onward through the speculations of Socrates, Plato, and Zeno ; underneath the systems of Seneca and Marcus Aurelius, and of Spinoza, Kant, Fichte, Hegel, and Comte ; in the utilitarianism of Hobbes, Locke, Hume, Bentham, the Mills, and Herbert Spencer, the one consistent practical aim which connects together all the widely different efforts and methods of philosophy has been to discover in the nature of things a rational sanction for individual conduct. George Henry Lewes notes the continued failure of philosophy to solve the capital problems of human existence, only, however, to attribute the result to the absence of the positive method associated with the name of Auguste Comte. But it would appear that all methods and systems alike, which have endeavoured to find in the nature of things any universal rational sanction for individual conduct in a progressive society, must be ultimately fruitless. They are all alike inherently unscientific in that they attempt to do what the fundamental conditions of existence render impossible. The positive system, no less than the others, and only all the more surely because it is positive, must apparently also be a failure.

The transforming fact which the scientific development of the nineteenth century has confronted us with is, that, as the interests of the social organism and of the individual are, and must remain, an-

tagonistic, and as the former must always be predominant, there can never be found any sanction in
individual reason for conduct in societies where the
conditions of progress prevail.   One of the first
results of the application of the methods and conclusions of the biological science* of our time to
social phenomena must apparently be to bring to a
close that long-drawn-out stage of thought in which
for 2300 years the human mind has engaged in a
task, the accomplishment of which fundamental
organic conditions of life render inherently impossible.[1]

[1] Mr. Herbert Spencer's conception of a state of society in which
the interests of the individual and those of society are reconciled (*Data
of Ethics*) is discussed in chapter x.   It must ever remain an incalculable loss to English science and English philosophy, that the author of
the *Synthetic Philosophy* did not undertake his great task later in the
nineteenth century.   As time goes on, it will become clearer what
the nature of that loss has been.   It will be perceived that the conception of his work was practically complete before his intellect had
any opportunity of realising the full transforming effect in the higher
regions of thought, and, more particularly, in the department of
sociology, of that development of biological science which began with
Darwin, which is still in full progress, and to which Professor
Weismann has recently made the most notable contributions.

CHAPTER IV

THE CENTRAL FEATURE OF HUMAN HISTORY

THE outlines of the great fundamental problem which underlies our social development are now clearly visible. We have a rational creature whose reason is itself one of the leading factors in the progress he is making ; but who is nevertheless subject, in common with all other forms of life, to certain organic laws of existence which render his progress impossible in any other way than by submitting to conditions that can never have any ultimate sanction in his reason. He is undergoing a social development in which his individual interests are not only subservient to the interests of the general progress of the race, but in which they are being increasingly subordinated to the welfare of a social organism possessing widely different interests, and an indefinitely longer life.

It is evident that we have here all the elements of a problem of capital importance—a problem quite special and entirely different from any that the history of life has ever before presented. On the one side we have the self-assertive reason of the individual necessarily tending to be ever more and more developed by the evolutionary forces at work. On the other, we have the immensely wider interests of the social organism, and behind it those of the race in general, demanding, nevertheless, the most absolute subordination of this ever-increasing rational self-assertiveness in the individual. We find, in fact, if progress is to continue, that the individual must be compelled to submit to conditions of existence of the most onerous kind which, to all appearance, his reason actually gives him the power to suspend—and all .to further a development in which he has not, and in which he never can have, *qua* individual, the slightest practical interest. We have, it would appear, henceforth to witness the extraordinary spectacle of man, moved by a profound social instinct, continually endeavouring in the interests of his social progress to check and control the tendency of his own reason to suspend and reverse the conditions which are producing this progress.

In the conflict which results, we have the seat of a vast series of phenomena constituting the absolutely characteristic feature of our social evolution. It is impossible to fully understand the spectacle presented by human history in the past on the one hand, or the main features of the social phenomena, now presenting themselves throughout our Western civilisation on the other, without getting to the heart of this conflict. It is the pivot upon which the whole drama of human history and human development turns.

If we could conceive a visitor from another planet coming amongst us, and being set down in the midst of our Western civilisation at the present day, there is one feature of our life which, we might imagine, could not fail to excite his interest and curiosity. If we could suppose him taken round London, Paris, Berlin, or New York, or any other great centre of population, by some man of light and leading amongst us, we might easily imagine the anxiety of his conductor to worthily explain to him the nature and the meaning of those aspects of our society which there presented themselves.   After all the outward features, the streets, the crowds, the buildings, and the means of traffic and communication had received attention, we might expect our man of science to explain to his visitor something of the nature of the wonderful social organisation of which the outward features presented themselves.   Our trades and manufactures, our commerce, our methods of government, the forces at work amongst us, and the problems, social and political, which occupy our minds, would doubtless all receive notice.   Something, too, of our history would be related, and our relations, past and present, to other nations, and even to other sections of the human race, would probably be explained.

But when our visitor had lived amongst us for a little time, he would probably find that there was one most obvious feature of our life about which he had been told nothing, yet respecting which he would, as an intelligent observer, sooner or later ask for information.   He would have noticed at every turn in our cities great buildings—churches, temples, and cathedrals—and he would have seen also that wherever men lived together in small groups they erected these buildings. He would have noticed the crowds which periodically frequented them ; and if he had listened to the doctrines taught therein he could not fail to be deeply interested. As his knowledge of us grew he would learn that these institutions were not peculiar to any particular place, or even to the people amongst whom he found himself ; that they were also a distinguishing feature of other cities and other countries ; that they existed throughout the greater part of the civilised world, and that similar institutions had been a characteristic feature of human life as far back as history extends.

If, at this stage, he had ventured to ask his guide for some explanation of these phenomena, he would not improbably begin to feel somewhat puzzled.   For if his guide had spoken as the spokesmen of science sometimes do speak nowadays, the information given would probably not have been altogether satisfying. The visitor would possibly have learned from him that the religious beliefs, which maintained these institutions, were by some held to represent the survival of an instinct peculiar to the childhood of the race ; that they were by others supposed to have had their origin in ancestor-worship and a belief in ghosts.   He might even have expressed his own opinion that they belonged to a past age, and that they were generally discredited by the intellectual class.   Pressed for any further information he might have added that science did not really pay much attention to the phenomena ; that she, in general, regarded them with some degree of contempt and even of bitterness, for, that, during many centuries, these religions had maintained a vast conspiracy against her, had persecuted her champions, and had used stupendous and extraordinary efforts to stifle and strangle her.   The guide, if he were a man of discrimination, might even have added that the feud was still continued under all the outward appearances of truce and friendliness ; that it was, in reality, only by her victories in applying her discoveries to the practical benefit of the race that science had finally been able to secure her position against her adversary ;

and that in its heart one of the parties still continued to regard the other as a mortal enemy which only the altered circumstances prevented it from openly assailing.

Such a visitor could not fail to find his interest continue to grow as he listened to such details. But if he had pressed for further information as to the nature of this conflict, and had sought to learn what law or meaning underlay this extraordinary. instinct which had thus driven successive generations of men to carry on such a prolonged and desperate struggle against forces set in motion by their own intellect, it is not improbable that his guide would at this point have shrugged his shoulders and changed the subject.

This is probably all the visitor would learn in this manner. Yet, as his perplexity increased, so also might his interest be expected to grow. As he learnt more of our history he would not fail to observe the important part these religions had played therein. Nay, as he came to understand it and to view it, as he would be able to do, without prepossession, he would see that it consisted to a large extent of the history of the religious systems he saw around him. As he extended his view to the history of other nations, and to that of our civilisation in general, he would be met with features equally striking. He would observe that these systems had exercised the same influence there, and that the history of our Western civilisation was largely but the life-history of a particular form of religion and of wide-extend-ing and deep-seated social movements connected therewith. He would see that these movements had deeply affected entire nations, and that revolu-

tions to which they gave rise had influenced national
development and even to a considerable extent
directed its course amongst nearly all the peoples
taking a leading part in the world around him.

As he inquired deeper he could not fail to be
struck by the extraordinary depth and dimensions
of the conflict to which his guide had incidentally
referred, namely, that waged between these religions
and the forces set in motion by human reason ; and
he would see also, that not only had it extended through
a great part of the history of Western civilisation, but
that it was quite true that it was still in progress.
Regarding this conflict impartially, he could not fail
also to be impressed profoundly by the persistence of
the instinct which inspired it, and he would doubtless
conclude that it must have some significance in the
evolution which we were undergoing.

His bewilderment would probably increase as he
looked beneath the surface of society. He would
see that he was in reality living in the midst of a
civilisation where the habits, customs, laws, and
institutions of the people had been influenced in
almost every detail by these religions ; that, although
a large proportion of the population were quite
unconscious of it, their conceptions of their rights
and duties, and of their relationship to each other,
their ideas of liberty, and even of government and
of the fundamental principles of society, had been
largely shaped by doctrines taught in connection
with them. Nay, more, he would see that those
who professed to entirely repudiate the teachings of
these religions, were almost as directly affected as
other sections of the community, and that whatever
their private opinions might be, they were quite

powerless to escape the influences of the prevailing tone and the developmental tendencies of the society in which they lived.

But the feature which would perhaps interest him most of all would probably attract attention later. He would observe that these forms of religious belief which his guide had spoken of as survivals, had nevertheless the support of a large proportion of perfectly sincere and earnest persons ; and that great movements in connection with the prevailing forms of belief were still in progress ; and that these movements, when they were studied, proved to have the characteristic features which had distinguished all similar movements in the past. He would find that they were not only independent of, but in direct conflict with the intellectual forces ; that although they not infrequently originated with obscure and uncultured persons, they spread with marvellous rapidity, profoundly influencing immense bodies of men and producing effects quite beyond the control of the intellectual forces of the time.

Such a visitor, at length, would not fail to be deeply impressed by what he had observed. He would be driven to conclude that he was dealing with phenomena, the laws and nature of which were little understood by the people amongst whom he found himself; and that whatever might be the meaning of these phenomena, they undoubtedly constituted one of the most persistent and characteristic features of human society, and not only in past ages but at the present day.

If, however, our visitor at last endeavoured to obtain for himself by a systematic study of the literature of the subject some insight into the

nature of the phenomena he was regarding, the
state of things which would meet his view would
excite his wonder not a little.   If at the outset he
endeavoured to discover what all these various
forms of religion admittedly had in common, that
is to say, the distinguishing characteristic they all
possessed, from the forms of belief prevalent
amongst men in a low social state up to those
highly-developed religions which were playing so
large a part in the life of civilised peoples, he would
be met by a curious fact.   He would find everywhere discussions on the subject of religion.   Be-
sides an immense theological literature, exclusively
devoted to the matter, he would encounter the term
at every turn in the philosophical and social
writings of the time.   He would find a vast number
of treatises, and innumerable shorter works and
articles in periodical publications, devoted to discussions connected with the subject and to almost
every aspect of the great number of questions more
or less intimately associated with it.   But for one
thing he would search in vain.   He would probably
be unable anywhere to discover any satisfactory
definition of this term "religion" which all the
writers are so constantly using, or any general
evidence that those who carried on the discussions
had any definite view as to the function in our
social development of the beliefs they disputed
about, if, indeed, they considered it necessary to
hold that they had any function at all.

He would probably find, at a very early stage,
that all the authorities could not possibly intend the
word in the same sense.   At the one extreme he
would find that there was a certain class of beliefs

calling themselves religions, possessed of well-marked characteristics, and undoubtedly influencing in a particular manner great numbers of persons. At the other he would find a class of persons claiming to speak in the name of science, repudiating all the main features of these, and speaking of a true religion which would survive all that they held to be false in them, *i.e.* all that the others held to be essential. Between these two camps, he would find an irregular army of persons who seemed to think that the title of religion might be properly applied to any form of belief they might hold, and might choose so to describe. He would hear of the religion of Science, of the religion of Philosophy, of the religion of Humanity, of the religion of Reason, of the religion of Socialism, of Natural Religion, and of many others. In the absence of any definite general conception as to what the function of a religion really was, it would appear to be held possible to apply this term to almost any form of belief (or unbelief), with equal propriety.

If he attempted at last to draw up a list of some representative definitions formulated by leading authorities representing various views, he would find the definitions themselves puzzling to an extraordinary degree. It might run somewhat as follows :—

CURRENT DEFINITIONS OF RELIGION

Seneca.—To know God and imitate Him.

Kant.—Religion consists in our recognising all our duties as Divine commands.

Ruskin.—Our national religion is the performance of Church ceremonies, and preaching of soporific truths (or untruths) to keep the mob quietly at work while we amuse ourselves.

Matthew Arnold.—Religion is morality touched by emotion.

Comte.—The Worship of Humanity.

Alexander Bain.—The religious sentiment is constituted by the Tender Emotion, together with Fear, and the Sentiment of the Sublime.

Edward Caird.—A man's religion is the expression of his ultimate attitude to the Universe, the summed-up meaning and purport of his whole consciousness of things.

Hegel.—The knowledge acquired by the Finite Spirit of its essence as an Absolute Spirit.

Huxley.—Reverence and love for the Ethical idea, and the desire to realise that ideal in life.

Froude.—A sense of responsibility to the Power that made us.

Mill.—The essence of Religion is the strong and earnest direction of the emotions and desires towards an ideal object, recognised as of the highest excellence, and as rightly paramount over all selfish objects of desire.

Gruppe.—A belief in a State or in a Being which, properly speaking, lies outside the sphere of human striving and attainment, but which can be brought into this sphere in a particular way, namely, by sacrifices, ceremonies, prayers, penances, and self-denial.

Carlyle.—The thing a man does practically believe ; the thing a man does practically lay to heart, and know for certain, concerning his vital relations to this mysterious Universe and his duty and destiny therein.

The Author of " Natural Religion."—Religion in its elementary state is what may be described as habitual and permanent admiration.

Dr. Martineau.—Religion is a belief in an everlasting God ; that is, a Divine mind and will, ruling the Universe, and holding moral relations with mankind.

The perplexity of our imaginary visitor at finding such a list grow under his hand (and it might be almost indefinitely prolonged) could well be conceived. It would seem almost inevitable that he must sooner or later be driven to conclude that he was dealing with a class of phenomena, the key to which he did not possess.

H

If we can now conceive such an observer able to
look at the whole matter from an outside and quite
independent point of view, there is a feature of the
subject which might be expected ultimately to impress itself upon his imagination. The one idea
which would slowly take possession of his mind
would be that underneath all these vast series of
phenomena with which he was confronted, he beheld
man in some way in conflict with his own reason.
The evidence as to this conflict would be unmistakable, and all the phenomena connected with
it might be seen to group themselves naturally under
one head. It would be perceived that it was these
forms of religious belief which had supplied the
motive power in an extraordinary struggle which
man had apparently carried on throughout his whole
career against forces set in motion by his own
mind—a struggle, grim, desperate, and tragic, which
would stand out as one of the most pronounced
features of his history.

From the point at which science first encountered
him emerging from the obscurity of prehistoric times,
down into the midst of contemporary affairs, it would
be seen that this struggle had never ceased. It had
assumed, and was still assuming, various forms, and
different symbols at different times represented, more
or less imperfectly, the opposing forces. Supersti-
tion and Knowledge, the Ecclesiastical and the Civil,
Church and State, Dogma and Doubt, Faith and
Reason, the Sacred and the Profane, the Spiritual
and the Temporal, Religion and Science, Super-
naturalism and Rationalism, these are some of the
terms which would be found to have expressed
sometimes fully, sometimes only partially, the forces

in opposition.   Not only would the conflict be perceived to be still amongst us, but its dominant
influence would be distinguished beneath all the
complex social phenomena of the time, and even
behind those new forces unloosed by the social
revolution which was filling the period in which the
current generation were living.

One of the most remarkable features which the
observer could not fail to notice in connection with
these religions would be, that under their influence
man would seem to be possessed of an instinct, the
like of which he would not encounter anywhere else.
This instinct, under all its forms, would be seen to
have one invariable characteristic.   Moved by it,
man would appear to be always possessed by the
desire to set up sanctions for his individual conduct,
which would appear to be *Super*-natural against
those which were natural, sanctions which would
appear to be *ultra*-rational against those which were
simply rational.   Everywhere he would find him
clinging with the most extraordinary persistence to
ideas and ideals which regulated his life under the
influence of these religions, and ruthlessly punishing
all those who endeavoured to convince him that
these conceptions were without foundation in fact.
At many periods in human history also, he would
have to observe that the opinion had been entertained by considerable numbers of persons, that a
point had at length been reached, at which it was
only a question of time, until human reason finally
dispelled the belief in those unseen powers which
man held in control over himself.   But he would
find this anticipation never realised.   Dislodged
from one position, the human mind, he would

observe, had only taken up another of the same kind which it continued once more to hold with the same unreasoning, dogged, and desperate persistence.

Strangest sight of all, the observer, while he would find man in every other department of life continually extolling his reason, regarding it as his highest possession, and triumphantly revelling in the sense of power with which it equipped him, would here see him counting as his bitterest enemies worthy of the severest punishment, all who suggested to him that he should, in these matters, walk according to its light. He would find that the whole department of speculative and philosophical thought which represented the highest intellectual work of the race for an immense period, furnished an extraordinary spectacle. It would present the appearance of a territory, along whose frontiers had been waged, without intermission, a war, deadly and desolating as any the imagination could conceive. Even the imperfect descriptions of this conflict from time to time by some of the minds which had taken part on one side in it would be very striking. "I know of no study," says Professor Huxley, "which is so unutterably saddening as that of the evolution of humanity as it is set forth in the annals of history. Out of the darkness of prehistoric ages, man emerges with the marks of his lowly origin strong upon him. He is a brute, only more intelligent than other brutes; a blind prey to impulses, which as often as not lead him to destruction; a victim to endless illusions which make his mental existence a terror and a burthen, and fill his physical life with barren toil and battle. He attains a certain degree of com-

fort, and develops a more or less workable theory of
life in such favourable situations as the plains of
Mesopotamia, or of Egypt, and then, for thousands
and thousands of years, struggles with varying fortunes, attended by infinite wickedness, bloodshed,
and misery, to maintain himself at this point against
the greed and the ambition of his fellow-men. He
makes a point of killing and otherwise persecuting
all those who first try to get him to move on ; and
when he has moved a step farther, foolishly confers
post-mortem deification on his victims. He exactly
repeats the process with all who want to move a
step yet farther." [1] This territory of the intellect
would, in fact, present all the appearances of a
battle-field, stained with the blood of many victims,
singed with the flames of martyrdom, and eloquent
of every form of terror and punishment that human
ingenuity had been able to devise.

And he would notice, as many of those who
fought in the ranks did not, the note of failure which
resounded through all that region of higher human
thought which we call philosophy, the profound air
of more or less unconscious melancholy which sat
upon many of the more far-seeing champions on the
side of human reason, and the—at times scarcely
concealed—sense of hopelessness of any decisive
triumph for their cause displayed by some of these
champions, even while their followers of less insight
were ever and anon hailing all the signs of final
victory.

There is not, it is believed, anything which is
unreal or exaggerated in this view of one of the
chief phases of human evolution. The aim has been

[1] " Agnosticism," *Nineteenth Century*, February 1889.

to look at the facts just as they might be expected
to present themselves to an observer who could thus
regard them from the outside, and with a mind quite
free from all prepossession. He would be able to
perceive the real proportions of this stupendous conflict; he would be able to see that both sides regarded it from merely a partisan standpoint, neither
of them possessing any true perception of its nature
or dimensions, or of its relationship to the development the race is undergoing. If it is profitless for
science to approach the examination of religious
phenomena from the direction in which it is usually
approached by a large class of religious writers, it
is also apparently none the less idle and foolish to
attempt to dismiss the whole subject as if it merely
furnished an exhibition of some perverse and meaningless folly and fury in man. Many of the ideas
concerning the origin of religions, insists De la
Saussaye truly, need only to be mentioned to have
their insufficiency realised. "Such is, for instance,
that formerly popular explanation which regarded
religion as a human discovery sprung from the
cunning deception of priests and rulers. Another
opinion not less insipid, though at present sometimes
regarded as the highest philosophy, is that which
declares religion to be a madness, a pathological
phenomenon closely allied with neurosis and
hysteria." [1] The phenomena in question are on such
a gigantic scale, and the instinct which finds an
expression therein is so general, so persistent, and so
deep-seated, that they cannot be lightly passed over
in this way. In the eyes of the evolutionist they

---

[1] *Manual of the Science of Religion,* by P. D. C. De La Saussaye,
translated from the German, by B. S. Colyer-Fergusson, 1891.

must have some meaning, they must be associated with some wide-reaching law of our social development as yet unenunciated.

The one fact which stands out clear above it all is that the forces against which man is engaged throughout the whole course of the resulting struggle are none other than those enlisted against him by his reason. As in Calderon's tragic story the unknown figure, which, throughout life, is everywhere in conflict with the individual whom it haunts, lifts the mask at last to disclose to the opponent his own features, so here underneath these religious phenomena we see man throughout his career engaged in a remorseless and relentless struggle in which the opponent proves to be none other than his own reason. Throughout all the centuries in which history has him in view we witness him driven by a profound instinct which finds expression in his religions unmistakably recognising a hostile force of some kind in his own reason.[1]

This is the spectacle which demands our attention. This is the conflict the significance of which in human evolution it is necessary to bring out into the fullest

---

[1] It is a remarkable and interesting fact that the two sides in this conflict, even under all the forms and freedom of modern life where the fullest scope is allowed for every kind of inquiry, still seem to recognise each other intuitively as opponents. Mr. Galton, as the result of his inquiries into the personal and family history of scientific men in England, says that it is a fact that, in proportion to the pains bestowed on their education, sons of clergymen rarely take the lead in science. The pursuit of science, he considers, must be uncongenial to the priestly character. He says that in his own experience of the councils of scientific societies it is very rare to find clergymen thereon. Out of 660 separate appointments clergymen held only sixteen, or one in forty, and these were in nearly every case attached to subdivisions of science with fewest salient points to jar against dogma.—*English Men of Science, their Nature and Nurture*, by F. Galton.

and clearest light.   It is a conflict, the meaning of
which has been buried for over two thousand years
under the fierce controversy (not less partisan and
unscientific on the one side than on the other) which
has been waged over it.   Goethe was not speaking
with a poet's exaggeration, but with a scientific insight in advance of his time when he asserted of it,
that it is " the deepest, nay, the one theme of the
world's history to which all others are subordinate." [1]

[1] Vide *The Social Philosophy and Religion of Comte,* by E. Caird,
LL.D., p. 160.

CHAPTER V

THE FUNCTION OF RELIGIOUS BELIEFS IN THE EVOLUTION OF SOCIETY

SINCE science first seriously directed her attention to the study of social phenomena, the interest of workers has been arrested by the striking resemblances between the life of society and that of organic growths in general. We have, accordingly, had many elaborate parallels drawn by various scientific writers between the two, and "the social organism" has become a familiar expression in a certain class of literature. It must be confessed, however, that these comparisons have been, so far, neither as fruitful nor as suggestive as might naturally have been expected. The generalisations and abstractions to which they have led, even in the hands of so original a thinker as Mr. Herbert Spencer, are often, it must be acknowledged, forced and unsatisfactory ; and it may be fairly said that a field of inquiry which looked at the outset in the highest degree promising has, on the whole, proved disappointing.

Yet that there is some analogy between the social life and organic life in general, history and experience most undoubtedly suggest. The pages of the historian seem to be filled with pictures of organic life, over the moving details of which the biologist instinctively lingers. We see social systems born in silence and obscurity. They develop beneath our eyes. They make progress until they exhibit a certain maximum vitality. They gradually decline, and finally disappear, having presented in the various stages certain well-marked phases which invariably accompany the development and dissolution of organic life wheresoever encountered. It may be observed too that this idea of the life, growth, and decline of peoples is deeply rooted. It is always present in the mind of the historian. It is to be met with continually in general literature. The popular imagination is affected by it. It finds constant expression in the utterances of public speakers and of writers in the daily press, who, ever and anon, remind us that our national life, or, it may be, the life of our civilisation, must reach, if it has not already reached, its stage of maximum development, and that it must decline like others which have preceded it. That social systems are endowed with a definite principle of life seems to be taken for granted. Yet: What is this principle? Where has it its seat? What are the laws which control the development and decline of those so-called organic growths? Nay, more: What is the social organism itself? Is it the political organisation of which we form part? Or is it the race to which we belong? Is it our civilisation in general? Or, is it, as some writers would seem to imply, the whole human family in process of evolution? It must be confessed that the literature of our time furnishes no satisfactory answers to a large class of questions of this kind.

It is evident that if we are ever to lay broadly

and firmly the foundations of a science of human society, that there is one point above others at which attention must be concentrated. The distinguishing feature of human history is the social development the race is undergoing. But the characteristic and exceptional feature of this development is the relationship of the individual to society. We have seen in the preceding chapters that fundamental organic conditions of life render the progress of the race possible only under conditions which have never had, and which have not now, any sanction from the reason of a great proportion of the individuals who submit to them. The interests of the individual and those of the social organism, in the evolution which is proceeding, are not either identical or capable of being reconciled, as has been necessarily assumed in all these systems of ethics which have sought to establish a rational sanction for individual conduct. The two are fundamentally and inherently irreconcilable, and a large proportion of the existing individuals at any time have, as we saw, no personal interest whatever in this progress of the race, or in the social development we are undergoing. Strange to say, however, man's reason, which has apparently given him power to suspend the onerous conditions to which he is subject, has never produced their suspension. His development has continued with unabated pace throughout history, and it is in full progress under our eyes.

The pregnant question with which we found ourselves confronted was, therefore: What has then become of human reason? It would appear that the answer has, in effect, been given. The central feature of human history, the meaning of which neither science nor philosophy has hitherto fully recognised, is, apparently, the struggle which man, throughout the whole period of his social development, has carried on to effect the subordination of his own reason. The motive power in this struggle has undoubtedly been supplied by his religious beliefs. The conclusion towards which we seem to be carried is, therefore, that the function of these beliefs in human evolution must be to provide a *super-rational* sanction for that large class of conduct in the individual, necessary to the maintenance of the development which is proceeding, but for which there can never be, in the nature of things, any *rational* sanction.

The fact has been already noticed that evolutionary science is likely in our day to justify, as against the teaching of past schools of thought, one of the deepest and most characteristic of social instincts, viz. that which has consistently held the theories of that large group of philosophical writers who have aimed at establishing a rational sanction for individual conduct in society——a school which may be said to have culminated in England in " utilitarianism" ——as being on the whole (to quote the words of Mr. Lecky) "profoundly immoral."[1] It would appear that science must in the end also justify another instinct equally general, and also in direct opposition to a widely prevalent intellectual conception which is characteristic of our time.

From the beginning of the nineteenth century, and more particularly since Comte published his *Philosophie Positive*, an increasingly large number of minds in France, Germany, and England (not necessarily, or even chiefly, those adhering to Comte's

[1] *History of European Morals*, vol. i. pp. 2, 3.

general views) have questioned the essentiality of the supernatural element in religious beliefs. In England a large literature has gradually arisen on the subject; and the vogue of books like *Natural Religion*, attributed to Professor J. R. Seeley, and others in which the subject has been approached from different standpoints, has testified to the interest which this view has excited. A large and growing intellectual party in our midst hold, in fact, the belief that the religion of the future must be one from which the super-rational element is eliminated.

Now, if we have been right so far, it would appear that one of the first results of the application of the methods and conclusions of biological science to human society must be to render it clear that the advocates of these views, like the adherents of that larger school of thought which has sought to find a rational basis for individual conduct in society, are in pursuit of something which can never exist. There can never be, it would appear, such a thing as a rational religion. The essential element in all religious beliefs must apparently be the *ultra*-rational sanction which they provide for social conduct. When the fundamental nature of the problem involved in our social evolution is understood, it must become clear that that general instinct which may be distinguished in the minds of men around us is in the main correct, and that :—

No form of belief is capable of functioning as a religion in the evolution of society which does not provide an ultra-rational sanction for social conduct in the individual.

In other words :—

A rational religion is a scientific impossibility,

representing from the nature of the case an inherent contradiction of terms.

The significance of this conclusion will become evident as we proceed. It opens up a new and almost unexplored territory. We come, it would appear, in sight of the explanation why science, if social systems are organic growths, has hitherto failed to enunciate the laws of their development, and has accordingly left us almost entirely in the dark as to the nature of the developmental forces and tendencies at work beneath the varied and complex political and social phenomena of our time. The social system which constitutes an organic growth, endowed with a definite principle of life, and unfolding itself in obedience to laws which may be made the subject of exact study, is something quite different from that we have hitherto had vaguely in mind. It is not the political organisation of which we form part ; it is not the race to which we belong ; it is not even the whole human family in process of evolution. It would appear that :—

The organic growth endowed with a definite principle of life, and unfolding itself in obedience to law, is the social system or type of civilisation founded on a form of religious belief.

It would also appear that it may be stated as a law that :—

Throughout the existence of this system there is maintained within it a conflict of two opposing forces ; the disintegrating principle represented by the rational self-assertiveness of the individual units ; the integrating principle represented by a religious belief providing a sanction for social conduct which is always of necessity ultra-rational, and the function of which is to secure in the stress of evolution the continual subordination of the interests of the individual units to the larger interests of the longer-lived social organism to which they belong.

It is, it would appear, primarily through these social systems that natural selection must reach and act upon the race. It is from the ethical systems upon which they are founded that the resulting types of civilisation receive those specific characteristics which, in the struggle for existence, influence in a preponderating degree the peoples affected by them. It is in these ethical systems, founded on super-rational sanctions, and in the developments which they undergo, that we have the seat of a vast series of vital phenomena unfolding themselves under the control of definite laws which may be made the subject of study. The scientific investigation of these phenomena is capable, as we shall see, of throwing a flood of light not only upon the life-history of our Western civilisation in general, but upon the nature of the developmental forces under-lying the complex social and political movements actually in progress in the world around us.

But before following up this line of inquiry, let us see if the conclusion to which we have been led respecting the nature of the element common to all religious beliefs can be justified when it is confronted with actual facts. Are we thus, it may be asked, able to unearth from beneath the enormous over-growth of discussion and controversy to which this subject has given rise, the essential element in all religions, and to lay down a simple, but clear and concise principle upon which science may in future proceed in dealing with the religious phenomena of mankind?

It is evident, from what has been said, that our definition of a religion, in the sense in which alone science is concerned with religion as a social phenomenon, must run somewhat as follows :—

A religion is a form of belief, providing an ultra-rational sanction for that large class of conduct in the individual where his interests and the interests of the social organism are antagonistic, and by which the former are rendered subordinate to the latter in the general interests of the evolution which the race is undergoing.

We have here the principle at the base of all religions. Any religion is, of course, more than this to its adherents: for it must necessarily maintain itself by what is often a vast system of beliefs and ordinances requiring acts and observances which only indirectly contribute to the end in question, by assisting to uphold the principles of the religion. It is these which tend to confuse the minds of many observers. With them we are not here concerned; they more properly fall under the head of theology.

Let us see, therefore, if this element of a super-rational sanction for conduct has been the characteristic feature of all religions, from those which have influenced men in a state of low social development up to those which now play so large a part in the life of highly civilised peoples; whether, despite recent theories to the contrary, there is to be discerned no tendency in those beliefs which are obviously still influencing large numbers of persons to eliminate it.

Beginning with man at the lowest stage at which

his habits have been made a subject of study, we are met by a curious and conflicting mass of evidence respecting his religious beliefs.   The writers and observers whose opinions have been recorded are innumerable ; but they may be said to be divided into two camps on a fundamental point under discussion.   In no stage of his development, in no society, and in no condition of society, is man found without religion of some sort, say one side. Whole societies of men and entire nations have existed without anything which can be described as a religion, say the other side.   In one of the Gifford Lectures, Mr. Max Müller well describes the confusion existing among those who have undertaken to inform us on the subject.   " Some missionaries," he says, " find no trace of religion where anthropologists see the place swarming with ghosts and totems and fetishes ; while other missionaries discover deep religious feelings in savages whom anthropologists declare perfectly incapable of anything beyond the most primitive sensuous perception." [1] He goes on to show how these two parties occasionally change sides.   " When the missionary," he declares, " wants to prove that no human being can be without some spark of religion, he sees religion everywhere, even in what is called totemism and fetishism ; while if he wants to show how necessary it is to teach and convert these irreligious races he cannot paint their abject state in too strong colours, and he is apt to treat even their belief in an invisible and nameless God as mere hallucination.   Nor is the anthropologist free from such temptations.   If he wants to prove that, like the child, every race of

[1] *Natural Religion* (Gifford Lectures), p. 85.

I

men was at one time atheistic, then neither totems, nor fetishes, nor even prayers or sacrifices are any proof in his eyes of an ineradicable religious instinct." [1]

The dispute is an old one, and examples of the differences of opinion and statement referred to by Mr. Max Müller will be found in books like Sir John Lubbock's *Origin of Civilisation* and *Prehistoric Times,* Tylor's *Primitive Culture* and *Researches into the Early History of Mankind,* Quatrefages' *L'Espèce Humaine,* and the more recent writings of Roskoff, Professor Gruppe, and others. In the considerable number of works which continually issue from the press, dealing with the habits and beliefs of the lower races of men, this feature is very marked. A recent criticism of one of these (Mr. H. L. Roth's *Aborigines of Tasmania*) in *Nature* concludes : " Such is the nature of the evidence bearing on the religious ideas of the Tasmanians, which Mr. Roth has collected so carefully and so conscientiously. Nothing can be more full of contradictions, more doubtful, more perplexing. Yet, with such materials, our best anthropologists and sociologists have built up their systems. . . . There is hardly any kind of religion which could not be proved to have been the original religion of the Tasmanians." And it is even added that the evidence would serve equally well to show that the Tasmanians were " without any religious ideas or ceremonial usages." [2] Underlying all this, there is, evidently, a state of chaos as regards general principles. Different writers and observers, when they speak of the religion of lower

---

[1] *Natural Religion* (Gifford Lectures), p. 87.
[2] Vide *Nature,* 18th September 1890.

races of men, do not refer to the same thing ; they
have themselves often no clear conception of what
they mean by the expression. They do not know,
in short, what to look for as the essential element in
a religion.

Now, there is one universal and noteworthy
feature of the life of primitive man which a comparative study of his habits has revealed. " No
savage," says Sir John Lubbock, " is free. All over
the world his daily life is regulated by a complicated
and apparently most inconvenient set of customs as
forcible as laws." [1]   We are now beginning to understand that it is these customs of savage man, strange
and extraordinary as they appear to us, that in great
measure take the place of the legal and moral codes
which serve to hold society together and contribute to
its further development in our advanced civilisations.
The whole tendency of recent anthropological science
is to establish the conclusion that these habits and
customs, " as forcible as laws," either have or had,
directly or indirectly, a utilitarian function to perform
in the societies in which they exist.   Mr. Herbert
Spencer and others have already traced in many
cases the important influence in the evolution of
early society of those customs, habits, and ceremonies
of savage man which at first sight often appear so
meaningless and foolish to us ; and though this
department of science is still young, there is no
doubt as to the direction in which current research
therein is leading us.

But if, on the one hand, we find primitive man
thus everywhere under the sway of customs which
we are to regard as none other than the equivalent

[1] *Origin of Civilisation*, p. 301.

of the legal and moral codes of higher societies; and if, on the other hand, we find these customs everywhere as forcible as laws, how, it may be asked, are those unwritten laws of savage society enforced? The answer comes prompt and without qualification. They are everywhere enforced in one and the same way. Observance of them is invariably secured by the fear of consequences from an agent which is always supernatural. This agent may, and does, assume a variety of forms, but one characteristic it never loses. It is always, supernatural. We have here the explanation of the conflict of opinions regarding the religions of primitive man. Some writers assume that he is without religion because he is without a belief in a Deity. Others because his Deities are all evil. But, if we are right so far, it is not necessarily a belief in a Deity, or in Deities which are not evil, that we must look for as constituting the essential element in the religions of primitive men. The one essential and invariable feature must be a supernatural sanction of some kind for acts and observances which have a social significance. This sanction we appear always to have. We are never without the supernatural in some form. The essential fact which underlies all the prolonged and complicated controversy which has been waged over this subject was once put, with perhaps more force than reverence, by Professor Huxley into a single sentence. " There are savages without God in any proper sense of the word, but there are none without ghosts,"[1] said he; and the generalisation, however it may have been intended, expresses in effective form the one fundamental

---

[1] *Lay Sermons and Addresses*, p. 163.

truth in the discussion with which science is concerned. It is the supernatural agents, the deities, spirits, ghosts, with which primitive man peoples the air, water, rocks, trees, his dwellings and his implements, which everywhere provide the ultimate sanction used to enforce conduct which has a social significance of the kind in question. Whatever qualities these agents may be supposed to possess or to lack, one attribute they always have ; they are invariably supernatural.

When we leave savage man, and rise a step higher to those societies which have made some progress towards civilisation, we find the prevailing religions still everywhere possessing the same distinctive features ; they are always associated with social conduct, and they continue to be invariably founded on a belief in the supernatural. In the religion of the ancient Egyptians, we encounter this element at every point. Professor Tiele says that the two things which were specially characteristic of it were the worship of animals and the worship of the dead. The worship of the dead took the foremost place. "The animals worshipped—originally nothing but fetishes which they continued to be for the great majority of the worshippers—were brought by the doctrinal expositions, and by the educated classes, into connection with certain particular Gods, and thus came to be regarded as the terrestrial incarnation of these Gods." The belief in the supernatural was the characteristic feature of the religion of the ancient Chinese, and this element has survived unchanged in it, through all the developments it has undergone down to our own day, as well as in the other forms of religious belief which influence

the millions of the Celestial empire at the present
time. The religion of the ancient Assyrians presents
the same essential features. It was a polytheism
with a large number of deities who were objects of
adoration. We already find in it some idea of a
future life, and of rewards and punishments therein,
the latter varying according to different degrees of
wickedness in this life.

In the religions of the early Greeks and Romans,
representing the forms of belief prevalent amongst
peoples who eventually attained to the highest state
of civilisation anterior to our own, we have features
of peculiar interest. The religion of the prehistoric
ancestors of both peoples was in all probability a
form of ancestor worship. The isolated family ruled
by the head, with, as a matter of course, absolute
power over the members, was the original unit alike
in the religious and political systems of these peoples.
At the death of some all-powerful head of this kind,
his spirit was held in awe, and, as generations went
on, the living master of the house found himself ruling simply as the vicegerent of the man from whom
he had inherited his authority. Thus arose the
family religion which was the basis of the Greek and
Latin systems, all outside the family religion being
regarded as aliens or enemies. As the family expanded in favourable circumstances into a related
group (the Latin *gens*), and the *gens* in turn into
clans (*phratriai*), and these again into tribes (*phylai*),
an aggregate of which formed the city state or *polis*,
the idea of family relationship remained the characteristic feature of the religion. All the groups,
including the *polis*, were, as Sir G. W. Cox points
out, religious societies, and the subordinate fellow-

ships were " religious with an intensity scarcely to
us conceivable."   In the development which such a
system underwent among the early Romans—a
system hard, cruel, and unpitying, which necessarily
led to the treatment of all outsiders as enemies or
aliens fit only to be made slaves of or tributaries—
we had the necessary religion for the people who
eventually made themselves masters of the world,
and in whom the military type of society ultimately
culminated.

But if it is asked, what the sanction was behind
the religious requirements of these social groups
" religious with an intensity scarcely to us conceivable," the answer is still the same.   There is no
qualification.   It is still invariably supernatural,
using this term in the sense of ultra-rational.   The
conception of the supernatural has become a higher
one than that which prevailed amongst primitive
men, and the development in this direction may be
distinguished actually in progress, but the belief in
this sanction survives in all its force.   The religions of
ancient Greece and Rome at the period of their highest
influence drew their strength everywhere from the
belief in the supernatural, and it has to be observed
that their decay dated from, and progressed *pari
passu* with, the decay of this belief.   The Roman
religion which so profoundly influenced the development of Roman civilisation derived its influence
throughout its history from the belief in the minds
of men that its rules and ordinances had a supernatural origin.   Summarising its characteristics Mr.
Lecky says : " It gave a kind of official consecration
to certain virtues and commemorated special instances in which they had been displayed ; its local

character strengthened patriotic feeling, its worship of the dead fostered a vague belief in the immortality of the soul ; it sustained the supremacy of the father in the family, surrounded marriage with many imposing ceremonies, and created simple and reverent characters profoundly submissive to an over-ruling Providence and scrupulously observant of sacred rites." [1]   A belief in the supernatural was in fact everywhere present, and it constituted the,essential element of strength in the Roman religion.

If we turn again to Mohammedanism and Buddhism, forms of belief influencing large numbers of men at the present day outside our own civilisation, we still find these essential features.   The same sanction for conduct is always present. ˙The essence of Buddhist morality Mr. Max Müller states to be a belief in *Karma*, that is, of work done in this or a former life which must go on producing effects. " We are born as what we deserve to be born ; we are paying our penalty or receiving our reward in this life for former acts.   This makes the sufferer more patient ; for he feels that he is wiping out an old debt ; while the happy man knows that he is living on the interest of his capital of good works, and that he must try to lay by more capital for a future life." [2]   We have only to look for a moment to see that we have in this the same ultra-rational sanction for conduct.   There is and can be no proof of such a theory ; on the contrary, it assumes a cause operating in a manner altogether beyond the tests of reason and experience.[3]

---

[1] *History of European Morals,* vol. i. pp. 176, 177.
[2] *Natural Religion,* p. 112.
[3] See Note, p. 73.

We may survey the whole field of man's religions in societies both anterior to, and contemporaneous with our modern civilisation, and we shall find that all religious beliefs possess these characteristic features. There is no exception. Everywhere these beliefs are associated with conduct, having a social significance ; and everywhere the ultimate sanction which they provide for the conduct which they prescribe is, a super-rational one.

Coming at last to the advanced societies of the present day, we are met by a condition of things of great interest. The facts which appeared so confusing in the last chapter now fall into place with striking regularity. The observer remarks at the outset that there exist now, as at other times in the world's history, forms of belief intended to regulate conduct in which a super-rational sanction has no place. But, with no want of respect for the persons who hold these views, he finds himself compelled to immediately place such beliefs on one side. None of them, he notes, has *proved* itself to be a religion ; none of them can so far claim to have influenced and moved large masses of men in the manner of a religion. He can find no exception to this rule. If he desired to accept any one of them as a religion he notes that he would be constrained to do so merely on the *ipse dixit* of the small group of persons who chose so to describe it.

When we turn, however, to these forms of belief which are unquestionably influencing men in the manner of a religion, we have to mark that they have one pronounced and universal characteristic. The sanction they offer for the conduct they prescribe is unmistakably always a super-rational one.

We may regard the whole expanse of our modern world and we shall have to note that there is no exception to this rule. Nay, more, we shall have to acknowledge, if we keep our minds free from confusion, that there is no tendency whatever to eliminate the super-rational element from religions. There is really no lesson of the history of the Christian religion clearer or more striking than that which illustrates this law. It has been correctly pointed out that whatever opinion we may hold of the decisions of Christianity respecting the ecclesiastical heresies of the early centuries "it is at least clear that they were not in the nature of explanations. They were, in fact, precisely the reverse. They were the negation of explanations. The various heresies which it combated were, broadly speaking, all endeavours to bring the mystery (of the Trinity) as far as possible into harmony with contemporary speculations, Gnostic, Neo-Platonic, or Rationalising, to relieve it from this or that difficulty : in short, to do something towards 'explaining' it." [1] But the Christian Church consistently rejected all rationalising explanations. It may be perceived, if we look closely, that we have to distinguish the same law underlying religious controversies down into our own time. Individuals may lose faith, may withhold belief, and may found parties of their own ; but among the religions themselves we shall find no evidence of any kind of movement or law of development in the direction of eliminating the ultra-rational. On the contrary, however these existing religious beliefs may differ from each other, or from the religions of the past, they have the

[1] A. J. Balfour, *Foundations of Belief,* p. 279.

one feature in common that they all assert uncompromisingly, that the essential doctrines which they teach are beyond reason, that the rules of conduct which they enjoin have an ultra-rational sanction, and that right and wrong are right and wrong by divine or supernatural enactment outside of, and independent of, any other cause whatever.

This is true of every form of religion that we see influencing men in the world around us. The supernatural element in religion, laments Mr. Herbert Spencer, "survives in great strength down to our own day. Religious creeds, established and dissenting, all embody the belief that right and wrong are right and wrong simply in virtue of divine enactment."[1] This is so : but not apparently because of some meaningless instinct in man. It is so in virtue of a fundamental law of our social evolution. It is not that men perversely reject the light set before them by that school of ethics which has found its highest expression in Mr. Herbert Spencer's theories. It is simply that the deep-seated instincts of society have a truer scientific basis than our current science.

Finally, if our inquiry so far has led us to correct conclusions, we have the clue to a large class of facts which has attracted the notice of many observers, but which has hitherto been without scientific explanation. We see now why it is that, as Mr. Lecky asserts, "all religions which have governed mankind have done so . . . by speaking, as common religious language describes it, to the heart,"[2] and not to the intellect ; or, as an advocate of Christianity has recently put it—A religion makes its way not by

[1] *Data of Ethics*, p. 50.
[2] *History of European Morals*, vol. i. p. 58.

argument, or by the rational sanctions which it offers,
" but by an appeal to those fundamental spiritual
instincts of men to which it supremely corresponds." [1]
We see also why, despite the apparent tendency to
the disintegration of religious belief among the intellectual classes at the present day, those who seek
to compromise matters by getting rid of that feature
which is the essential element in all religions make
no important headway ; and why, as a prominent
member of one of the churches has recently remarked,
the undogmatic sects reap the scantiest harvest, while
the dogmatic churches still take the multitude. We
are led to perceive how inherently hopeless and misdirected is the effort of those who try to do what
Camus and Grégoire attempted to make the authors
of the French Revolution do—reorganise Christianity
without believing in Christ. A form of belief from
which the ultra-rational element has been eliminated
is, it would appear, no longer capable of exercising
the function of a religion.

Professor Huxley, some time ago, in a severe
criticism of the " Religion of Humanity " advocated
by the followers of Comte,[2] asserted, in accents which
always come naturally to the individual when he
looks at the drama of human life from his own
standpoint, that he would as soon worship " a wilderness of apes " as the Positivist's rationalised conception of humanity. But the comparison with which
he concluded, in which he referred to the considerable
progress made by Mormonism as contrasted with
Positivism, has its explanation when viewed in the
light of the foregoing conclusions. Mormonism may

---

[1] W. S. Lilly, *Nineteenth Century*, September 1889.
[2] *Nineteenth Century*, February 1889.

be a monstrous form of belief, and one which is undoubtedly destined to be worsted in conflict with the forms of Christianity prevailing round it; yet it is seen that we cannot deny to it the characteristics of a religion. Although, on the other hand, the " Religion of Humanity " advocated by Comte may be, and is, a most exemplary set of principles, we perceive it to be without these characteristics. It is not, apparently, a religion at all. It is, like other forms of belief which do not provide a super-rational sanction for conduct, but which call themselves religions, incapable, from the nature of the conditions, of exercising the functions of a religion in the evolution of society.[1]

[1] It is very interesting to notice how clearly G. H. Lewes, himself a distinguished adherent of Comte, perceived the inherent antagonism between religion and philosophy (the aim of the latter having always been to establish a rational sanction for conduct), and yet without realising the significance of this antagonism in the process of social evolution the race is undergoing. Speaking of the attempt made in the past to establish a " Religious philosophy," he remarks upon its innate impossibility because the doctrines of religion have always been held to have been *revealed*, and therefore beyond and inaccessible to reason. " So that," he says, "metaphysical problems, *the attempted solution of which by Reason constitutes Philosophy*, are solved by Faith and yet the name of Philosophy is retained ! But the very groundwork of Philosophy consists in reasoning, as the groundwork of Religion is Faith. There cannot, consequently, be a Religious Philosophy : it is a contradiction in terms. Philosophy may be occupied about the same problems as Religion ; but it employs altogether different criteria, and depends on altogether different principles. Religion may, and should call in Philosophy to its aid ; but in so doing it assigns to Philosophy only the subordinate office of illustrating, reconciling, or applying its dogmas. This is not a Religious Philosophy, it is Religion *and* Philosophy, the latter stripped of its boasted prerogative of deciding for itself, and allowed only to employ itself in reconciling the decisions of Religion and of Reason" (*History of Philosophy*, vol. i. p. 409). These are words written with true scientific insight. But a clearer perception of the fundamental problem of human evolution might have led the writer to see that the universal instinct of mankind which has recognised that the essential element in a religion is that its doc-

In the religious beliefs of mankind we have not simply a class of phenomena peculiar to the childhood of the race. We have therein apparently the characteristic feature of our social evolution. *These beliefs constitute, in short, the natural and inevitable complement of our reason;* and so far from being threatened with eventual dissolution they are apparently destined to continue to grow with the growth and to develop with the development of society, while always preserving intact and unchangeable the one essential feature they all have in common in the ultra-rational sanction they provide for conduct. And lastly, as we understand how an ultra-rational sanction for the sacrifice of the interests of the individual to those of the social organism has been a feature common to all religions, we see, also, why the conception of sacrifice has occupied such a central place in nearly all beliefs, and why the tendency of religion has ever been to surround this principle with the most impressive and stupendous of sanctions.[1]

trines should be inaccessible to reason, has its foundation in the very nature of the problem our social evolution presents; and that the error of Comte has been in assuming that a set of principles from which this element has been eliminated is capable of performing the functions of a religion.

[1] It is the expression of the antagonism between the interests of the individual and those of the social organism in process of evolution that we have in Kant's conception of the opposition between the inner and outer life, in Green's idea of the antagonism between the natural man and the spiritual man, and in Professor Caird's conception of the differences between self and not self. We would not be precluded from accepting religion in Fichte's sense—as the realisation of universal reason—*if we can understand universal reason involving the conception that the highest good is the furtherance of the evolutionary process the race is undergoing.* But once we have clearly grasped the nature of the characteristic problem human evolution presents we see how absolutely individual rationalism has been precluded from attaining this position: it can only be reached as Kant contemplated—"by a faith of reason which postulates a God to realise it" (*i.e.* the ultra-rational).

To the consideration of the results flowing from this recognition of the real nature of the problem underlying our social development we have now to address ourselves. If we have, in the social system founded on a form of religious belief, the true organic growth with which science is concerned, we must, it would appear, be able then to discover some of the principles of development under the influence of which the social growth proceeds. If it is in the ethical system upon which a social type is founded that we have the seat of a vast series of vital phenomena unfolding themselves in obedience to law, then we must be able to investigate the phenomena of the past and to observe the tendencies of the current time with more profit than the study of either history or sociology has hitherto afforded. Let us see, therefore, with what prospect of success the biologist, who has carried the principles of his science so far into human society, may now address himself to the consideration of the history of that process of life in the midst of which we are living, and which we know under the name of Western Civilisation.

Individuals repudiating ultra-rational sanctions may feel it possible to willingly participate in the cosmic process in progress ; but conclusions often drawn from this involve an incomplete realisation of the fact that the feelings which render it possible are—like our civilisations themselves—the direct product of ethical systems founded on ultra-rational sanctions. We live and move in the midst of the influences of these systems, and it is only by a mental effort of which only the strongest minds are capable that we can even imagine what our action, or the action of others, would be if they were non-existent.

CHAPTER·VI

WESTERN CIVILISATION

To obtain even a general idea of that vast organic growth in the midst of which we are living, and which for want of a better name we call Western Civilisation, it is absolutely necessary that the point of view should be removed to some distance. When this is done the resulting change in aspect is very striking. We are apt to imagine that many of the more obvious features of the society in which we live go to constitute the natural and normal condition of the world ; that they have always existed, and that it is part of the order of things that they should always continue to exist. It is far more difficult than might be imagined for the average mind to realise that the main features of our modern society are quite special in the history of the world ; that institutions which seem a necessary part of our daily life and of our national existence are absolutely new and exceptional ; and that under the outward appearance of stability they are still undergoing rapid change and development.

We have only to look round us to immediately perceive how comparatively recent in origin are many of the most characteristic features of our social life.

Our trades, commerce, and manufactures, our bank-
ing systems, our national debts, our huge systems
of credit, are the growth of scarcely more than two
centuries. The revolution in methods of travel and
means of communication, and our systems of universal
education, are the products of the century in which
we are still living. The capitalism and industrialism
of to-day, and the world market which they seek
to supply, are but recent growths. The immense
revolution which applied science has made in the
modern world dates its beginning scarcely more
than a century back, is still in full progress, and is
yet far from having reached a point at which any
limits whatever can be set to it. Yet all these things
are brought before the mind only with an effort. " It
is," says Sir Henry Maine, " in spite of overwhelming evidence, most difficult for a citizen of Western
Europe to bring thoroughly home to himself the
truth that the civilisation which surrounds him is a
rare exception in the history of the world." [1] It is
a still more difficult task for the observer to realise
that, in point of time, it is all a growth occupying a very small space in the period with which
history deals, and an almost infinitesimal span of
time in the period during which the human race has
existed.

When we bring ourselves to look, from this point
of view, at the times in which we live, we begin to
perceive that no just estimate of the tendencies of
our civilisation, or of the nature of the forces at work
therein, can be arrived at by merely taking into
account those new forces which have been unloosed
amongst us during the last century or two. One of

[1] *Ancient Law*, p. 22.

K

the most characteristic features of the social literature
of our time is, nevertheless, the attempt which is
often made therein to consider our social problems
as if they were the isolated growths of a short period.
It would appear that those who think about these
problems, while rightly perceiving that we in reality
live in the midst of the most rapid change and
progress, forthwith become so impressed with the
magnitude of the change, that they overlook the
connection between the present and the past, and
form no true conception of the depth and strength
of the impression which the centuries, that have
preceded our own, have produced on the age in
which we are living.   The essential unity and continuity of the vital process which has been in progress
in our civilisation from the beginning is almost
entirely lost sight of.   Many of the writers on social
subjects at the present day are like the old school of
geologists ; they seem to think that progress has
consisted in a series of cataclysms.   Some there are
who would almost have us believe that society was
created anew at the period of the French Revolution ;
and in the French nation of the present day we have
the extraordinary spectacle of a whole people who
have cut themselves off from the past in the world
of thought almost as completely as they have done
in the world of politics.   Others see the same destructive, transforming, and recreative influences in
universal suffrage, universal education, the rule of
democracy, and modern socialism, instead of only
the connected features of a vast orderly process of
development unfolding itself according to law.

If then our civilisation is a rare exception in the
history of the world, and if at the same time it is,

and has been from the beginning, in a state of change
and constant development, the question which presents itself at the outset is : What are the characteristics in which this civilisation differs from that
of other peoples, and from the civilisations of the
past ?

When such a comparison is instituted the most
striking and obvious features immediately present
themselves in the great advances which have been
made in the arts of life, in trade, manufactures, and
commerce, in the practical appliances of science, and
the means of communication. But we may, nevertheless, put these features entirely aside for the
present. A little reflection suffices to make it clear
that the civilisation around us does not owe its
existence to these ; but that, on the contrary, these
features, like many others, have had their cause and
origin in certain principles inherent in our civilisation
existing apart in themselves, and serving to distinguish it from the civilisations of other peoples and
other times.

If we look round us we may perceive that,
although the system of civilisation to which we belong
has a clearly defined place amongst the peoples of
the earth, it has really no definite racial or national
boundaries. It is not Teutonic or Celtic or Latin
civilisation. Nor is it German or French or Italian
or Anglo-Saxon. So far as we have any right to
connect it with locality, it might be described as
European civilisation, although this definition would
still be incomplete if not inaccurate. The expression
which is applied most suitably to describe the social
system to which we belong is that in general use,
viz. " Western Civilisation."

Now, viewing this civilisation as a single continuous growth, there can be little doubt as to the point at which its life-history begins. We must go back to the early centuries of our Era. This extraordinary period in the world's history possesses the deepest interest for the scientific mind. At that time a civilisation, not only the most powerful and successful which man had so far evolved, but in which all previous civilisations had found their highest type and expression, had already commenced to die, even though it still possessed all the outward appearance of strength and majesty. It had culminated in a period of extraordinary intellectual activity. Into the century before and that immediately following the Christian era, there are crowded the names of an altogether remarkable number of men who did work of the very highest order in nearly every sphere of intellectual activity then open to the world. Cicero, Varro, Virgil, Catullus, Horace, Lucretius, Ovid, Tibullus, Sallust, Cæsar, Livy, Juvenal, the two Plinys, Seneca, Quintilian, and Tacitus in literature alone are all included in this brief period. They have all left work by which they are still remembered, some of it probably reaching the highest degree of intellectual excellence to which the human mind has ever attained. But the Roman genius had passed its flowering period. Roman civilisation had reached its prime. The organism had ceased to grow, and the vigorous life which had flowed in so many diverse channels throughout the vast body had begun to wane.

We have to note that for some time previously the ethical system upon which the Roman dominion had been built up had begun to decay. It no longer controlled men's minds. "The old religions," says Mr. Froude, speaking of Cæsar's time, "were dead, from the Pillars of Hercules to the Euphrates and the Nile, and the principles upon which human society had been constructed were dead also."[1]   The efforts of successive emperors, beginning with Augustus, to restore old forms, to prop up declining religion, and to revive the spirit of a defunct ethical system, were utterly vain.   Henceforward, amid all the intellectual systems for regulating conduct which the time produced, we have only to watch the progress of those well-marked and well-known symptoms of decay and dissolution which life at a certain stage everywhere presents.

But underneath all this history of death the observer has, outlined before him, a remarkable spectacle.   It is the phenomenon of a gigantic birth. To the scientific mind, there can be no mistaking the signs which accompany the beginning of life, whether it be the birth of the humblest plant, or of a new solar system ; and in the fierce ebullition of life which characterised that little understood period of the world's history, commencing with the first centuries of our era, we have evidently the beginning of a series of vital phenomena of profound scientific interest.

The new force which was born into the world with the Christian religion was, evidently, from the very first, of immeasurable social significance.   The original impetus was immense.   The amorphous vigour of life was so great that several centuries have to pass away before any clear idea can be obtained of even the outlines of the growth which it was

[1] *Cæsar*, by J. A. Froude.

destined to build up out of the dead elements around it. From the beginning the constructive principle of life was unmistakable ; men seemed to be transformed ; the ordinary motives of the individual mind appeared to be extinguished. The new religion evoked, "to a degree before unexampled in the world, an enthusiastic devotion to its corporate welfare, analogous to that which the patriot bears to his country."[1] There sprang from it "a stern, aggressive, and at the same time disciplined enthusiasm, wholly unlike any other that had been witnessed upon earth."[2]

Amid the corruption of the time the new life flourished as a thing apart ; it took the disintegrated units and built them up into the new order, drawing strength from the decay which was in progress around it. When the state at length put forth its influence against it in the persecutions which followed, it only exhibited the altogether uncontrollable nature of the force which was moving the minds of men. The subordination of the materials to the constructive principle of life which was at work amongst them was complete. "There has probably never existed upon earth a community whose members were bound to one another by a deeper or purer affection than the Christians in the days of the persecution," says Mr. Lecky.[3] Self seemed to be annihilated. The boundaries of classes, and even of nationalities and of races, went down before the new affinities which overmastered the strongest instincts of men's minds.

We have to note also that the new force was in

---

[1] W. E. H. Lecky, *History of European Morals*, vol. i. *vide* p. 409, etc.   [2] *Ibid.*   [3] *Ibid.*

no way the product of reason or of the intellect. No impetus came from this quarter. As in all movements of the kind, the intellectual forces of the time were for the most part directly in opposition. The growing point where all the phenomena of life were actively in progress, was buried low down in the under-strata of society amongst the most ignorant and least influential classes. The intellectual scrutiny which had undermined the old faiths saw nothing in the new. So ignorant were men of the nature of the physiological laws to which the social organism is subject, that the intellectual classes were altogether unconscious, both of the nature and of the destiny of the movement which was unfolding itself underneath their eyes. They were either actively hostile or passively contemptuous. There is no fact in the history of the human mind more remarkable, says Mr. Lecky, than the complete unconsciousness of the destinies of Christianity, manifested by writers before the accession of Constantine. " That the greatest religious change in the history of mankind should have taken place under the eyes of a brilliant galaxy of philosophers and historians who were profoundly conscious of the decomposition around them ; that all these writers should have utterly failed to predict the issue of the movement they were observing, and that during the space of three centuries they should have treated as simply contemptible an agency which all men must now admit to have been, for good or evil, the most powerful moral lever that has ever been applied to the affairs of men, are facts well worthy of meditation in every period of religious transition." [1]

[1] *Op. cit.*, vol. i. p. 359.

When the mists with which prejudice and controversy have surrounded this remarkable epoch in the
world's history disappear, it must become clear to
science that what we have in reality to note in the
events of these early centuries is not the empty and
barren fury of controversy and fanaticism, but the
uncontrollable vigour and energy of a social movement of the first magnitude in its initial stage.
There was no suggestion of maturity, or of the vast
consequences which were inherent in the vital process
which was at work.   Scarcely anything can be distinguished at first save the conception of the supernatural constitution of society being launched with
enormous initial energy, and the absolute subordination of the materials to the constructive forces which
were at work amongst them.   The extraordinary
epidemic of asceticism, which at the beginning over-
ran the world, merits much more than the mere
painful curiosity with which so many philosophical
and controversial writers have regarded it.   It marks
in the most striking manner, not only the strength
of the conception of the supernatural, but the extent
of that spirit of utter self-abnegation which had been
born into the world, and which was destined to find
its characteristic social expression only at a later
stage.

The contrast which the ideals of the time presented when compared with those of the past is so
striking that many writers of philosophical insight
still altogether misunderstood the social significance
of this movement; and, looking only upon that
aspect which most readily attracts notice, can scarcely,
even at the present time, bring themselves to speak
tolerantly of it.   Says Mr. Lecky, " A hideous,

sordid, and emaciated maniac without knowledge, without patriotism, without natural affection, passing his life in a long routine of useless and atrocious self-torture, and quailing before the ghastly phantoms of his delirious brain, had become the ideal of nations which had known the writings of Plato and Cicero, and the lives of Socrates and Cato."[1]   No greater mistake can be made than the common one of judging this development, and the larger movement of which it formed a phase, by contemporaneous results. It cannot be properly regarded from such a narrow standpoint.   Its real significance lies in the striking evidence it affords, even at this early stage, of the unexampled vigour of the immature social forces at work.   The writer just quoted has elsewhere shown a truer appreciation of the nature of these forces in speaking of them as those which were subsequently to "stamp their influence on every page of legislation, and direct the whole course of civilisation for a thousand years."

As the development continues we note the growing organisation of the Church, the utter and willing subordination of reason, the slow extinction of every form of independent judgment, the gradual waning, and, with the complete predominance of one of the two conflicting factors in our evolution, the almost entire cessation of every form of intellectual activity in the presence of the tremendous supernatural idea which held possession of the minds of men throughout the Western world.

We reach at length the twelfth century.   All movement, so far, has been in one direction. Western Europe has become a vast theocracy.

[1] *Op. cit.* vol. ii. p. 114.

Implicit obedience to ecclesiastical authority, un-questioning faith in the ultra-rational, the criminality of doubt and of error, is the prevailing note through-out every part of the organisation.   Human history is without any parallel to the life of these centuries, or to the state which society had now reached.   The Church is omnipotent ; her claim is to supremacy in all things, temporal as well as spiritual ; emperors and kings hold their crowns from God as her vassals ; the whole domain of human activity, moral, social, political, and intellectual, is subject to her.   The attainments of the Greek and Roman genius are buried out of sight.   The triumphs of the ancient civilisations are as though they had never existed : they are not only forgotten ; there is simply no organic continuity between the old life and that which has replaced it.

This transformation had been no rapid and fitful development.   A period, longer by some centuries than that separating the present time from the date of the Norman Conquest of England, had passed away ; and in the interval the characters of men and every human institution had been profoundly modified by the movement that had filled the world. With the twelfth and thirteenth centuries, as the other factor in our social evolution begins to assert itself, we have the first stirrings heralding the coming revolution.   In the fifteenth century we at length take our stand, in the period of the Renaissance, on the great watershed which divides the modern world from the old.   No one can have caught the spirit of the evolutionary science of the latter half of the nineteenth century, who can from this point look back over the history of the gigantic movement

which absorbed the entire life of the world for
fourteen centuries, and then forward over its history
in the centuries that intervene between the Renaissance and our own time, without realising the utter
futility of attempting to formulate the principles
which are working themselves out in our modern
civilisation, without taking this religious movement
into account. The evolutionist perceives that it,
in reality, dwarfs and overshadows everything else.
Whatever we may, as individuals, think of the belief
in which it originated, or of the principles upon which
it was founded and upon which it still exists, we are
all alike the product of it; the entire modern world
is but part of the phenomena connected with it.
Science must, sooner or later, recognise that in this
movement we have, under observation, the seat, the
actual vital centre, of that process of organic development which is still unfolding itself in what is called
Western Civilisation.

So far, fourteen centuries of the history of our
civilisation had been devoted to the growth and
development of a stupendous system of other-world-
liness. The conflict against reason had been successful to a degree never before equalled in the
history of the world. The super-rational sanction
for conduct had attained a strength and universality
unknown in the Roman and Greek civilisations.
The state was a divine institution. The ruler held
his place by divine right, and every political office
and all subsidiary power issued from him in virtue of
the same authority. Every consideration of the
present was overshadowed in men's minds by conceptions of a future life, and the whole social and
political system and the individual lives of men

had become profoundly tinged with the prevailing ideas.[1]

To ask at this stage for the fruit of these remarkable centuries, and in the absence thereof to speak of the time as one of death and barrenness, and of the period as the most contemptible in history, is to totally misunderstand the nature of the movement we are dealing with. The period was barren only in the sense that every period of vigorous but immature growth is barren. The fruit was in the centuries to come. Science has yet scarcely learned to look at the question of our social evolution from any standpoint other than that of the rationalism of the individual; whereas, we undoubtedly have in these centuries a period in the lifetime of the social organism when the welfare, *not only of isolated individuals, but of all the individuals of a long series of generations*, was sacrificed to the larger interests of generations at a later and more mature stage. As we turn now to the period which intervenes between the Renaissance and our own time, we have to watch the gradual reassertion of the other factor in our social development. The successive waves of revolution, set in motion by the intellect, which follow each other rapidly from the fourteenth century onwards, have all one feature in common.

The Christian religion possessed from the outset two characteristics destined to render it an evolu-

---

[1] Bluntschli, in his *Theory of the State* (translation published by Clarendon Press) well brings out, in the tables showing the differences between the modern, mediæval, and ancient state, the prevailing features of the Mediæval Theocracy in which the authority of the state was held to be derived from God, and in which it descended from the vicegerent through the various subsidiary authorities to whom it was delegated.

tionary force of the first magnitude. The first was the extraordinary strength of the ultra-rational sanction it provided, which was developed throughout the long period we have been considering. The second was the nature of the ethical system associated with it, which, as we shall see, was at a later stage in suitable conditions calculated to raise the peoples coming under its influence to the highest state of social efficiency ever attained, and to equip them with most exceptional advantages in the struggle for existence with other peoples.

Now, it will have been evident from the last chapter, if the conclusions there arrived at were correct, that we may state it as an historical law that :—

The great problem with which every progressive society stands continually confronted is : How to retain the highest operative ultra-rational sanction for those onerous conditions of life which are essential to its progress ; and at one and the same time to allow the freest play to those intellectual forces which, while tending to come into conflict with this sanction, contribute nevertheless to raise to the highest degree of social efficiency the whole of the members.

From the fifteenth century onwards, the movement we watch in progress amongst the races of Western Europe is in this respect two-sided. Henceforward we have, on the one hand, to note the human mind driven by forces set in motion by itself, ever endeavouring to obtain the fullest opportunity for the utilisation of those advantages with which it was the inherent function of the ethical system upon which our civilisation is founded to equip society. On the other hand we have to watch in conflict with this endeavour a profound instinct of social self-preservation, ever struggling to maintain intact that ultra-rational sanction for social conduct with which the life of every social system is ultimately united.

The first great natural movement, born in due time, of the conflict between these two developmental tendencies was that known in history as the Reformation. But to bring ourselves into a position to appreciate to the full the exceptional importance, from the evolutionist's standpoint, of the development which has been in progress in our civilisation from the sixteenth century onwards, it is desirable, if possible, to get a clear view of those essential features in which our civilisation differs from all others.

It will be remembered that in Chapter II emphasis was laid on the fact that in the period of the Roman Empire we had that particular epoch in the history of society, in which a long-drawn-out stage of human evolution culminated. In the civilisation there developed, we had the highest and most successful expression ever reached of that state of society, in which the struggle for existence is waged mainly between communities organised against each other on a military footing. The natural culminating period of such a stage was that in which universal dominion was obtained, and held for a long period, by one successful community.

It is a curious feature of European history that it should present to us the clearest evidence of the survival amongst the Western peoples, down almost into the time in which we are living, of those ideals of empire which found their natural expression in the ancient civilisations. To the period of the Napoleonic wars, the Roman ideal of empire and conquest can hardly be said to have been regarded by the statesmen or the people of any of the nationalities included in the European family as other than a perfectly legitimate national aspiration. Yet nothing can be clearer to the evolutionist when he comes to understand the nature of the process, in progress throughout our history, than that those ideals have been, and are quite foreign to our civilisation. They are utterly inconsistent with the tendency of the development which is proceeding therein. Let us, therefore, in order to understand the better the nature of the change which is taking place in our modern societies, briefly glance once more at the characteristic features of that type of social life which reached its highest phase in the Roman Empire.

Now, from the beginning it may be noticed that those societies which existed under stress of circumstances as fighting organisations, presented everywhere certain strongly marked features. In their early stage the social relations may be summed up briefly. The individual is of little account ; the men are the warriors of the chief or the state ; the women are the slaves of the men, and the children are the property of the parents. Infanticide is a general custom ; the society is of necessity rudely communistic or socialistic, and the population is kept within due bounds by the simple plan of killing off all undesirable accessions to it.[1] The individual *per se* has few rights " natural " or acquired ; he holds his property and even his life at the mercy of a despotism tempered only by religious forms and customs.

---

[1] Even in the Greek states and amongst the Romans, infanticide generally prevailed, and the act excited no public reprobation.

The high state of civilisation eventually attained to in some of these societies has given rise to many specious comparisons between them and our modern democratic states. But such comparisons are most misleading. The Greek city states were essentially military units, each cherishing its own independence, and, as a rule, seldom remaining long free from war with its neighbours. They preserved unchanged, down to the end, the leading characteristics which the Greek communities presented at the period when history brings us first into contact with them. "Homer," says Mr. Mahaffy, "introduces us to a very exclusive *caste* society, in which the key to the comprehension of all the details depends upon one leading principle—that consideration is due to the members of the caste and even to its dependents, but that beyond its pale even the most deserving are of no account saving as objects of plunder." [1] At a later period the independent organisations of the city states embraced almost every shade of political constitution. In some, what was called a "pure democracy" held rule ; in others, power was in the hands of a narrow oligarchy ; in others, it was exercised by a ruling aristocracy ; in still others it was in the hands of tyrants. But in all of them the ruling classes had a single feature in common—their military origin. They represented the party which had imposed its rule by force on the rest of the community, at best at a comparatively remote period, at worst within living memory. The difference between the ruling class, even in an aristocracy and democracy, was, as Professor Freeman has remarked, simply that in one case the legislative power and

[1] *Social Life in Greece*, by J. P Mahaffy, p. 44.

eligibility to high office was extended to the whole, and in the other confined to a part, *of a class of hereditary burghers.* " In no case did it extend beyond that class ; in no case could the freedman, the foreigner, or even the dependent ally, obtain citizenship by residence, or even by birth in the land. He who was not the descendant of citizen ancestors, could be enfranchised only by special decree of the sovereign assembly." [1] Even in Athens, the citizen " looked down upon the vulgar herd of slaves, freedmen, and unqualified residents, much as his own plebeian fathers had been looked down upon by the old Eupatrides in the days before Kleisthenês and Solôn." [2] As for any conception of duty or responsibility to others outside the community, it did not exist. Morality was of the narrowest and most egotistical kind. It never, among the Greeks, embraced any conception of humanity ; no Greek, says George Henry Lewes, ever attained to the sublimity of such a point of view.[3]

This feature of a large excluded class with a basis of slavery beneath the whole political fabric must never be lost sight of in these ancient military societies. The Greek writers seemed, indeed, to be unable to imagine a condition of social organisation in which there should not be either a large excluded class, or slaves or barbarians, to relieve the ruling class of what they considered the menial and inferior duties of existence.[4]

---

[1] *History of Federal Government* (Greek Federations), vol. i. chap. ii.
[2] *Ibid.*
[3] *History of Philosophy*, vol. i. p. 408.
[4] Professor Freeman held this to be the really weak point of Greek Democracy. " The real special weakness of pure Democracy is that it

In the Roman Empire again we have only the highest example of the military state. Ancient Rome, as already noticed, was a small city state which attained the position it eventually occupied in the world by a process of natural selection, its career from the beginning being a record of incessant fighting, in which at several points its very existence seemed to be at stake. In the Roman Empire, as in the Greek states, an immense proportion of the population were slaves without rights of any kind. Gibbon calculated that in the time of Claudius the slaves were at least equal in numbers to the free inhabitants in the entire Roman world.[1] The highest ambition amongst the leading citizens in the remainder of the Roman population was to serve the state in a military capacity, and to bring about the subjugation of other states and peoples. Universal conquest was the recognised and unquestioned policy of the state. The subjugation of rivals implied something very different from what we have come to understand by the term : it meant compelling other peoples to pour their tribute into Rome. The national policy was in reality but the organised exploitation by force and violence of weaker peoples. Trade and commerce as we know them were unknown to the Romans, and they could not have attained any large development under such an organisation of society. Such

almost seems to require slavery as a necessary condition of its existence. It is hard to conceive that a large body of men, like the qualified citizens of Athens, can ever give so large a portion of their time, as the Athenians did, to the business of ruling and judging, without the existence of an inferior class to relieve them from at least the lowest and most menial duties of their several callings. Slavery, therefore, is commonly taken for granted by Greek political thinkers."

[1] *Vide* chap. ii. *Decline and Fall of the Roman Empire.*

agriculture and manufactures as existed were carried
on mainly by slaves, and occupations connected with
them were regarded as unworthy of free men.   The
higher classes in Rome looked with contempt upon
trade of any kind, and passed laws forbidding their
members to engage therein.   It was the same even
in the freest of the Greek democracies.   One of the
leading features of Attic culture, says Mr. Mahaffy,
" was the contempt of trade, or indeed of any occupation which so absorbed a man as to deprive him
of ample leisure.   Though architects were men of
great position, and obtained large fees, yet in Plato's
Gorgias we have so intellectual a trade as that of
an engineer despised ; and in Aristotle's *Politics*
(p. 1340) we find the philosopher, with deeper wisdom,
censuring the habit of aiming at perfection in instrumental music as lowering to the mind, and turning
the free gentleman into a slavish handicraftsman."
Possibly, he continues, " we may have this feeling
rather strongly represented by aristocratic writers
like Plato and Aristophanes, who felt hurt at trades-
men coming forward prominently in politics ; but
the tone of Athenian life is too marked in this
respect to let us mistake the fact." [1]   The free men
of Rome could hardly be said to work ; they fought
or lived on the produce of fighting.   The rich and
their dependents had obtained their wealth or their
positions directly or indirectly through the incessant
wars ; the rest during a prolonged period lived on
the corn sent as tribute to Rome and distributed
by public demand amongst the citizens.
    As might have been expected in a military com-
munity of the kind, the relationship of the individual

[1] *Social Life in Greece*, by J. P. Mahaffy, chap. ix.

to the state was one of complete subordination—
individual freedom as against the state was unknown.
Religion lent its aid to ennoble the duty of the individual to a military society rather than to his fellows,
and all its authority, like all the best ability of the
community, was pressed into the immediate service of
a military organisation. The military virtues were
predominant; the priesthood was a political office;
patriotism occupied a position in public estimation
which it is difficult nowadays to realise. Cicero but
gave expression in its best form to the spirit which
pervaded the whole fabric of the ancient state, when
he asserted that no man could lay claim to the title
of good who would hesitate to die for his country;
and that the love owed thereto by the citizen was
holier and more profound than that due from him
to his nearest kinsman.

Now what we have to notice in such states is that
as they all originated in successful military enterprise,
it always happened that relatively small communities
or organisations, having at the beginning obtained
power and extended their influence over other peoples,
the members of these original castes thenceforward
regarded themselves as distinct ruling classes within
the social organisation. They secured to themselves
special privileges, and were considered superior to
the great majority of their fellows, whom they forthwith thrust out as an inferior class apart. These
latter, with the immense number of slaves continually
being made in war and by other means, constituted
the foundation upon which the social fabric rested.
The inevitable tendency of successful military enterprise to concentrate power in the hands of a few did
not act to check the organisation of society in the

direction in which it was thus set from the beginning, but served to continually strengthen the position of the ruling classes. The evolutionary forces which we shall have to observe at work amongst ourselves, and affecting to such an extraordinary degree the further development of society, could not operate to any extent in such communities. The great mass of the people under the sway of restrictive laws invented by these military oligarchies in their own interests, were artificially penned off beyond the reach of such forces, and so came in time to accept their reputed inferiority, their restricted rights, and their oppressed condition, as part of the natural order of things.

Progress was, therefore, strictly limited in the military state. All the outward magnificence which was attained by the Roman Empire at the period of its maximum development was, in effect, but the result of the most ruthless centralisation, the most direct and impoverishing exploitation, and the most unbridled individual and class aggrandisement at the expense of immense oppressed populations, largely comprised of slaves. Mr. Frederic Harrison has recently attempted, in an eloquent passage, to describe what Rome must have looked like some seventeen or eighteen hundred years ago when viewed from the tower of the Capitol,[1] and the picture is helpful and suggestive in enabling us to realise more vividly the nature of that social type which culminated in the empire. " This earth," he concludes, " has never seen before or since so prodigious an accumulation of all that is beautiful and rare. The quarries of the world had been emptied to find precious marbles. Forests of exquisite

[1] Vide *Fortnightly Review*, No. cccxvii., New Series.

columns met the gaze, porphyry, purple and green, polished granite, streaked marbles in the hues of a tropical bird, yellow, orange, rosy, and carnation, ten thousand statues, groups of colossi of dazzling Parian or of golden bronze, the work of Greek genius, of myriads of slaves, of unlimited wealth and absolute command. Power so colossal, centralisation so ruthless, luxury so frantic, the world had never seen, and, we trust, can never see again."

There are two leading questions which now present themselves. First, What is the real significance of that developmental process at work in our modern societies which is carrying us so far away from that social type we have outlined before in the Greek States and the Roman Empire? Second, What is the nature of the evolutionary force which has thus so completely changed the current of social development among those who are now the leading peoples of the world?

We have already, in Chapter II., referred to that movement of modern societies noticed by Sir Henry Maine, the effect of which has been to gradually substitute the individual for the group as the unit of which our civil laws take account. Now this progress towards individual liberty, which is known to the student of jurisprudence as the movement from *status* to *contract*, and which has thus, as it were, become registered in our laws, has a deeper meaning than at first sight appears. Closely regarding, as a whole, the process of change which has been going on in our Western civilisation, the evolutionist begins to perceive that it essentially consists in the slow breaking-up of that military type of society which reached its highest development in, although it did not disappear with, the Roman Empire. Throughout the history of the Western peoples there is one central fact which underlies all the shifting scenes which move across the pages of the historian. The political history of the centuries so far may be summed up in a single sentence : it is the story of the political and social enfranchisement of the masses of the people hitherto universally excluded from participation in the rivalry of existence on terms of equality. This change, it is seen, is being accomplished against the most prolonged and determined resistance at many points, and under innumerable forms of the power-holding classes which obtained under an earlier constitution of society the influence which they have hitherto, to a large extent, although in gradually diminishing measure, continued to enjoy. The point at which the process tends to culminate is a condition of society in which the whole mass of the excluded people will be at last brought into the rivalry of existence on a footing of equality of opportunity.

The steps in this process have been slow to a degree, but the development has never been interrupted, and it probably will not be until it has reached that point up to which it has always been the inherent tendency of the principle of our civilisation to carry it. The first great stage in the advance was accomplished when slavery, for the first time in history, became extinct in Europe somewhere about the fourteenth century. From this point onward the development has continued under many forms amongst the peoples included in our civilisation —locally accelerated or retarded by various causes, but always in progress. Amongst all the Western peoples there has been a slow but sure restriction of the absolute power possessed under military rule by the head of the State. The gradual decay of feudalism has been accompanied by the transfer of a large part of the rights, considerably modified, of the feudal lords to the landowning, and later to the capitalist classes which succeeded them. But we find these rights undergoing a continuous process of restriction, as the classes which inherited them have been compelled to extend political power in ever-increasing measure to those immediately below. As the rights and power of the upper classes have been gradually curtailed, the great slowly formed middle class has, in its turn, found itself confronted with the same developmental tendency. Wider and wider the circle of political influence has gradually extended. Whether the progress has been made irregularly amid the throes of revolution, or more regularly in the orderly course of continuous legislative enactment, it has never ceased. The nineteenth century alone has witnessed an enormous extension of political power to the masses amongst most of the advanced peoples included in our civilisation. In England the list of measures aiming directly or indirectly at the emancipation and the raising of the lower classes of the people, that have been placed on the statute-book in the lifetime of even the present generation, is an imposing one, and it continues yearly to be added to. Last of all, it may be perceived that in our own day, amid all the conflict of rival parties, and all the noise and exaggeration of heated combatants, we are definitely entering on a stage when the advancing party is coming to set clearly before it, as the object of endeavour, the ideal of a state of society in which there shall be at last no law-protected power-holding

class on the one side, and no excluded and disinherited masses on the other—a stage in which, for a
long period to come, legislation will aim at securing to
all the members of the community the right to be
admitted to the rivalry of life, as far as possible, on
a footing of equality of opportunity.

As the evolutionist ponders on this process of
development, its immense significance is gradually
perceived.   He observes that it is only our familiarity
with the process which obscures from us the fact that
it is one which is absolutely unique in the history of
the race.   Its inherent tendency he sees is not really
to suspend the rivalry of life, but to raise it to the
highest possible degree of efficiency as a cause of
progress.   So far from our civilisation tending to
produce an interruption of, or an exception to, the
cosmic process which has been in progress from the
beginning of life, its distinctive and characteristic
feature, he observes, must be found in the exceptional
degree to which it has furthered it.   The significance
of the entire order of social change in progress
amongst the Western peoples consists, in short, in
the single fact that this cosmic process tends thereby
to obtain amongst us the fullest, highest, and completest expression it has ever reached in the history
of the race.

It has been noticed that in that state of society
which flourished under the military empires, the extent to which progress could be made was strictly
limited.   In a social order comprising a series of
hereditarily distinct groups or classes, and resting
ultimately on a broad basis of slavery, the great
majority of the people were penned off apart, and
excluded from all opportunity of developing their

own personalities. Those forces which have created
the modern world could, therefore, have little opportunity for action or for development. In Eastern
countries, where the institution of caste still prevails,
we have, indeed, only an example of a condition of
society in which (in the absence of that developmental force which we shall have to observe at work
amongst ourselves) these groups and classes have
become fixed and rigid, and in which, consequently,
progress has been thwarted and impeded at every
turn by innumerable barriers which have for ages
prevented that free conflict of forces within the community which has made so powerfully for progress
among the Western peoples.[1]

When we follow the process of development
gradually proceeding throughout European history,
we can be in no doubt as to its character. We see
that the energies of men, instead of being, as in the
earlier societies, either stifled altogether, or absorbed
in the service of the state to be utilised largely in
the exploitation of other peoples by violence, have
continually tended to find a freer outlet. But the

---

[1] Castes had their place and meaning in an earlier stage of social
evolution ; they were an inevitable incident accompanying a certain
stage of military expansion. Probably, as Professor Marshall has remarked, the feature was at the time probably well suited to its environment, as "in early times . . . all the nations which were leading
the van of the world's progress were found to agree in having adopted
a more or less strict system of caste." "One peculiarity invariably
distinguishes the infancy of societies," remarks Sir Henry Maine.
"Men are regarded and treated, not as individuals, but always as
members of a particular group. Everybody is first a citizen, and then,
as a citizen, he is a member of his order,—of an aristocracy or a
democracy, of an order of patricians or of plebeians ; or, in those
societies which an unhappy fate has afflicted with a special perversion in
their course of development, of a caste ; next, he is a member of a gens,
house, or clan ; and, lastly, he is a member of his family."—*Ancient
Law*, p. 183.

process, we observe, has been accompanied by a
steady increase of energy, enterprise, and activity
amongst the peoples most affected.   As the movement which is bringing the excluded masses of the
people into the competition of life on a footing of
equality has continued, its tendency, while humanising
the conditions, has unmistakably been to develop in
intensity, and to raise in efficiency the rivalry in
which, as the first condition of progress, we are all
engaged.   As the opportunity has been more and
more fully secured to the individual to follow without
restraint of class, privilege, or birth wherever his
capacity or abilities lead him, so also have all those
features of enterprise and activity which distinguish
the leading branches of the European peoples become more marked.   As the rivalry has become
freer and fairer, the stress has become greater and
the results more striking.   All those remarkable
features of the modern world which impress the
imagination, which serve to distinguish our times so
effectively from the past, and which have to a large
extent contributed to place the European peoples
outside the fear of rivalry from any other section
of the race, are, in effect, but the result of those
strenuous conditions of life which have accompanied
the free play of forces in the community, this latter
being in its turn the direct product of the movement
which is bringing the masses of the people into the
rivalry of existence on conditions of equality.

It may be perceived, in short, that the characteristic process of development, which is carrying us so
far away from that social type which reached its
highest expression in the ancient civilisations, is only
another phase of that process already noticed, which

has been throughout history gradually shifting the seat of power northwards into regions where the struggle for existence is severest. In the process of social. expansion which the Western races are undergoing, they are being worked up to a high state of efficiency in the rivalry of life. The resulting energy, activity, vigour, and enterprise of the peoples most deeply affected by this process has given them the commanding place they have come to occupy in the world. It is in the extent to which it has contributed to further this development and to increase the stress of life that we must recognise the significance of that broadening down throughout the centuries of individual liberty, observable alike in our laws, our political institutions, and our social and domestic relations. It is as an aspect of this development that we must regard the importance of that progress towards economic freedom, which political economists are coming to look upon as characteristic of modern times.[1] And it is as a necessary accompaniment of the same development that we must recognise the significance of that movement which, having at length almost completed the political enfranchisement of the masses, has in our own day, amid much misconception and misapprehension, already began their social emancipation.

So far we have attempted to answer the question as to the significance in the eyes of the evolutionist of that developmental process in progress in our civilisation. To answer the question as to what is the nature of the evolutionary force which has been behind it, we must now return to the consideration of the ethical system upon which our civilisation is founded.

[1] *Vide* Professor Marshall's *Principles of Economics*, vol. i. p. 8.

CHAPTER VII

WESTERN CIVILISATION—(*continued*)

IT is not improbable, after the sanguine expectations which have been entertained throughout the greater part of the nineteenth century, as to the part which the intellect is destined to play in human evolution, that one of the most remarkable features of the age upon which we are entering will be the disillusionment we are likely to undergo in this respect. There has been for long abroad, in the minds of men, an idea, which finds constant expression (although it is not perhaps always clearly and consistently held) that this vast development in the direction of individual, economic, political, and social enfranchisement which has been taking place in our civilisation, is essentially an intellectual movement. Nothing can be more obvious, however, as soon as we begin to understand the nature of the process of evolution in progress around us, than that the moving force behind it is not the intellect, and that the development as a whole is not in any true sense an intellectual movement. Nay, more, we may distinguish, with some degree of clearness, the nature of the part taken therein by the intellect. It is an important part certainly, but it is also beyond doubt a subordinate one, strictly limited and circumscribed. The intellect is employed in developing ground which has been won for it by other forces. But it would appear that it has by itself no power to occupy this ground ; it has not even any power to continue to hold it after it has been won when these forces have spent and exhausted themselves.

We have seen that, to obtain a just conception of our Western civilisation, it is necessary to regard it from the beginning as a single continuous growth, endowed with a definite principle of life, subject to law, and passing, like any other organism, through certain orderly stages of development. If we look back once more over that ethical movement which we have regarded as the seat of the vital phenomena we are witnessing, and which projects itself with such force and distinctness through the history of the European peoples, it may be perceived that it is divided into two clearly defined stages. In the preceding chapter our attention was confined exclusively to the first of these stages. The second stage began with the Renaissance, or, more accurately speaking, with the Reformation, and it continues down into the period in which we are living.

It will be remembered that in the last chapter it was insisted that the dominant and determinative feature of the first period was the development of an ultra-rational sanction for the constitution of society ; which sanction attained, in the European Theocracy of the fourteenth century, a strength and influence never before known. All the extraordinary series of phenomena peculiar to the centuries which have become known as " the ages of faith " are in this light to be regarded, it was maintained, as constituting the early and immature aspects of a movement endowed from the beginning with enormous vital energy. The process, as a whole, was to reach fruition only at a later stage. In the second period, as the other factor in our evolution begins slowly to operate, we see the revolutionary and transforming forces which from the outset constituted the characteristic element in the religious system upon which our civilisation is founded, but which during the period of growth were diverted into other channels, now finding their true social expression. We witness in this period the beginning, and follow through the centuries the progress, of a social revolution unequalled in magnitude and absolutely unique in character, a revolution the significance of which is perceived to lie, not, as is often supposed, in its tendency to bring about a condition of society in which the laws of previous development are to be suspended ; but in the fact that it constitutes the last orderly stage in the same cosmic process which has been in progress in the world from the beginning of life. Let us see if we can explain the nature of the force that has been behind this revolution, and the manner in which it has operated in producing that process of social development which the Western peoples are still undergoing.

If the mind is carried backwards and concentrated on the first period of the religious movement which began in the early centuries of our era, it will be noticed that there was one feature which stood out with great prominence. It is a matter beyond question that this movement involved from its inception the very highest conception of the Altruistic

ideal to which the human mind has in any general
sense ever attained.   At this distance of time this
characteristic is still unmistakable.   "Any impartial
observer," says Mr. Lecky, " would describe the most
distinctive virtue referred to in the New Testament
as love, charity, or philanthropy." [1]   It is the spirit
of charity, pity, and infinite compassion which
breathes through the gospels.   The new religion
was, at the outset, actually and without any figurative
exaggeration what the same writer has called it elsewhere, "a proclamation of the universal brotherhood
of man."   We note how it was this feature which
impressed the minds of men at first.   The noble
system of ethics, the affection which the members
bore to each other, the devotion of all to the corporate welfare, the spirit of infinite tolerance for
every weakness and inequality, the consequent
tendency to the dissolution of social and class
barriers of every kind, beginning with those between
slave and master, and the presence everywhere of
the feeling of actual brotherhood, were the outward
features of all the early Christian societies.

Now it seems at first sight a remarkable fact, even
at the present day, that the adherents of a form of
belief apparently so benevolent and exemplary should
have been at an early stage in the history of the
movement subjected to the persecutions which they
had to endure under the Roman Empire.   It is not,
in fact, surprising that many writers should have
followed Gibbon, in search of a satisfactory explanation, into an elaborate analysis of the causes that
led the Roman state, which elsewhere exercised so
contemptuous a tolerance for the religions of the

[1] *History of European Morals*, vol. ii. p. 130.

peoples whom it ruled, to have undertaken the
rigorous measures which it from time to time
endeavoured to enforce against the adherents of the
new movement. " If," says Gibbon, " we recollect
the universal toleration of Polytheism, as it was
invariably maintained by the faith of the people, the
incredulity of the philosophers, and the policy of the
Roman senate and emperors, we are at a loss to
discover what new offence the Christians had com-
mitted, what new provocation could exasperate the
mild indifference of antiquity, and what new motives
could urge the Roman princes who beheld without
concern a thousand forms of religion subsisting in
peace under their gentle sway, to inflict a severe
punishment on any part of their subjects who had
chosen for themselves a singular but an inoffensive
mode of faith and worship. The religious policy of
the ancient world seems to have assumed a more
stern and intolerant character to oppose the progress
of Christianity." [1]

A peculiar feature of the persecutions under the
Roman Empire was that they were not to any
extent originated by the official classes. Particular
emperors or magistrates may have used for their own
purposes the prejudices which existed in the popular
mind against the new sect ; but these prejudices
were already widespread and general. The enlightened classes were, indeed, rather puzzled than
otherwise at the deep-seated feelings which they
found in existence against the adherents of the
movement. They, for the most part, knew very
little, and scarcely troubled to inquire, about the real
nature of the new doctrines. Even Tacitus saw in

[1] *Decline and Fall of the Roman Empire*, vol. i. chap. xvi.

M

the Christians only a sect peculiar for their hatred
of humankind, who were, in consequence, branded
with deserved infamy ; while Pliny was content with
asserting that whatever might be the principle of
their conduct, their unyielding obstinacy was deserving of punishment.

What it is, however, of the highest importance to
note here is that it was those same altruistic ideals,
which seem so altogether exemplary in our eyes, that
filled the minds of the lower classes of the Roman
population (who were not permeated with the intellectual scepticism of the educated classes) with vague
but deep-seated distrust and hatred of the new
religion and its adherents.   The profound social
instincts of the masses of the people—then, as nearly
always, possessing a truer scientific basis than the
merely intellectual insight of the educated classes—
recognised, in fact, in the new ideals which were
moving the minds of men, a force, not only different
in nature and potentiality to any of which the
ancient world had previous experience, but one
which was fundamentally antagonistic to the forces
which had hitherto held together that organisation of
society which had culminated in the Empire.

Hence it was that this popular feeling found
expression in accusations, many of which appear so
strange to us.   The adherents of the new faith were
accused, not only of dissolving the sacred laws of
custom and education and of abhorring the gods of
others, but of " undermining the religious constitution
of the empire," of being " a society of atheists, without patriotism," who obstinately refused to hold
communion with the gods of Rome, of the empire,
and of mankind.   The populace of the ancient world,

in fact, rightly regarded as a public danger the
adherents of a religion, in the altruistic conceptions
of which all the bonds of race, nationality, and class
were dissolved ; and treated them consequently as
outcasts to be branded with infamy by all men, of
whatever creed or nationality, in a world where the
universal constitution of society had hitherto been
that which had found its highest expression in the
epoch in which men were living.

We must keep clearly in mind, therefore, that it
was the nature of the altruistic ideals of the new
religion which from the beginning differentiated it in
so marked a manner from all other faiths ; and that
while it was this characteristic which formed one of
the most powerful causes of its spread and influence,
it was also the feature which was instinctively recognised as constituting a danger to the universal
social order of the ancient world, and which caused
the religion to be early singled out for the exceptional
treatment it received at the hands of the Roman
state.

As the movement progressed it must be noticed
that the altruistic ideals which thus, from the outset,
formed the distinctive feature of the new faith were
not extinguished, but that, in the period of intense
vitality which ensued, they became, as the religious
principle developed, overshadowed by, and merged in,
the supernatural conceptions with which they were
necessarily associated.   In the epidemic of asceticism
which overspread the world, every consideration of
the present became dominated by conceptions of
another life ; but in these conceptions we still
perceive that self-abnegation and self-sacrifice in this
life were held to be the proper preparation for the

next, and that they constituted the very highest ideal of acceptable conduct the world could then comprehend.   As the ascetic period was succeeded by the monastic period, there is no essential distinction to be made ; for in the latter we have only the organised expression of the former.   Throughout all this prolonged period we have to note that self-sacrifice and the unworthiness of every effort and ambition centred in self or in this life was the ideal the Church consistently held before the minds of men.   Nor was this the standard of the cloister only ; throughout every section of the European Theocracy the minds and lives of men were profoundly imbued with the spirit of this teaching.   Whatever may have been the faults and excesses of the Church, there can be no question as to the tendency of its doctrine to exalt the altruistic ideal ; and, either directly or indirectly, to raise the conduct prescribed by it to the highest level of human reverence it had ever reached.   At a time when the military organisation of society still outwardly retained a scarcely diminished influence over the Western mind, the act which became typical of the higher life was to wash the feet of social inferiors and beggars.   At a period when the history of the ancient empires still formed a kind of lustrous background, in the light of which the deeds of men continually tended to be judged, the vision of the Church was of the soldier who in sharing his cloak with the outcast beggar found that he had shared it with Christ.   In an age of turbulence and war, and while force continued to be everywhere triumphant, the uncompromising doctrine of the innate equality of men was slowly producing the most pregnant and remarkable change that has ever passed over the minds of a large section of the race. Even the all-powerful ruling classes could not remain permanently unaffected by a voice which, taking them generation after generation in their triumphs and pleasures as well as in their most impressionable moments, whispered with all the weight of the most absolute and unquestioned authority that they were in reality of the same clay as other men, and that in the eyes of a higher Power they stood on a footing of native equality with even the lowest of the earth.

We now come to the beginning of the second stage which is reached in the great social movement known in history as the Reformation. The importance of this movement, as we shall better understand later, is very great, much greater indeed than the historian, with the methods at his command, has hitherto assigned to it. Its immediate significance was, that while, as already explained, it represented an endeavour to preserve intact the necessary super-rational sanction for the ethical ideals of the Christian religion, it denoted the tendency of the movement which had so far filled the life of the Western peoples to find its social expression. It liberated, as it were, into the practical life of the peoples affected by it, that immense body of altruistic feeling which had been from the beginning the distinctive social product of the Christian religion, but which had hitherto been, during a period of immaturity and intense vitality, directed into other channels. To the evolutionist this movement is essentially a social development. It took place inevitably and naturally at a particular stage which can never recur in the life of the social organism. In his eyes its significance consists in the greater development which the altruistic feelings must

attain amongst the peoples where the development
was allowed to proceed uninterrupted in its course.
It is, it would appear, amongst these peoples that
the great social revolution which our civilisation is
destined to accomplish must proceed by the most
orderly stages, must find its truest expression, and
must produce its most notable results.

Before following the subject farther, let us, however, first see what is the real function in the evolution
we are undergoing of this great body of humanitarian
feeling which distinguishes our time ; for there is
scarcely any other subject connected with the progress
we are making upon which so much misconception
appears to prevail.   So far from the doctrine of
evolution having shed light thereon, it has, apparently,
in some respects only deepened the darkness, so that
from time to time we find observers who, failing to
reach the essential meaning of the evolutionary
process as a whole, or fixing their eyes on some
incidental detail, give currency to the doctrine that
the most important result of the development which
the humanitarian feelings have attained, is to largely
secure at the present day the survival of the unfittest
in society.

There can be no doubt that one of the most
marked features of our times is the development
which has taken place of the feelings that, classed
together under the head of altruistic, represent in
the abstract that willingness to sacrifice individual
welfare in the cause of the welfare of others.   Yet
there are probably few students of social progress
familiar with the explanations currently given as to
the function of these feelings in our modern civilisation who have not felt at one time or another that

such explanations are to a considerable extent unsatisfactory. The functions assigned to the feelings are simply not sufficiently important to account for the magnitude of the phenomenon we are regarding. We seem to feel that there must be some larger process of evolution behind, the nature of which remains unexplained, but which should serve to group together, as the details of a single movement, all the extraordinary phenomena connected with the humanitarian feelings which the modern world presents.

It is, of course, easy to understand the explanations currently given of the part which the altruistic feelings have played in a stage of development anterior to our own. Their function in the type of civilisation which culminated in the Roman Empire is clear enough ; the devotion of the individual to the corporate welfare was one of the first essentials of success in societies which existed primarily for military purposes, where the struggle for existence was carried on mainly between organised bodies of men. We had, accordingly, in this stage of society an extreme sense of devotion to clan or country. Sentiment, education, and religion all lent their aid to ennoble the idea of absolute self-sacrificing devotion to the state ; so that virtue amongst the ancients seemed always to be indissolubly associated with the idea of patriotism in some form.

But, although we live in an age in which the altruistic feelings have attained a development previously unexampled in the history of the race, the conditions under which they exercised so important a function at an earlier stage seem to be slowly disappearing. Patriotism, not of the modern kind, but of the type which prevailed during the Roman period, has long been decaying amongst us, and the tendency of the present time undoubtedly points in the direction of a continuous decline in the strength of this feeling.   Again, our civilisation would appear, at first sight, to be distinctly unfavourable to the cultivation of the altruistic feelings, or to their utilisation as a developmental force. From time to time, as already mentioned, we are even informed that the teaching of Darwinian science is that these feelings are actually injurious to society, and that in their operation now they tend largely to promote amongst us the survival of the unfittest. We have seen how, in some respects, the tendency of progress from ancient to modern societies has apparently been to promote individual selfishness, a leading feature of this progress having been the change in the base from which the struggle for existence takes place, so that it has come to be waged less and less between the societies, and more and more between the individuals comprising them.   We have observed also how the emancipation of the individual, enabling him to utilise to the fullest advantage, in a free rivalry with his fellows, every ability with which he has been endowed, has been the object of all modern legislation ; and we have had to note that the ideal towards which all the advanced nations are apparently travelling is a state of society in which every individual shall, without disadvantage in respect of birth, privilege, or position, start fair in this rivalry, and obtain the fullest possible development of his own personality.

All this, it would appear, must tend to exalt the individual's regard for himself, and must denote an accompanying tendency to weaken rather than to strengthen the altruistic feelings. Attention is indeed not infrequently directed to this feature by a certain class of writers who profess to view it with apprehension and alarm, and individual and class selfishness is not infrequently spoken of as the great evil of the age which casts an ominous shadow over the future.

Yet, making due allowance for all these considerations, we are, nevertheless, met by the fact that there undoubtedly has been a great development of the humanitarian feelings amongst us. The strengthening and deepening which they have undergone has also all the appearance of being one of the vital processes in progress in our civilisation. No student of European history can fail to observe that throughout the whole period there has been a gradual but continuous growth of these feelings amongst the Western races ; that they have reached their highest development in the period in which we are living ; and that this development, and the change in character which has accompanied it, has proceeded farthest amongst the most advanced races.

The nature and meaning of the process which is going on appears, however, to be little understood, even by writers of authority. The confusion of ideas to which the tendencies of the time give rise finds remarkable expression in Mr. Herbert Spencer's writings. In the *Data of Ethics*, the author, in attempting to reconcile the undoubted tendency to the development of the altruistic feelings in our civilisation on the one hand, with the equally undoubted tendency to the development of the individualistic feelings on the other, presents the curious spectacle of providing one party with a set of arguments in favour of socialism, and another party with an equally good set of arguments in favour of individualism; while he has himself pictured the reconciliation of the two tendencies in a future society which the Darwinian, it must be confessed, can only imagine as existing in a state of progressive degeneration.[1]

The evidence as to the extent of this development of the humanitarian feelings is in itself remarkable. The growth of the benevolent institutions is a characteristic of the age, and, although it is not as convincing as other evidence, it is a very striking feature. England, the United States, and other countries, are overspread with a network of institutions founded or supported by the contributions of private individuals. The annual revenue of the private charities of London alone is close on £5,000,000, or equal to the entire public revenue of some of the smaller states. Associations and corporations for giving effect to philanthropic purposes are innumerable, and scarcely a week passes that fresh additions are not made to their number. It is to a large extent the same in other countries included in our Western civilisation, and appearances would seem to indicate that the most progressive

---

[1] See, in particular, chapters xiii. and xiv. of his *Data of Ethics.* Mr. Spencer recognises clearly " that social evolution has been bringing about a state in which the claims of the individual to the proceeds of his activities, and to such satisfactions as they bring, are more and more positively asserted." The other tendency is equally unmistakable. " If we consider what is meant by the surrender of power to the masses, the abolition of class privileges, the efforts to diffuse knowledge, the agitations to spread temperance, the multitudinous philanthropic societies, it becomes clear that regard for the wellbeing of others is increasing *pari passu* with the taking of means to secure personal wellbeing " (chap. xiii.)

societies are not behind the others in this respect, but that, on the contrary, they have made most advance in this direction also.

Still, it is not these results, noteworthy though they be, which furnish the most important evidence as to the development which the altruistic feelings have attained in our time. This is to be marked more particularly in a widespread interest in the welfare of others, which exhibits itself in a variety of less obtrusive forms. There may be noticed in particular the extraordinary sensitiveness of the public mind amongst the advanced peoples to wrong or suffering of any kind. One of the strongest influences prompting the efforts which the British nation has persistently (although quite thanklessly and un-obtrusively) made towards the suppression of the slave trade, has been the impression produced by accounts of the cruelties and degradation imposed on the slaves. In like manner the effect produced on the minds of the British people by descriptions of the wrongs and sufferings of oppressed nationalities has been one of the most powerful influences affect-ing the foreign policy of England throughout the nineteenth century ; and any close student of our politics during this period would have to note that this influence, so far as the will of the people found expression through the government in power, has been a far more potent factor in shaping that policy than any clear conception of those far-reaching political motives so often attributed to the British nation by other countries.

Evidence still more conclusive, although of a different kind, is to be found in that mirror of our daily life which the press furnishes. No one can closely follow from day to day that living record, so faithfully reflecting the feelings and opinions of the period, without becoming profoundly conscious of the strength and importance of the altruistic feelings at the present time. Appeals in respect of injury, outrage, or wrong suffered by any particular class have become one of the strongest political forces, and may sometimes be observed to be more effective than even direct appeals to private selfishness. We may notice too, that when, from time to time in the daily life of the people, the feelings to which such appeals are made become focussed on individual cases, the habits of restraint acquired under free institutions are often insufficient to prevent the humanitarian impulses from overmastering those habits of sober judgment so readily exercised in other circumstances by large masses of the people.

In smaller but not less important matters the indications are equally striking. The record in the press of a case of death from starvation sends a tremor which may almost be felt through the community. It is not that the sensitiveness of the public mind in such cases is shown by noisy denunciation ; it is those hesitating heart-searching comments—frequently so pathetically misdirected— which the circumstance oftenest evokes, that are so eloquent and so significant. We have become, too, not only sensitive to physical suffering, but to the mental suffering which the moral degradation of our fellows implies. One of the most remarkable movements of the period, in some respects, has been the agitation successfully carried on in England against the laws requiring the state regulation of vice ; and one of the leading factors which gave strength to this agitation, and which tended to render it eventually successful, was undoubtedly the feeling of abhorrence produced in the minds of a large section of the public by the degradation which these laws publicly imposed on a section of our fellow-creatures.

Moreover, this extreme sensitiveness to misery or suffering in others appears to be extending outwards in a gradually widening circle. We do not allow unmerited suffering to be imposed even on animals ; bear - baiting, dog - fighting, badger - baiting, cock-fighting, have one after another disappeared from amongst us within recent times, suppressed, like duelling, by public sentiment rather than by law. The action of these feelings may also be traced more or less directly in many of the movements peculiar to our time. The opinion in favour of vegetarianism has drawn its strength, to a consider-able extent, from the feeling of repugnance which the idea of the infliction of death or suffering on the animals which provide us with food inspires in many minds. The century has seen the rise of the well-known and successful British Society for the Pre-vention of Cruelty to Animals ; and similar associations have been founded and have taken root all over the English-speaking world, and to some extent elsewhere. We have even to note how the same feelings have, within the lifetime of the present generation, proved sufficiently strong in England to secure the passing of a law against vivi-section, forbidding (except in duly authorised cases and under certain restrictions) the infliction of suffer-ing upon animals even in the cause of science ; and, what is perhaps more remarkable, we have seen public opinion moved, as it often is, by an instinct sounder than the arguments used in support of it, insisting on the strict enforcement of this law in the face of authoritative protests which have been made against it.[1]

The contrast which all this presents to the utter indifference to suffering which prevailed amongst the ancients, and which survived, to some extent, among ourselves down to a comparatively recent date, is very striking. Amongst the early Greeks and Romans the utmost callousness and brutality were displayed towards persons outside the ties of relationship or dependency. We can hardly realise the brutal selfishness which prevailed even within those ties. Infanticide was a general practice. Even old age was not, as a rule, respected amongst the Greeks. Says Mr. Mahaffy, "The most enlightened Greeks stood nearer, I fear, to the savages of the present day, who regard without respect or affec-

[1] The arguments which have been used on both sides of this question have a special interest, inasmuch as they serve to bring out in a striking light that general absence, already remarked upon, of any clear conception as to what the function of the altruistic feelings really is. The opponents of vivisection have hitherto largely based their case on the peculiar ground of the alleged absence of any considerable benefit to medical science from the practice. The advocates of vivisection on the other hand have based their case on the equally precarious ground that, because the benefits to medical science have been large, obstacles should not be placed in the way of vivisection. It is evident, however, that neither side touches what is the real question at issue. If society is asked to permit vivisection, the only question it has to decide is, whether the benefits it may receive from the practice through the furtherance of medical science (even admitting them to be considerable) outweigh the injury it may receive through the weakening of the altruistic feelings which it tends to outrage. The reason, however, why the question is not usually put thus directly and simply in the controversial literature which the subject so plentifully provokes, is, apparently, that we have no clear apprehension as to what the real function of the altruistic feelings is. Their immense importance is accordingly justified by instinct rather than by reason, and consequently such justification comes almost exclusively from that section of the population where the social instincts are healthiest.

tion every human being who has become useless in
the race of life or who even impedes the course of
human affairs. We know that at Athens actions of
children to deprive their parents of control of property were legal and commonly occurring, nor do
we hear that medical evidence of imbecility was
required. It was only among a few conservative
cities like Sparta, and a few exceptionally refined
men like Plato, that the nobler and kindlier sentiment prevailed." [1] Compared with ours even the
noblest Greek ethics were of the narrowest kind ;
and Greek morality, as already observed, at no period
embraced any conception of humanity.

Finally, we have to remark that there is no justification for regarding the change in progress in our
time as indicating that we are undergoing a kind of
deterioration, or as evidence that we are becoming
effeminate and less able to bear the stress of life
than formerly. There are no real grounds for such
a supposition. We show no signs of effeminacy in
other respects. On the contrary it is amongst the
peoples who are most vigorous and virile, and
amongst whom the stress is severest, that the change
is most noticeable. It is amongst the races that are
winning the greatest ascendency in the world that
this softening process has proceeded farthest. The
phenomenon of the development of the altruistic
feelings presents well-marked features ; it has been
persistent and continuous throughout a prolonged
period ; it has progressed farthest amongst the most
advanced peoples ; and it has all the appearance of
being closely associated in some way with the progress we are making in other directions. What

[1] *Social Life in Greece*, by J. P. Mahaffy, chap. v.

then, it may be asked, is the import of this development ?   What is the function of the humanitarian
feelings in that process of expansion which is
peculiar to our civilisation ?   In what lies the significance of that deepening and softening of character
which has long been in progress amongst the Western
peoples ?

At the risk of repetition, it is essential to once
more briefly recall the distinguishing features of that
social transformation which has been slowly taking
place in our Western civilisation.   The clue to this
process we found to lie in the fact that it has consisted essentially in the gradual breaking down of
that military organisation of society which had
previously prevailed, and in the emancipation and
enfranchisement of the great body of the people
hitherto universally excluded under that constitution
of society from all participation on equal terms in
the rivalry of existence.   From a remote time down
into the period in which we are living, we have
witnessed a continuous movement in this direction.
The progress may not have been always visible to
the current generation amongst whom the rising
waves surge backwards and forwards ; but, looking
back over our history, we mark unmistakably the
unceasing onward progress of the slowly advancing
tide.   This movement we have seen resulting in
that free play of forces within the community which
has produced the modern world.   And it tends to
culminate in a condition of society in which there
shall be no privileged classes, and in which all the
excluded people shall be at last brought into the
rivalry of life on a footing of equality of opportunity — the significance of the whole process

consisting in its tendency to raise the rivalry of existence to the highest degree of efficiency as a cause of progress to which it has ever attained in the history of life.

Now the prevailing impression concerning this process of evolution is that it has been the product of an intellectual movement, and that it has been the ever-increasing intelligence and enlightenment of the people which has constituted the principal propelling force. It would appear, however, that we must reject this view. From the nature of the case, as we shall see more clearly later on, the intellect could not have supplied any force sufficiently powerful to have enabled the people to have successfully assailed the almost impregnable position of the power - holding classes. So enormous has been the resistance to be overcome, and so complete has been the failure of the people in similar circumstances outside our civilisation, that we must look elsewhere for the cause which has produced the transformation. The motive force we must apparently find in the immense fund of altruistic feeling with which our Western societies have become equipped ; this being, with the extraordinarily effective sanctions behind it, the characteristic and determinative product of the religious system upon which our civilisation is founded. *It is the influence of this fund of altruism in our civilisation that has undermined the position of the power-holding classes.* It is the resulting deepening and softening of character amongst us which alone has made possible that developmental movement whereby all the people are being slowly brought into the rivalry of life on equal conditions. And in the eyes of the evolu-

N

tionist, it is by contributing the factor which has rendered this unique process of social development possible, that the Christian religion has tended to raise the peoples affected by it to the commanding place they have come to occupy in the world. Let us see how this remarkable development has proceeded.

The first great epoch in the history of this process was that which marked the extinction of slavery. There is scarcely any one feature of our modern civilisation of greater significance to the evolutionist than the absence of this institution. The abolition of slavery has been one of the greatest strides forward ever taken by the race. The consequences, direct and indirect, have been immense, and even now we habitually under-rate rather than over-rate its effects and importance. Slavery became extinct in Europe about the fourteenth century, but had the institution continued unchanged after the break-up of the Roman Empire, modern civilisation would never have been born; we should still be living in a world with the fetters of militancy hopelessly riveted upon us; social freedom and equality would be unknown; trade, commerce, and manufactures, as they now exist, could not have been developed, and the few engaged in such occupations would have been despised. The friction of mind against mind which has produced modern science and its multifarious applications to the needs of life would never have arisen; industrialism would have been unknown; and the degrading and retarding influences of a rule of brute force would have been felt in every department of life.

Yet, although it is difficult to realise it in the

midst of our civilisation, slavery is one of the most natural and, from many points of view, one of the most reasonable of institutions. Professor Freeman regarded it almost as a necessary condition of a pure democracy of the Greek type, in which the individual free citizen was " educated, worked up, and improved to the highest possible pitch."[1] What may be called the intellectual case against slavery has nearly always run on the same lines. From this point of view it is capable of the clearest proof that slavery is hurtful in the long-run to the welfare of the people amongst whom it prevails. But it must not be forgotten that such arguments have never been of the slightest practical importance ; for, as already maintained elsewhere, men in such circumstances are everywhere dominated, not by calculations of the supposed effects of their acts or their institutions on unborn generations, but by more immediate considerations of their own personal advantage. It must be remembered also that the tendency of intellectual progress must always be to make it clear that, under all the forms of the highest civilisation, the process tending to the survival of the fittest, and the worsting of the least efficient, goes on as surely and as steadily as under any other system of social organisation. The intellect alone can, in such circumstances, never be expected to furnish any strong condemnation of those who, knowing themselves to be the stronger and more efficient, and feeling their interest in the conditions of existence to be bounded by the limited span of individual human life, should take this short and direct road and utilise the superiority with which they have been equipped to their

[1] Vide *History of Federalism*, vol. i. chap. ii.

own immediate advantage, rather than to that of unknown and unborn generations.

In dealing with inferior races when removed from the environment of Western civilisation, it has, indeed, been the consistent experience of all European peoples that the influence of inherited conceptions, and of centuries of training, has not been sufficient to keep in check this feeling as to the inherent naturalness of slavery. We must not forget that the institution has flourished down almost into our own times under the auspices of, and in the midst of an Anglo-Saxon community in the Southern States of the North American continent; and the subsequent painful history of the negro question in the United States only brings out in strong light the strength and even reasonableness of the feeling upon which slavery was founded—always, of course, restricting our view to the immediate local interests of the stronger of the two parties envisaged.

We are apt to consider the abolition of slavery as the result of an intellectual movement. But he would be a bold man who, with a clear apprehension of the forces that have been at work, would undertake to prove that slavery was abolished through the march of the intellect. It is not held in check even at the present time by forces set in motion by the intellect. Its extinction is, undoubtedly, to be regarded as one of the first of the peculiar fruits of that ethical movement upon which our civilisation is founded. The two doctrines which contributed most to producing the extinction of slavery were the doctrine of salvation and the doctrine of the equality of all men before the Deity—both being essentially ultra-rational. The doctrine of salvation, in parti-

cular, proved at an early stage to be one of the most
powerful solvents ever applied to the minds of men.
The immense and incalculable importance that the
welfare of even the meanest creature acquired for his
soul's sake possessed an unusual social significance.
It tended from the beginning to weaken degrading
class distinctions, and it immediately raised even the
slave to a position of native dignity. The conception of the equality of all men before the Deity,
which such a doctrine supplemented, was also of
profound importance and in an even wider sense.
The theoretical conception to which it gave rise that
all men are born equal (an assumption which, it must
be remembered, receives no sanction from science
or experience) has been throughout one of the
most characteristic products of our civilisation,
and it has played a large part in that process of
expansion through which the Western peoples have
passed.

The abolition of slavery was, however, only the
first step in the evolutionary process. The others
possess even greater interest. We may observe in
European history the peculiar manner in which the
development which is gradually bringing all the
people into the rivalry of life on conditions of equality
has proceeded. In the countries where it has taken
place in a regular manner, it is not so much the
concentration and determination of the advance of
the people that is noticeable. We observe rather
how the classes in power have been steadily retreating, and extending the privileges of their own position in greater measure to larger and larger numbers
of the outside classes. The change has taken place
slowly at first, but more rapidly as we approach our

own times, and it is proceeding most rapidly of all in the period in which we are living. Our histories are filled with descriptions of phases of this movement, and with theories and explanations of the causes which have been at work in producing these local manifestations. But the evolutionist sooner or later sees that the influences which have produced these merely subsidiary eddies are not the prime cause, and that there must be one common cause operating progressively and over a prolonged period in which all these subordinate phenomena have their origin.

There can scarcely be any doubt as to where we must look for this. It arises from the development of the same influence that abolished slavery. It is to be found in that great fund of altruistic feeling generated by the ethical system upon which our civilisation is founded. It is this which provides the prime motive force behind the whole series of political and social phenomena peculiar to our civilisation which we include together under the general head of "progress." But the manner in which the cause operates is little understood.

It is in the main a correct insight which has led so many writers of the advanced school to regard the French Revolution as the objective starting-point of the modern world. It is not that the Revolution has in any way added to or taken from the developmental forces that are shaping this world. It is simply that causes, for the most part local and exceptional, which did not occur amongst peoples whose development had taken a more regular course, there contributed to bring face to face the old spirit and the new in extreme contrast and opposition,

and in a situation fraught to the most extraordinary
degree with human interest.

No one can rise from the study of this remarkable
period without feeling, however dimly, that he has
been watching the operation of a force utterly unlike
any of which the ancient world had experience—a
force which, though peculiar to our civilisation from
the beginning, here for the first time manifested
itself in a striking and clearly defined manner in
European history. Not to realise the nature of this
force is to misunderstand, not only the Revolution,
but all current political and social history amongst
ourselves and all other sections of the advanced
European peoples. At the time of the Revolution
nothing so powerfully impressed the spectator as the
irresistible advance of the people ; at this distance of
time nothing causes so much wonder as their weakness. They were without weapons, without organisation, without definite aims. Even their leaders
were but the representatives of different and, in many
cases, utterly antagonistic currents of thought which
met and surged wildly together, and which, while
struggling amongst themselves for mastery, were
swept onwards by deeper and obscurer forces over
which these leaders had no control, and which they
did not themselves understand.

The strength of the people apparently lay in their
enthusiasm. This, in its turn, was the product of the
sense of pity for themselves and for each other in the
state of profound misery and degradation in which
they found themselves ; and it was rendered the more
intense by the contrast their lives presented in comparison with those of the classes above them in the
social scale. But although this situation, and the

state of things which led up to it, has been ably and accurately described by many writers, we do not reach, through details of this kind, however accurate and exhaustive, the inner significance of the Revolution. It was no new spectacle in history for the people to rise against their masters. They had often done so before, and they had almost invariably been driven back to their tasks. The odds which might have been utilised against them were enormous. Why, therefore, were they successful on this occasion; and why is the Revolution to all appearance, and for this reason, the beginning of a new world? It is not until we look at the other side that we begin to understand the nature of the force on the side of the people which is peculiar to our civilisation.

The most striking spectacle in all that memorable period was, undoubtedly, the weakness and disorganisation of the party representing the ruling classes. It has been the custom to attribute the success of the Revolution to the decay, misrule, and corruption of these classes ; but history, while recognising these causes, will probably regard them as but incidental. Its calmer verdict must be, that it was in the hearts of these classes and not in the streets that the cause of the people was won. It is impossible, even at this distance of time, to observe without a feeling of wonder and even of awe, the extent to which the ideas of the Revolution had undermined the position of the upper classes. Effective resistance was impossible ; they could not utilise their own strength. We begin to understand this slowly. We look for any inspiriting appeal ; for any rally against the forces arrayed against them ; for any of that conscious devotion to a worthy cause which has made even forlorn hopes successful, and which here, in the presence of overpowering odds against the people, would have rendered their opponents irresistible. But we look in vain. The great body of humanitarian feeling which had been slowly accumulating so long had done its work; it had sapped the foundations of the old system. Elsewhere the transforming agent had operated by degrees, and the result, at any time, had been less noticeable; here, where the fabric had outwardly held, it had all gone down suddenly and completely, because the columns which had supported it were deeply affected by the disintegrating process. The conceptions of which the Revolution was born had given enthusiasm to the people, and even a certain cohesion to the most intractable material. But their natural opponents were without either enthusiasm or cohesion; they were indirectly almost as profoundly affected as the people by the force which was reconstituting the world.

A fuller and franker recognition of the true position occupied at this period by the nobility and power-holding classes in France must apparently be one of the features of the work of the future historian who would do justice to the Revolution. They occupied a position almost unique in history, large numbers of them being, as Michelet has expressed it, at once the heirs and the enemies of their own cause. "Educated in the generous ideas of the philosophy of the time, they applauded that marvellous resuscitation of mankind, and offered up prayers for it, even though it cost their ruin." [1] It is easier to be ironical, like Carlyle, than to attempt to do justice, like

[1] *Historical View of the French Revolution*, Book 2, chap. iv.

Michelet, to the remarkable spectacle presented by the meeting of the Assembly on the night of the 4th August 1789, when feudalism, "after a reign of a thousand years, abdicates, abjures, and condemns itself." The subject lent itself admirably to Carlyle's sarcastic pen. "A memorable night, this Fourth of August: Dignitaries temporal and spiritual; Peers, Archbishops, Parlement-President, each outdoing the other in patriotic devotedness, come successively to throw their now untenable possessions on the 'altar of the fatherland.' Louder and louder vivats—for indeed it is 'after dinner' too—they abolish Tithes, Seignorial Dues, Gabelle, excessive Preservation of Game; nay Privilege, Immunity, Feudalism root and branch, then appoint a *Te Deum* for it, and so finally disperse about three in the morning striking the stars with their sublime heads."[1] The evolutionist sees, however, no cause for regarding such a spectacle as any other than one of the most remarkable that human history presents. It was one of the earlier scenes of the Revolution. But never before had the power-holding classes regarded in such a spirit the movement which threatened to engulf and overwhelm them. We must recognise that beneath these incidents, however they may appear to move the irony of the recorder, we are in the presence of a force different in character from any that moved the ancient world, a force which had indeed rendered the ancient constitution of society no longer possible.

But to understand the significance of the Revolution and the real nature of the forces which produced it, our proper standpoint is not in history, nor in the events of the past, but rather in the midst of the

[1] *The French Revolution*, vol. i. Book 6, chap. ii.

strenuous conflict of contemporary life. Nay, more, we shall not find a more profitable post of observation from which to study the cause that produced the French Revolution, and in which to convince ourselves of the continuity and unity of the process of development which the Western peoples are undergoing, than in the very thick of the current political life of the British nation. For here, in the midst of a people whose history has been, so far, to a large extent one of orderly development, we stand continuously in the actual presence of the same cause, and observe on every side, when we understand the nature of the process which is proceeding, the potency and promise of further development of the most vigorous and transforming character.

It may be noticed, if we observe closely the political and social life of our time, that most of the complex forces at work in reality range themselves on the side of one or the other of two great opposing parties. On one side we have that party which is but the modern liberalised representative of that power-holding class already referred to. In the transition from the military to the industrial type of society in England it has become largely transformed into the capitalist class. It is still the party of wealth, prestige, leisure, and social influence and position. On the other side we have a party comprised to the largest extent of those lower in the social scale, and including the greater part of those who lead toilsome, strenuous lives for the least reward. In England, where the course of social development has been less interrupted by disturbing influences than in many other countries, these opponents correspond more or less closely to the two great historic parties in the state. In France, in the United States, in Germany, and in other countries we have, in reality, the same two parties no less distinctly in opposition, although local and particular causes to some extent prevent them from thus clearly confronting each other continuously and all along the line as organised political forces.

If we inquire now what the history of progressive legislation has been during a long period extending down into our own times, we shall find that it presents remarkable features. It may be summed up in a few words. It is simply the history of a continuous series of concessions, demanded and obtained by that party which is, undoubtedly, through its position, inherently the weaker of these two from that power-holding party which is equally unmistakably the stronger. There is no break in the series ; there is no exception to the rule. The record of the past is undeniable ; but the promise of the future is not the less significant, for the programmes of all advancing parties consist simply of further demands, which in due time we may expect to see met in like manner with further concessions. This is the manner in which progress is being made. But what, it may be asked, is the meaning of this peculiar and noteworthy relationship of the two parties, for it undoubtedly presents a spectacle which is altogether exceptional in the history of the world ?

One of the explanations most frequently offered is that the situation arises from the unscrupulous bidding of politicians for power and office under our system of popular government. When, however, we look into the matter this explanation is perceived to be insufficient to account for the facts of the situation.

Politicians can, in the first place, obtain power only from those who have it to bestow ; and, if this explanation was correct, the series of concessions referred to could only have been obtained—had the party conceding them been resolutely unwilling to grant them—by a continuous series of political betrayals by this party's own representatives. We do not, however, find in political history any such series of betrayals on record. Nor is it to be expected that such a condition could continue as one of the normal features of public life. Another explanation, currently offered, is that the result is caused by the growing strength and intelligence of the people's party which render the attack irresistible. But we may readily perceive that the increasing strength and intelligence of the lower classes of the community is the *result* of the change which is in progress, and that it cannot, therefore, be by itself the cause. It must always be remembered too that the party from which the concessions are being won is, in the nature of things and from its entrenched position, even still immeasurably the stronger of the two ; and that elsewhere, outside the modern period, where the two classes have confronted each other, the record of history is emphatic to the effect that this party has always ruthlessly overmastered the other. There must evidently be some other operating cause, large, deep-seated, and constant, which is producing this gradual orderly change in the relationship of the two opponents.

If we look back through the present century at the great movements in English political life, which have resulted in the carrying, one after another, of the numerous legislative measures that have had for their object the emancipation and the raising of the lower classes of the people, it will be perceived that the method in which progress has been produced has always been the same. The first step has invariably been the formation of a great body of feeling or sentiment in favour of the demand. To describe this body of opinion as the product simply of class selfishness would show lack of insight. It is always something much more than this. If it be closely scrutinised, it will generally be found to be in a large degree the result of that extreme sensitiveness of the altruistic feelings to stimulus which has been already noticed. The public mind has become so intolerant of the sight of misery or wrong of any kind that, as the conditions of the life of the excluded masses of the people are gradually brought under discussion and come into the light, this feeling of intolerance slowly gathers force, until at last it finds expression in that powerful body of opinion or sentiment which has been behind all the great social and political reforms of our time.[1]

Even amongst those classes of the people who must immediately profit by the change, the impulses which move them cannot, with truth, be described as simply selfish. We have to observe that the feeling which is, at the present time, stirring the lower classes in most lands included in our Western civilisation is largely a sense of pity for each other and for them- selves as a class in the toilsome, cheerless conditions in which their lives are cast; this feeling being strengthened to an extraordinary degree by that

[1] The press and all the machinery of communication and of modern social life are, of course, powerful factors in concentrating this body of opinion, and in enabling it to find expression.

sense of the innate equality of all men which has entered so deeply into the minds of the advanced European peoples, and by the consciousness of the contrast their lives nevertheless present to those at the other end of the social scale.   Into the body of opinion in which these feelings find expression, the element of sordid private selfishness enters to a far less degree than is commonly supposed.   It is, as a whole, and in the best sense, the product of the altruistic feelings.   It is primarily the result of that deepening of character which has been in progress amongst us, and it is for this reason that the demands of the masses are now made, and must continue to be made, with a depth of conviction, a degree of resolution, and a sense of courage which mere private selfishness could not inspire, and which render them in the highest degree significant.

But it is only when we come to fix our attention on the other side, on that party from which the concessions are being obtained, and which is in retreat before the advancing people, that we become fully conscious of the peculiar and exceptional nature of the phenomenon we are regarding.   It must be borne in mind that this party is the present-day representative of the class which has for ages successfully held the people in subjection, which has erected impregnable barriers against them, which has throughout history consistently reserved in its own hands all power and influence, so as to render any assault on its position well-nigh hopeless. Nay, more, it is the party which, as we have seen, still possesses a reserve of strength which renders it inherently immeasurably stronger than its opponent. Yet by a long list of legislative measures, we now behold this same party educating, enfranchising, and equipping its opponent in the struggle against itself. The record of public life for the past one hundred and fifty years is an extraordinary spectacle in this respect, and it is only our familiarity with the currents of thought in our time which could lead us to forget that the movement we are witnessing is one which is quite unique in the history of the world.

If we come to examine closely the causes at work in producing this result, we shall find that they all have their root in the phenomenon we have been considering. It must be observed that the fact of most significance is the extent to which this deepening and softening of the character has progressed *among the power-holding class.* This class is even more affected than the opposing party. The result is peculiar. It is thereby rendered incapable of utilising its own strength, and consequently of making any effective resistance to the movement which is undermining its position. All heart is, in fact, taken out of its opposition ; men's minds have become so sensitive to suffering, misery, wrong, and degradation of every kind that it cannot help itself. As light continues to be let in on the dark foundations of our social system, the developmental forces do their work silently but effectively in strengthening the attack on one side it is true ; but to a far greater and more significant extent in weakening the defence on the other—by disintegrating the convictions and undermining the faith of the defending party.

We may note clearly in English public life the different effects produced on different sections of the retreating party. In the first place, a considerable number of the best and most generous minds are affected.   The.effect produced on these is such that, instead of siding with the class to which by tradition and individual interest they undoubtedly belong, they take their places in the ranks of the opponents.[1] But those who remain are not less significantly affected.   It may be noticed that they hardly attempt to deny the force of the case brought against them by their opponents ; they mostly confine their defence to arguing that things are not really so bad as they are represented to be, that there is exaggeration and misrepresentation.   And at worst, and as a last resource, they tend to fall back upon science to say that even the remedy proposed would not be effective in the long-run, and that matters are, in the nature of things, ultimately irremediable.

And so our modern progress towards the equalisation of the conditions of life continues to be made. It is not so much the determination of the attack, although it is both firm and determined as far as may be ; it is rather that, through the all-pervading influence in our civilisation of that immense fund of altruism with which it has been equipped, the occupying party finds its faith in its own cause undermined.   It possesses no firm conviction of the

---

[1] The leaders of the masses do not always realise the nature of the forces which are working on their side, and they sometimes overlook how much they owe to those who are naturally members of the party to which they are opposed.   Mr. Grant Allen has lately pointed out that the chief reformers have not, as a rule, come from the masses. "Most of the best Radicals I have known," he says, "were men of gentle birth and breeding," although others, just as earnest, just as eager, just as chivalrous, sprang from the masses.   It is, he says, a common taunt on the one side to say that the battle is one between the Haves and the Have-nots.   But that is by no means true.   "It is between the selfish Haves on the one side, and the unselfish Haves who wish to see something done for the Have-nots on the other."—*Westminster Gazette*, 26th April 1893.

justice of its position of the kind necessary to
maintain that position successfully against attack;
it has agreed upon an orderly retreat; it is abandon-
ing its outworks, surrendering its positions, evacuating
its entrenchments one after the other and all along
the line.   This is the real significance of the remarkable and altogether exceptionable spectacle presented
throughout our Western civilisation at the present
day.

If we look round now at all the great social and
political movements which are in progress, it may be
perceived that we possess the key to our times.   It
is in this softening of the character, in this deepening
and strengthening of the altruistic feelings, with their
increased sensitiveness to stimulus, and the consequent
ever-growing sense of responsibility to each other,
that we have the explanation of all the social and
political movements which are characteristic of the
period.   In the times in which we are living, the
most remarkable product of this spirit is that widespread movement affecting the working classes
throughout Europe and America, which has been
described as the "revolt of labour."   Of all the
developments in progress at the end of the nineteenth century, it is the most important because
the most characteristic.   But, like all other social
movements that have preceded it, it is the direct
product of the change in character we are undergoing, born of it in due time, intimately and
vitally associated with it at every point, incapable of
any success or even of any existence apart from it.
It has been the custom to attribute the progress and
the success of the movement by which the working
classes have already obtained a large share of political

power and through which they are now laying the
foundation of a more equal social state, to a variety
of causes,—to the spread of education, to the growth
of intelligence, to the development of the influence of
the press, to the progress of industrialism, to the
annihilation of space by the improved means of
communication and the increased opportunities for
organisation resulting, and, generally, to "economic
tendencies" of all kinds.   But it is primarily due to
none of these things.   It has its roots in a single
cause, namely, the development of the humanitarian
feelings, and the deepening and softening of character
that has taken place amongst the Western peoples.

The manner in which the cause acts will be
immediately perceived on reflection.   The working
classes are indeed themselves keenly alive to the
method of its operation.   It may be constantly
noticed in the course of the struggle in which labour
is engaged against the terms of the capitalist class,
and more particularly in those pitched battles which
occur from time to time in the form of strikes, that
the determining factor is always in reality public
opinion ; and, in Great Britain at least, public
opinion tends to be more and more on the side of
the working classes when the battle is fairly conducted.   This public opinion, it must be remarked
also, is by no means merely the opinion of those
sections of the population which might be expected
to sympathise with the lower masses through class-
feeling or motives of class-selfishness ; it includes the
opinions of large numbers of individuals of all classes,
not excepting many whose interests, so far as they
are concerned, would tend to be favourably affected
by the success of the other party engaged.

It is the same if we look round in other directions. It is the action of this fund of altruistic feeling in the community, its all-pervading influence on every one of us, and the resulting sensitiveness of individual and public character to misery or wrong inflicted on any one, however humble, which alone renders that process of social development which is going on around us possible. Without it our laws would be absurd, and our democratic institutions impossible. Mr. Herbert Spencer has lately objected [1] to the English and American system of party government, on the ground that it is capable of lending itself to a one-man or a one-party tyranny. And if we leave out of account the special circumstances of our times, such a system of government does seem in theory one of the most ridiculous that ever existed. Yet, with all its faults, and despite the features Mr. Spencer objects to, it proves to be, in practice, one of the most perfect. A system which, in England, allows a bare majority to rule absolutely would appear to commit small minorities holding opinions differing from those of the great majority of their fellows to the most hopeless form of tyranny. A system which allows a bare majority, when it attains to power, to reverse all the acts of its opponents, would, in a community where party feeling runs high, seem to be an ideal system for securing political chaos. Yet the opinions of minorities are treated with respect, unknown in ancient history, and, in Great Britain at least, the acts of one party are never reversed by its successor. But the reason does not exist in State Constitutions; it is to be found in this extreme sensitiveness of the public

[1] *Principles of Ethics.*

conscience to wrong or unfairness. Acts which are considered wrong could not be attempted with impunity by any party, for it would find itself immediately deserted by its own supporters.

It is here, and here only, that we stand in the real presence of the force that is moving, regulating, and reconstructing the world around us, without which our progress would cease, and our forms of government be unworkable. It must be remembered that, as in the case of slavery, the intellect alone can never furnish any sanction to the power-holding classes for surrendering to the people the influence and position which they have inherited. If the teaching of the intellect is merely that the process tending to secure the survival of the fittest, and the elimination of the least efficient, goes on as efficiently under all the forms of the highest civilisation as elsewhere, then, to repeat the argument already used, individual reason alone cannot be expected to furnish any condemnation of those who, being the strongest, and regarding their interests enclosed within the span of a single lifetime, or at best within the lifetime of a few generations, should utilise their strength to their own advantage. They could do so with courage and conviction. The conception of the native equality of men which has played so great a part in the social development that has taken place in our civilisation is essentially irrational. It receives no sanction from reason or experience; it is the characteristic product of that ultra-rational system of ethics upon which our civilisation is founded.

We have only to imagine the development of the altruistic feelings which has taken place as non-existent to realise forcibly the immense part which it plays in our modern societies. If we can picture the power-holding classes throughout our Western civilisation again filled with that firm belief in their own cause and their own privileges, and that contempt for large masses of their fellow-creatures which prevailed among the "pure democracies" of ancient Greece, and under the Roman Republic and Empire, we shall have no difficulty in realising what a feeble barrier all the boasted power to which the people have attained would be against class rule, even of the most ruthless and intolerant kind. The rich and the power-holding classes would be able even now, in the freest and most advanced communities, to restrain, arrest, and turn back the tide of progress. All the liberties and securities of the most extended constitutional Democracy would be no more than the liberties and securities of the Roman Republic were to Marius or to Sylla before the rise of the Empire. All the power of the press ; all the appliances of science ; all the developments of industrialism ; all the "economic tendencies" which are now held to make for the influence of the people, would, in such circumstances, prove, each and every one, but effective weapons of offence and defence in the hands of an oppressive oligarchy.

If the mind is carried a short distance backwards, it will be seen, now, that the more essential conclusions to which we have been led in the present chapter are as follows. First, that the process of social development which has been taking place, and which is still in progress in our Western civilisation, is not the product of the intellect, but that the motive force behind it has had its origin in, and is still sustained by, that fund of altruistic feeling with which our

civilisation has become equipped.   Second, that this
altruistic development, and the deepening and softening of character which has accompanied it, are the
direct and peculiar product of the religious system
on which our civilisation is founded.   Third, that to
science the significance of the resulting process of
social evolution, in which all the people are being
slowly brought into the rivalry of existence on equal
conditions, consists in the single fact that this rivalry
has tended to be thereby raised to the highest degree
of efficiency as a cause of progress it has ever attained.
The peoples affected by the process have been thereby
worked up to a state of social efficiency which has
given them preponderating advantages in the struggle
for existence with other sections of the race.

   If we are to regard our civilisation as a single
organic growth, and if, for the seat of these vital
forces that are producing the movements in progress
around us, we must look to the ethical development
which has projected itself through the history of the
Western races, it is evident that it is from the epoch
of the Renaissance and the Reformation that we
must, in a strictly scientific sense, date the modern
expansion of society.   From the point of view of
science the pre-Reformation and the post-Reforma-
tion movement is an unbroken unity seen in different
stages of growth.   But it is in the period of the post-
Reformation development that it became the destiny
of the religious system, upon which our civilisation is
founded, to release into the practical life of the world
the characteristic product which constitutes such a
powerful motive influence enlisted in the cause of
progress.   The development which took place at
this stage in the life of the social organism could

only take place then.   The time for it can never
recur.   The subsequent course of social development must be different amongst the peoples where
it was retarded or suppressed, and amongst those
where it was allowed to follow its natural course.[1]
The nature of this difference, caused by the greater
development of the humanitarian feelings, and the
greater extent to which the deepening and softening
of the character has proceeded amongst the peoples
most affected by the Reformation, will be dealt with
at a later stage.[2]

It has been the aim of a certain class of writers,
which has one of its most distinguished representatives
in Mr. Herbert Spencer, to lead us to regard the
altruistic sentiments as a kind of product which is
being accumulated, as it were, by use in our civilisation, and which we tend, therefore, to transmit in
ever-increasing ratio to our descendants.   In course

[1] Mr. Lecky has followed Macaulay (Essay on Ranke's *History*) in
noticing that the later movements of opinion amongst peoples who have
not accepted the principles of the Reformation have been, not towards
those principles, but towards Rationalism (*History of Rationalism*, vol.
i. pp. 170-173).   It is so; but the conclusions often drawn from this
fact, disparaging to the Reformation, have arisen from an incomplete
sense of the nature of the progressive development we are undergoing.
The time for the development which then took place has for ever gone
by; it cannot be repeated at a later stage in the life of the organism.
But the subsequent course of social progress amongst the peoples where
the movement followed its natural order, will be profoundly different
from elsewhere.   It is amongst these peoples, as will be seen in a
later chapter, that the social revolution which it is the destiny of our
civilisation to accomplish must proceed by the most orderly stages,
and must reach its completest expression.

[2] The vital connection between the modern industrial expansion and
the Reformation is recognised by many socialists.   See, for instance,
the section on "the Modern Revolution" in Mr. Belfort Bax's *Religion
of Socialism*.   It is, of course, treated of from the author's peculiar
standpoint; but in this, as in many other matters, socialistic writers
show a sense of the essential unity and interdependence of the various
phases of our social phenomena which is often wanting in their critics.

of time, according to this view, we may expect to be
born ready to act naturally and instinctively in a
manner conducive to the good of society. The
exercise of the altruistic feelings would, in such circumstances, be independent of all religious sanctions,
including that larger class which operate indirectly
through producing satisfactions of the kind which
most people, whatever their opinions, derive from
acting in accordance with standards which general
feeling holds to be right. This party, as we shall see
farther on, must, however, sooner or later, find itself
ranged in opposition to the progressive tendencies
of modern biological science, as, indeed, Mr. Spencer
has already found himself to be in the controversy
which he has recently undertaken against the
Weismann theories.[1] The aim throughout the preceding pages has been to show that the peculiar
feature in which human evolution differs from all
previous evolution consists in the progressive development of the intellect, rendering it impossible that
instincts of the kind indicated should continue to
act as efficient sanctions for altruistic conduct.
Before the advent of man the cause of progress was
always served by the forms of life which preceded
him being endowed with instincts rendering them subservient to the end which the process of evolution was
working out. A difference in his case is, that by the
possession of reason he has become equipped with the
power to obtain satisfaction of such instincts without
entailing the consequences. He has at many points

---

[1] Vide *Contemporary Review*, February 1893, "The Inadequacy of
Natural Selection, I."; *Ibid.* March 1893, "The Inadequacy of
Natural Selection, II."; *Ibid.* May 1893, "Professor Weismann's
Theories."

in his career, and more particularly in his declining civilisations, engaged in the attempt to circumvent some of the most imperative of them. The intellect, uncontrolled by ethical forces of the kind we have been considering, must, in society, be always individualistic, disintegrating, destructive ; even, as we shall have to observe later, to the extent of suspending the operation (in the interests of the evolution the race is undergoing) of fundamental feelings like the parental instincts, which have behind them, not only the infinitesimal period during which society has existed, but the whole span of time since the beginning of life.[1] Hence the characteristic feature of human evolution, ever growing with the growth and developing with the development of the intellect, and forming the natural complement of its growth and development ; namely, the phenomenon of our religions—the function of which is to provide the necessary controlling sanctions in the new circumstances. Hence also the success of those forms which have provided sanctions that have contributed most effectively to the working out of that cosmic process which has been in progress from the beginning of life. Human reason alone can never, in the nature of things, provide any effective sanction to the individual for conduct which contributes to the furtherance of this process, for one of the essential features of the cosmic process is the sacrifice of the individual himself, not merely in the interest of his fellows around him, but in the interests of generations yet unborn.[2]

[1] See pp. 313-319, chap. x.
[2] The common but short-sighted objection that there exists amongst us a considerable number of persons of the highest motives

In conclusion, it may be remarked that nothing
tends to exhibit more strikingly the extent to which
the study of our social phenomena must in future be
based on the biological sciences, than the fact that
the technical controversy now being waged by
biologists as to the transmission or non-transmission
to offspring of qualities acquired during the lifetime
of the parent, is one which, if decided in the latter
sense, must produce the most revolutionary effect
throughout the whole domain of social and political
philosophy.   If the old view is correct, and the
effects of use and education *are* transmitted by
inheritance, then the Utopian dreams of philosophy
in the past are undoubtedly possible of realisation.
If the individual tends to inherit in his own person at
birth the result of the education and mental and moral
culture of past generations, then we may venture to
anticipate a future society which will not deteriorate,
but which may continue to make progress, even though
the struggle for existence be suspended, the population
regulated exactly to the means of subsistence, and
the antagonism between the individual and the social
organism extinguished, even as Mr. Herbert Spencer
has anticipated.[1]   But if, as the writer believes, the
views of the Weismann party are in the main correct ;
if there can be no progress except by the accumulation
of congenital variations above the average to the
exclusion of others below ; if, without the constant
stress of selection which this involves, the tendency

who are not consciously affected by the religious movement to which
we have been attributing so much importance, who regard themselves
as outside its influence, but who are nevertheless affected by, and in
full sympathy with the altruistic influences which are making for
progress, will be found discussed in its proper place in the next chapter.
   [1] Vide *Data of Ethics*, chap. xiv.

of every higher form of life *is actually retrograde ;*
then is the whole human race caught in the toils of
that struggle and rivalry of life which has been in
progress from the beginning. Then must the rivalry
of existence continue, humanised as to conditions it
may be, but immutable and inevitable to the end.
Then also must all the phenomena of human life,
individual, political, social, and religious, be considered
as aspects of this cosmic process, capable of being
studied and understood by science only in their
relations thereto.

CHAPTER VIII

MODERN SOCIALISM

BEFORE proceeding now to the further consideration of the laws which underlie the complex social
phenomena that present themselves in the civilisation
around us, it will be well to look for a moment
backwards, so as to impress on the mind the more
characteristic features of the ground over which we
have travelled.

We have seen that progress from the beginning
of life has been the result of the most strenuous and
imperative conditions of rivalry and selection, certain
fundamental physiological laws rendering it impossible, in any other circumstances, for life to continue along the upward path it has taken. Man being
subject like other forms of life to the physiological
laws in question, his progress also was possible only
under the conditions which had prevailed from the
beginning. The same process, accordingly, takes its
course throughout human history. But it does so
accompanied by phenomena quite special and peculiar.
The human intellect has been, and must necessarily
continue to be, an important factor in the evolution
which is proceeding. Yet the resulting self-assertiveness of the individual must be absolutely subordinated

to the maintenance of a process in which the individual himself has not the slightest interest, but to the furtherance of which his personal welfare must be often sacrificed.   Hence the central feature of human history, namely the dominance of that progressively developing class of phenomena included under the head of religions whereby this subordination has been effected.   Hence, also, the success of those forms which have contributed to the fullest working out of that cosmic process which is proceeding throughout human existence, just as it has been proceeding from the beginning of life.

What we have, therefore, specially to note before advancing farther is, that it is this cosmic process which is everywhere triumphant in human history. There has been no suspension of it.   There has been no tendency towards its suspension.   On the contrary, throughout the period during which the race has existed, the peoples amongst whom the process has operated under most favourable conditions have always been the most successful.   And the significance of that last and greatest phase of social development which has taken place in our Western civilisation, in which all the people are being slowly brought into the rivalry of life, consists simply in the fact that this process tends to reach therein the fullest and completest expression it has ever attained.

Keeping these facts in mind, let us now proceed to consider the significance of that great social movement which is beginning to exert a gradually deepening influence on the political life of our period. The uprising known throughout Europe, and in America, as the Socialist movement is the most characteristic product of our time.   Nothing is, however, more remarkable than the uncertainty, hesitation, and even bewilderment with which it is regarded, not only by those whose business lies with the practical politics of the current day, but by some of those who, from the larger outlook of social and historical science, might be expected to have formed some conception of its nature, its proportions, and its meaning.

In attempting to examine this movement, it is a matter of no small importance to carefully consider the environment in which it is to be studied ; for a very brief reflection makes it clear that many of the phenomena associated with it in various parts of our civilisation are due to local causes that have no essential connection with the movement in general. Thus, if France is chosen as the locality in which to study the movement, it sooner or later becomes clear that that country, despite its early and trenchant experiments in democratic government, is not by any means a favourable one in which to observe the progress of modern socialism.   The process of social development therein, although rapid, has been too irregular, and its people have too completely broken with the past to allow of an exact comparison of the relationship to each other of the developmental forces at present at work.   In the recent history of the country, the old spirit and the new have tended to confront each other in extremes ; and we must remember that, despite the genuine triumph which democracy obtained in the period of the Revolution, it is in France that we have witnessed within the nineteenth century attempts to revive, on a most ambitious scale, that ancient spirit of military Cæsarism which is altogether foreign to our civilisation.

In Germany, again, we have a country which in many respects must be considered the true home at the present day of social democracy. Yet it may be noted that even there the causes which have contributed most effectively to swell the proportions of the existing movement are largely local and peculiar. Placed, as the German people are, between a neighbour like France on the one side, and a country like Russia in a far earlier stage of social evolution on the other, they have developed, through force of circumstances, an extensive militaryism which, while essentially defensive and therefore characteristically different from the older type, tends, nevertheless, to retard the process of social expansion which is in progress, and to develop features which are incompatible with the spirit underlying this expansion. In many of its social features, Germany is still backward, although it is difficult to believe, as M. Leroy-Beaulieu asserts, that it remains, despite the rapid advance made by socialism therein, the one country in Europe, excluding Russia, which is most under the sway of old influences.[1] Social development in Germany is, in fact, proceeding unevenly. It is advanced as regards ideas, but in arrear as regards practice ; and such a situation does not offer the most favourable conditions for estimating the character and the destiny of the movement with which the extreme party in that country is identified.

Again, in the United States of America, where we have the most typical Democracy our civilisation

---

[1] Vide *Economiste Français*, " Influence of Civilisation on the Movement of Population," by P. Leroy-Beaulieu, 20th and 27th September 1890.

has produced, we are also under some disadvantage in the study of the forces that lie behind modern socialism. The social question in America is, in all essential respects, the same question as in any other part of our Western civilisation. It is probable too that nowhere else will the spirit which is behind socialism measure itself with greater freedom from disturbing influences against certain opposing forces which are the peculiar product of our modern free communities, than in that country. Yet the special conditions of " newness " which are present largely interfere to prevent the essential character of the social question as a phase of an orderly development which has been long in progress, from being so clearly distinguished in the United States, and, therefore, from being so profitably studied there as elsewhere.

Taking all these considerations into account we shall probably not be able to do better than to follow the lead of Marx in choosing England as the best country in which to study the developments of the modern spirit. We may do so, not only for the reason which influenced Marx, namely, that it is the land in which modern capitalism and in-dustrialism obtained their earliest and fullest ex-pression ; but also because, in this country, the process of social development has been less obscured by local causes and less interrupted by disturbing events. It has, on the whole, proceeded by regular, orderly, and successful stages in the past, and it shows no signs of weakening or cessation in the present. For these reasons it would appear that the relationship of the present to the past and the future may be more profitably studied in England than in anywhere else in our Western Civilisation.

P

Now there is an aspect of English political life at
the end of the nineteenth century which will, not
improbably, at a later period, absorb the attention of
the historian.   This is the remarkable change that
at the present time is slowly and silently taking
place within that great political party which has led
the van of progress during the past one hundred and
fifty years, and which, during the lifetime of the last
few generations, has added to the statute-book a
list of progressive measures that, taken all together,
constitutes in effect one of the greatest revolutions
through which any country has passed in so brief a
period.   At first sight the change in progress has all
the appearance of being a process of disintegration,
and one of its results for the time being must undoubtedly be to strengthen, in some measure, the
opposing ranks.   It is not that the party of progress
has been rent with feuds, or that its strength has
been undermined by malign influences.   On the
contrary, not only has it fought a good fight, but it
has kept the faith.   It is rather that events appear
to have outgrown the faith ; and slowly and almost
imperceptibly the depressing and dispiriting feeling
has spread throughout the ranks that the old watch-
words are losing their meaning, and that the party
is at length confronted with problems which the
well-tried formulæ of the past have no power to
solve.

The unusual and exceptional nature of the crisis
through which political life in England is passing at
the present time, is only brought into greater prominence on a closer view.   It may be observed that
the development which the Liberal party has been
working out in English public life throughout the

nineteenth century has been but the latest phase of
that great social movement, the progress of which
we traced in the last chapter throughout the history
of our Western civilisation ; and in this stage it has
at length almost accomplished the emancipation of
the individual and the establishment of political
equality throughout the entire social organisation.
Since the early part of the century we have had, for
instance, in England a series of measures following
each other at short intervals extending the political
franchise until it now nearly includes the adult male
population.   Side by side with these we have had a
number of measures emancipating trade and commerce from the control of the privileged classes, who,
under the cover of protective laws, made largely in
their own interests, were enabled to tax the community for their benefit.

In like manner, during the century, a long list of
measures has aimed at the curtailment and abolition of class privileges.   Local popularly-elected
bodies of all kinds have been everywhere created,
the tendency of which has been to greatly restrict,
and even to extinguish, the undue local influence
previously exercised by wealth.   The voting power
of the property-owning classes has been gradually
curtailed until it has been reduced almost to the
level of the humblest class of citizens.   The state
services have been thrown open, instead of being
practically reserved for the friends of the privileged
classes ; all comers have been placed on a footing
of equality, and unexampled purity of administration
has been secured throughout the public services.
There has been also a great number of measures
which have aimed at rendering this state of political

equality, not only theoretical, but real and effective. The extension of the franchise has been accompanied by measures like the Ballot Act and the Bribery Acts, intended to protect the weakest and poorest class of people from being interfered with in the exercise of their political rights ; and, lastly, we have had a succession of Education Acts which have aimed at qualifying every citizen to understand and value for himself his rights and position as a member of a free community.

It has to be specially noted now that the political doctrine which lay behind all this extensive list of reforms in England has had certain clearly defined limitations. The acknowledged aim of the political party, under whose influence or direction most of these measures were carried, has always been kept clearly in the foreground. It has been to secure *equal political rights* for all. The first article of faith behind this programme was that, this end being secured, the highest good of the community was then to be secured by allowing the individuals to work out their own social salvation (or damnation) amid the free and unrestricted play of natural forces within the community, hampered by the least possible inter-ference from government. It has been held in England by the progressive party, as a fundamental principle, that " a people among whom there is no habit of spontaneous action for a collective interest —who look habitually to their government to command or prompt them in all matters of joint-concern, who expect to have everything done for them in all matters of joint-concern, who expect to have everything done for them except what can be made an affair of mere habit and routine—have their

faculties only half developed ; their education is de-
fective in one of its most important branches." [1]
The end consistently aimed at was, therefore, the
" restricting to the narrowest compass the interven-
tion of a public authority in the business of the community." [2]   Mill urged with emphasis that the *onus*
of making out of a strong case in respect of this in-
tervention, should further be placed, not on those
who resisted it, but on those who recommended it,
and he insisted without compromise that " letting
alone should be the general practice," and that
" every departure from it, unless required by some
great good, is a certain evil." [3]

Such has been the great English political doctrine
of *laissez-faire.*   To the development, expansion,
and application thereof, one of the most distinguished
group of political leaders and social, political, and
philosophical writers that any country has ever produced, has for a long period contributed.   Under it
the unexampled English expansion of the nineteenth
century has taken place, and it has undoubtedly been
an important factor in producing that expansion.
Taken with all its faults and limitations, it has been
one of the most characteristic products of the political
genius of the English-speaking peoples.   Its spirit
still pervades the entire political life of all the lands
into which these peoples have carried their institutions.   In what respect, therefore, have we outgrown
it ?   What is the import in relation thereto of that
socialistic movement which is now so deeply affecting the minds of certain sections of the population
amongst the Western peoples ?   Whither beyond it

---

[1] *Principles of Political Economy*, J. S. Mill, Book v. chap. xi.
[2] *Ibid.*   [3] *Ibid.*

is that evolution which we have traced throughout the history of these peoples now carrying us?

In order to answer these questions it is necessary to scrutinise the forces at work in English political life at the present time. We have already found that the real impelling force which lies behind the political advance that we, in common with most European peoples, have been making in recent times, has its seat in the development the altruistic feelings have attained amongst us, and in the deepening and softening of character which has accompanied the change. It is these feelings that have found a vehicle for expression in that body of public opinion which, moving slowly in the past but more quickly in our own time, has brought about the gradual political emancipation of the individual from the rule of the privileged classes. What we have, however, now to particularly note, is that the movement which has carried us thus far shows no signs of staying or abating; the same feelings continue to supply an impelling force that threatens to drive us, and that actually *is* driving us, onwards far beyond the limits which the political doctrines of the recent past prescribed.

It may be noticed in England that the political emancipation of the masses, the last stage of which in this country has occupied almost an entire century, is now well-nigh accomplished. The shreds of political measures necessary to complete it—which are all that those who adhere to the progressive faith of the past have to offer—form so slender a programme as scarcely to excite any real enthusiasm amongst the followers of those leaders whose mental horizon is still bounded by the old ideals of the political enfranchisement of the people. On the other hand, an immense number of larger and greatly more important questions have arisen which press for attention. In the unparalleled expansion which has taken place, new and vast problems that the old leaders did not foresee have been born, and it may be noticed that the free and unrestricted play of forces within the community is producing results against which the public conscience, still moved by the altruistic feelings, has been slowly but surely rising in revolt.

In England, within the last decade, descriptions of how the poor live in our great cities, and the revelations made through inquiries like that conducted by the Sweating Commission, or more recently through that instituted on so extensive a scale by Mr. Charles Booth into the condition of the London poor, have deeply stirred the public mind. It is being gradually realised that there are great masses of the people who, amid the unrestricted operation of social and economic forces, and under a régime of political liberty, have never had any fair opportunity in life at all, and who have been from the beginning inevitably condemned to the conditions of a degraded existence. It seems to be already generally felt that something more than mere political liberty is demanded here.

Again, trade and commerce have been to a large extent freed from the control of the privileged classes of the past; but, in the unrestricted expansion which has followed, the capitalist classes appear to have inherited a very large share of the rights and powers of their predecessors. They have even become possessed of others in addition, while the personal sense of relationship, which introduced a modifying sense of duty in the past, tends to become more and more attenuated. Political liberty has not enabled the poorer classes to make headway against the enormous influence which these classes wield, to the extent to which many of the old reformers expected. By the combination of the capitalist classes into rings, trusts, syndicates, and like associations for the universal control of production and the artificial keeping up of prices, the community finds the general welfare threatened by a complication which the reformers of the past can scarcely be said to have counted upon. We have also great organisations and combinations of labour against these capitalist classes whereby the life of the community is disturbed and disorganised to a serious extent, and to which it seems to be increasingly difficult to apply the old doctrine of the restricted nature of the duty of the state. It is evident, moreover, that in these recurring struggles the combatants, if left to themselves, are often unequally matched ; for the weapon on one side is merely the power to reduce profits, while on the other it is the right to impose actual want and hunger on large numbers of our fellow-creatures. We have, therefore, public opinion tending more and more to side with the inherently weaker cause, and, under the stimulus of the altruistic feelings, coming to propose measures that leave the *laissez-faire* doctrine of the past far behind.

It may be observed also, that the public opinion, which earlier in the century regarded with suspicion (as tending to the infringement of the prevailing theories as to the restricted nature of the duty of the state) even the attempt to regulate the hours of women and children in factories and mines, has already come to view as within the realm of reasonable discussion proposals to strengthen the position of the working classes by enforcing a legal eight hours day and even a minimum wage in certain occupations. The public conscience, which is moving fast in these matters, has all the appearance of being destined to move far. We are not without growing evidence that our education laws will not stop with providing the bare rudiments of education for the people, nor with providing them on the grounds mentioned by Mill :—that others are liable to suffer seriously from the consequences of ignorance and want of education in their fellow-citizens.[1] Nor would indications seem to show that we have reached finality in our poor laws in simply guaranteeing the bare necessities of existence.

We have evidence everywhere along the line, not only of a movement towards the general abandonment of the doctrine of the non-interference of the state in social matters, but of a more significant tendency that seems to be associated with it—*a tendency to strengthen and equip at the general expense the lower and weaker against the higher and wealthier classes of the community.* We have, it is evident, already progressed a considerable distance beyond the doctrine, that the end of endeavour is to secure political equality for all. Yet whither are we travelling ?

Another feature of the times which we may notice is that, under the outward appearance of action, the great political party which has carried progress so far in England stands in reality doubting

[1] Vide *Principles of Political Economy*, Book v. chap. xi.

and confused in mind. It moves, it is true, but rather because it is thrust forward ; the enthusiasm, the robust faith, the clearly defined conviction that marked its advance through the early and middle decades of the nineteenth century seem to be wanting. The ranks move ; but irresolutely. They still appear to wait for the vibrant call of a leader upon whom a larger faith has descended.

While the party of progress in England advances thus falteringly, and with eyes cast backwards rather than forwards, the most remarkable political phenomenon of the time is rising into prominence in another quarter. The socialist movement which has languished through various phases, and fitfully occupied attention in various parts of Europe since the beginning of the century, has entered on a new stage, and has taken the field with a definite political programme. The leaders of the movement, no longer ignoring politics and political methods, now appear to have set before themselves the task of reforming the state through the state. The Utopian projects which distinguished the writings of its earlier advocates have disappeared, and even the essential ideals of the movement tend to be kept in the background, to be discussed amongst the faithful as the ultimate goal rather than with the adversary as the immediate end of endeavour. We have not now to deal with mere abstract and transcendental theories, but with a clearly defined movement in practical politics appealing to some of the deepest instincts of a large proportion of the voting population, and professing to provide a programme likely in the future to stand more and more on its own merits in opposition to all other programmes whatever.

Yet more remarkable still, one of the signs of the times in England is the attitude of the advanced wing of the great progressive party of the past to this new movement. It appears to be slowly wheeling its forces into line with those of this socialist party. To the bewilderment of many of the old leaders, that party whose central article of political faith in the past, namely, the untrammelled freedom of the individual, has given a distinctive colouring to the political life of the whole English-speaking world, is now asked apparently to turn its face in a direction opposite to that in which it has been previously set, and contrary to that in which the evolution of our civilisation has, so far, progressed. The advance in the new direction, it appears to those who still hold to the old faith, must inevitably involve the weakening, if not the ultimate abandonment, of the principles for which the party has fought so long and so sturdily in the past. The individualism which they held so highly, and which has been so markedly associated with the stress and energy of life amongst the advanced peoples, must apparently, if the new views are to prevail, be given up. The play of the competitive forces which has so largely contributed to the extraordinary expansion of the past, must be, it appears to them, not only restricted, but perhaps ultimately suspended in an era of soul-deadening and energy-restricting socialism on the one side, and general confusion and political insolvency on the other.

The question which now presents itself is :— What is the significance of this situation, and of that remarkable period of transition through which political life in England, as in most countries where our civilisation has reached an advanced stage, is passing? Let us, as a means of throwing light on the subject, proceed to examine the leading features of the most prevalent and influential form of socialism at the present day, namely, the "scientific socialism" of the German school more particularly associated with the names of two of its exponents, Marx and Engels.

One of the first things to be noticed by any one who undertakes an examination of the socialistic phenomena of our time, is the remarkable number of schemes, projects, and measures, loosely described as socialist or socialistic, that have nothing whatever of an essentially socialist character about them. Without going so far as to accept Proudhon's definition of socialism as all aspiration towards the improvement of society, a large number of persons appear to make only a slight reservation, and to regard it as all aspiration towards the improvement of society *by* society. True socialism has, however, one invariable characteristic by which it may be always recognised, whether it take the form advocated by the more prevalent German school, or by that anarchist section represented by Proudhon and Bakunin, whose ideal, despite their title and methods, is really a morally perfect state in which government, law, and police would be unnecessary. True socialism has always one definite object in view, up to which all its proposals directly or indirectly lead. This is the final suspension of that personal struggle for existence which has been waged, not only from the beginning of society, but, in one form or another, from the beginning of life.[1]

[1] The existence of an inherent principle of antagonism betweer

Although Marx prudently abstained from putting forward any detailed scheme of the social order which he held was to supersede the present capitalist and competitive era, he, as we shall presently see, deliberately leads us up to this culmination. The attainment of the same object is clearly put forward by Engels as the avowed end of endeavour. As a later example we have the same idea in Mr. Bellamy's artistic model of a socialist community in working order, — a community in which children are to become entitled to an equal share of the national wealth in virtue of being born, in which the prices of staples are to grow less year by year, in which there is to be no state legislature and no legislation, in which there are to be no police and no criminal classes, but in which it can be said at last that "society rests on its base, and is in as little need of support as the everlasting hills."[1]

Now, directly we come to examine these schemes, a somewhat startling admission has to be made, an admission, however, for which those who have followed the argument developed through the preceding chapters will be prepared. It is that the arguments

true socialism and that class of proposals which currently pass under the name of "State Socialism" was uncompromisingly maintained by Herr Leibknecht in his speech at the Social Democratic Congress held at Berlin in November 1892. "Social democracy," said Herr Leibknecht, "has nothing in common with the so-called state socialism, a system of half-measures dictated by fear, and aiming merely at undermining the hold of social democracy over the working classes by petty concessions and palliatives. Such measures social democracy has never disdained to promote and to approve, but it accepts them only as small instalments, which cannot arrest its onward march towards the regeneration of the state and of society on socialistic principles. Social democracy is essentially revolutionary : state socialism is conservative. As such they are irreconcilably opposed."

[1] Vide *Looking Backward*, by Edward Bellamy.

by which their advocates lead up to them are unanswered, and even unanswerable from the point of view from which the greater number of their critics have assailed them. This admission may appear the more remarkable, when it has to be asserted in the same breath that it is probably true that in all the literature which socialism has produced, no serious attempt has been made, and that probably no serious attempt can be made, to deal with even the initial difficulties in the way of the continued success of a society organised on a socialist basis.

At the outset, underneath all socialist ideals, there yawns the problem of population. Progress so far in life has always been, as we have seen, necessarily associated with the inexorable natural law over which man has no control, and over which he can never hope to have any control, which renders selection necessary; and which, therefore, keeps up the stress of life by compelling every type, as the first condition of progress, to continually press upon and tend to outrun the conditions of existence for the time being. One of the fundamental problems which has, therefore, confronted every form of civilisation that has arisen, and which must confront every form that will ever exist, is that arising from the tendency of human reason to come into conflict with nature over this requirement. Under the Utopias of socialism one of two things must happen : either this increase must be restricted or not. If it be not restricted, and selection is allowed to continue, then the whole foundations of such a fabric as Mr. Bellamy has constructed are bodily removed. Even if we imagine the competitive forces suspended for a time between the members of the community, the society as a

whole must, sooner or later, come into active competition with other societies, and so begin once more
one of the phases through which human society has
already passed.

But if, on the other hand, the increase of population is to be restricted, a difficulty no less important
presents itself. A considerable number of persons
have contemplated the action of a new restrictive
influence (although it operated widely in the ancient
civilisations) in public opinion and the conditions of
life under the new order, anticipating, with a lady
writer who has given attention to the subject in
England, the growth of a feeling of intellectual
superiority to " this absurd sacrifice to their children
of generation after generation of grown people." [1]
But in whatever way restriction which would limit
the population to the actual conditions of life might
be effected, it is not necessary, after what has been
said in previous chapters as to the physiological conditions of the process which has been working itself
out throughout life—and nowhere more effectively
and thoroughly than in human history—to deal at
length with the fate of any people amongst whom
the restriction was practised. The conditions of
selection being suspended, such a people could not
in any case avoid progressive degeneration even if
we could imagine them escaping more direct consequences. In ordinary circumstances they would
indubitably receive short shrift when confronted with
the vigorous and aggressive life of societies where,
other things being equal, selection and the stress and
rivalry of existence were still continued.

Again, a class of objections, now being temperately

[1] Mrs. Mona Caird, *Nineteenth Century*, May 1892.

discussed in England and Germany, according to which a state organised on a socialist basis would find more immediate difficulties, hindrances, and drawbacks, which would place it at a manifest disadvantage with other communities, have never been seriously dealt with by socialist writers. The enormous pressure, capable of being exercised by the competitive system at its best, operating continually to ensure the most economic and efficient system of production ; the accompanying tendency of the best men to find the places for which they are best fitted ; the tendency towards the free utilisation of the powers of such men to the fullest degree in the direction of invention, discovery, and improvement, coupled with the difficulty of finding (human nature being what it is) any thoroughly efficient stimulus for the whole of the population to exert itself to the highest degree when the main wants of life were secure, these are all considerations which would, in an earlier stage, tell enormously against a socialist community when matched in the general competition of life against other communities where the stress of life was greater.

It will not help us even if there are to be no competing societies, and if, in the contemplated era of socialism, the whole human family without distinction of race or colour is to be included in a federation within which the competitive forces are to be suspended. We may draw such a draft on our imagination, but our common-sense, which has to deal with materials as they exist, refuses to honour it. We are concerned, not with an imaginary being, but with man as he exists, a creature standing with countless æons of this competition behind him ; every quality of his mind and body (even including, it must always be remembered, that very habit of generous thought for others which gives heart to the modern socialistic movement) the product of this rivalry, with its meaning and allotted place therein, and capable of finding its fullest and fittest employment only in its natural conditions.

But these are the mere commonplaces which only bring us to the crux of the subject. Impressive as such considerations may be to those who have caught the import of the evolutionary science of the time, no greater mistake can be made than to think that they form any practical answer to the arguments of those who would lead us on to socialism. Why? For the simple reason that, as we have throughout insisted, men are not now, and never have been, in the least concerned with, or influenced by, the estimates which scientists or any other class of persons may form of the probable effects of their present conduct on unborn generations. The motives which inspire their present acts are of quite a different kind. But it is these motives which are shaping the course of events, and it is consequently with these, and these only, that we have to deal if we would gauge the character and dimensions of the modern socialist movement. Let us see, therefore, in what way the conception, of what is called scientific socialism—of modern society developing towards socialism as the result of forces now actually at work amongst us— is justified or the contrary.

According to Marx the dominant factor in the evolution through which we are passing is the economic one. The era in which we are living began in the mediæval period with the rise of

Q

capitalism.   To understand what capitalism is—and
few writers have grasped more thoroughly than Marx
some of the ultimate facts which underlie the institution in the form in which he attacked it—we have
to get behind the superficial phrases, and some of
the errors of the political economists of the old
school.   When we reach the heart of the matter we
find it to be, according to Marx, a system by which
the capitalist is enabled to appropriate the *surplus
value* of the work of the labourers, these being able
to retain as wages only what represents the average
subsistence necessary for themselves and their children
in keeping up this supply of labour.   There is thus
an inherent antagonism between the two classes.

As the conflict takes shape it begins to develop
remarkable features.   At the one pole we have the
continued appropriation and accumulation of surplus
value, with the ever-increasing wealth and power of
those in whose hands it is concentrated.   At the
other end we have the progressive enslavement and
degradation of the exploited classes.   As the development continues, the workers, on the one hand,
gradually come to recognise their position as a class
and become possessed of a sense of their common
interests.   On the other hand, the competition
amongst the capitalist class is great and continually
growing ; the larger capitalists gradually extinguish
the smaller ones, and wealth becomes accumulated
in fewer and fewer hands.   To quote Marx's words :—
" Along with the constantly diminishing number of
the magnates of capital, who usurp and monopolise
all advantages of this process of transformation, grow
the mass of misery, oppression, slavery, degradation,
exploitation ; but with this, too grows the revolt

of the working class, a class always increasing in numbers and disciplined, united, organised by the very mechanism of the process of capitalist production itself. The monopoly of capital becomes a fetter upon the mode of production, which has sprung up and flourished along with and under it. Centralisation of the means of production and socialisation of labour, at last, reach a point when they become incompatible with their capitalist integument. This integument is burst asunder. The knell of capitalist private property sounds."[1] That is to say, the state of things becomes at length intolerable; there is anarchy in production, accompanied by constantly recurring commercial crises; and the incapacity of the capitalist classes to manage the productive forces being manifest, public opinion at last comes to a head. The organised workers seize possession of the means of production, transforming them into public property, and socialistic production becomes henceforward possible.

The transformation supposed to be effected in the latter stage of the movement is thus described by Frederick Engels: "With the seizing of the means of production by society, production of commodities is done away with, and, simultaneously, the mastery of the product over the producer. Anarchy in social production is replaced by systematic, definite organisation. The struggle for individual existence disappears. Then, for the first time, man, in a certain sense, is finally marked off from the rest of the animal kingdom, and emerges from mere animal conditions of existence into really human ones. The

---

[1] *Capital*, by Karl Marx, English translation (Swan Sonnenschein & Co., 1887), vol. ii. pp. 788, 789.

whole sphere of the conditions which environ man, and which have hitherto ruled man, now comes under the dominion and control of man, who now, for the first time, becomes the real conscious lord of Nature, because he has now become master of his own social organisation. . . . It is the ascent of man from the kingdom of necessity to the kingdom of freedom." [1]

This is the Marx-Engels theory of our modern civilisation, and of the denouement to which it is hastening, so far as justice can be done to it in so brief a summary. It is a conception, whatever its shortcomings, of power and originality—displaying, despite its errors, a deep knowledge of social forces and a masterful grasp of some of the first principles underlying our complex modern life.

Now, the first fact which it is necessary to keep clearly before the mind in dealing with this theory of society is, that this relationship of capital to labour which Marx has described is nothing more than the present-day expression of a social relationship which has existed throughout the greater part of human history. There is nothing new or special about the fact which underlies the theory of surplus value ; nor is it peculiar to the capitalist era any more than to any other era. We had what corresponds to the appropriation of the surplus value of the work of the lower masses of the people by the ruling classes in all the early military societies, in the Greek States, and under the Roman Republic and Empire. We had it in a marked form under the institution of slavery, and it continued under the feudal system which preceded the rise of modern capitalism. With the

[1] *Socialism, Utopian and Scientific*, by Frederick Engels, translated by Edward Aveling, 1892.

discoveries of science, and their application to the wants of life, we have it only under another phase in the resulting era of expansion and capitalism in which we are now living.[1]

But while this fact must never be lost sight of, it must, at the same time, be noticed that there *is* a development taking place in this relationship of labour to capital, a development of the most significant kind which is likely, as time goes on, to control and dominate the entire political outlook. Although Marx, it appears to the writer, has been quite mistaken as to the nature of the development which is taking place in our civilisation, and as to the direction in which it is carrying us ; it will, nevertheless, in all probability be recognised in the future that he has been much nearer the truth in regarding, as he did, the prevailing relationship of the workers to the capitalist classes, than the hitherto dominant school of political economists have been in regarding it as the natural and normal condition of

---

[1] The younger school of economists in England have not yet quite done justice to Marx's conception of the state of capitalistic society which he describes. It is quite true, as Professor Marshall remarks ("Some Aspects of Competition," *Journal Roy. Stat. Soc.* December 1890), that socialist schemes founded thereon "seem to be vitiated by want of attention to the analysis which the economists of the modern age have made of the functions of the undertaker of business enterprises," and that they "seem to think too much of competition as the exploiting of labour by capital, of the poor by the wealthy, and too little of it as the constant experiment by the ablest men for their several tasks, each trying to discover a new way in which to attain some important end." But it must also be kept well in mind—and the rising school of economic science can do nothing but good in keeping the fact always clearly in view—that the rights and privileges of capital and wealth have hitherto been much more than those which necessarily attach to "the function of the undertaker of business enterprises" in order to attain the highest possible efficiency. Marx went much too far, but the idea underlying his conception of the exploitation of labour in the past is, in the main, sound and scientific.

the two parties, any disturbance of which must involve the dislocation of the entire social machinery of the modern world. Not the least important part of the work which Marx has already accomplished (for to the influence of the socialist party the change is undoubtedly due) is the tendency already visible amongst the younger and rising school of political economists, particularly in England, to question whether this relationship *is* natural and normal, and whether the extraordinary powers and privileges which capital has inherited from a past order of society—powers begetting, to use words of Professor Marshall, "the cruelty and waste of irresponsible competition and the licentious use of wealth," [1]— constitute any necessary feature of the institution of private capital in enabling it to discharge the beneficial function it is held to be capable of performing for society

Now, the development which Marx contemplated is, it may be observed, thoroughly materialistic ; it takes no account of those prime evolutionary forces which lie behind the whole process of our social development. The phenomenon which underlies what has been called the exploitation of labour is, as we have seen, in no way new or special to our time. What then is the special factor in modern life which has enabled Marx to anticipate the growing power of the workers, and as a result to picture with some degree of verisimilitude a stage at which it will become irresistible, and at which they will proceed to seize and socialise the means of production ? His followers may

[1] *Journal of the Royal Statistical Society*, December 1890, p. 643. Reprint of Address as President of Economic Section, British Association, Meeting September 1890.

reply that it is the inherent tendency of the process of economic evolution actually in progress. Yet it is nothing of the kind. If any of Marx's followers really hold this view, they are deceiving themselves. The economic problem *per se* has no inherent tendency whatever which it did not possess under any other phase of society, and from the beginning. The new factor in the problem is one altogether outside of and independent of the economic situation.

If we look round at the position of the workers at the present day, and note their relations to the state and to the capitalist class, it will be seen that the one absolutely new and special feature which distinguishes these relationships now, as compared with all past periods, is, that the exploited classes, as the result of an evolution long in progress, and still continuing with unabated pace, have been admitted to the exercise of political power on a footing which tends more and more to be one of actual equality with those who have hitherto held them in subjection. This evolution has its causes exclusively in that ethical development, the course of which has been traced in the previous chapter. It is the cardinal and essential feature of the situation dominating the entire outlook, but remaining entirely independent of the economic question.

It will help materially towards the clearer understanding of the position if this feature of the situation is kept well in view. We may perceive the importance of the factor at once if it is taken away. The materialistic evolution of Marx is left without its motive power. For, if we are to have only the frank selfishness of the exploiting classes on the one side, and the equally materialistic selfishness of the exploited classes on the other, "the inherent tendency of modern society" disappears. There would remain nothing , whatever in the present constitution of society, economic or otherwise, which would lead us to expect any progress towards the culmination which Marx describes, but everything which would lead us to anticipate the repetition of a well-worn tale of history. If we are to have nothing but materialistic selfishness on the one side leagued against equally materialistic selfishness on the other, then the power-holding classes, being still immeasurably the stronger, would be quite capable of taking care of themselves, and would indeed be very foolish if they did not do so. Instead of enfranchising, educating, and raising the lower masses of the people (as they are now doing as the result of a development which Marx has not taken into account), they would know perfectly well, as they have always done in the past, "how to keep the people in their places," *i.e.* in ignorance and political disability, all the modern tendency of capital towards competition and concentration notwithstanding.

But, it will be answered, the feature of our times, which there is no gainsaying, is the humanitarian tendency in the contrary direction. The situation with which we have to deal is one in which this materialistic selfishness does not exist. Never in human history have the minds of men been moved with nobler or more generous ideas towards each other ; and the whole tendency of our civilisation has been, and continues to be, to develop this disposition. Quite so. This is, indeed, the reason why we are only likely to misinterpret, as Marx has undoubtedly done, the nature and tendency of the

economic development we are undergoing, by regarding it apart in itself as the key to the whole
situation, instead of as only a subordinate phase of
an immensely wider evolutionary process. From the
larger outlook the view is immeasurably widened. The
development that will fill the history of the twentieth
century will certainly be the change in the relations
of capital, labour, and the state ; but once we have
grasped the fundamental laws behind that development as a whole, it becomes clear that the change,
vast and significant as it undoubtedly promises to
be, will, nevertheless, be one essentially and profoundly different both in character and results from
that which Marx anticipated.

To understand the nature of this change, it is
desirable now to call to mind once more the leading
features of that remarkable process of social development which has been in progress throughout the
history of our civilisation. We found this process
to consist essentially in the slow disintegration of
that military type of society which reached its
highest development in the Roman Empire. The
change has been gradually accomplished against the
prolonged resistance encountered under innumerable
forms of those privileged classes which obtained,
under this constitution of society, the influence they
have in considerable measure, although to a gradually
diminishing extent, continued to enjoy down into
the time in which we are living. Let us see then, in
the first place, what have been the tendencies of this
process so far, for this must evidently be a most important consideration in endeavouring to form an
estimate of the direction in which it is carrying us.

If we look at this process as a whole, it will be

seen that, so far as it has proceeded, it presents two easily recognised features. There have been two distinct tendencies displayed therein, each constant, growing, unmistakable. In the first place, there can be no doubt that, allowing for all disappointments and drawbacks, the social progress, moral and material, which the masses of the people have made since the process commenced has been great, and has been, although interrupted at times, practically continuous. It must be remembered that, at the period at which we take up the process, the lower masses of the people amongst the present European nations possessed scarcely any social or political rights. Great numbers of them lived continually on the brink of starvation ; military force was almost the only law society recognised ; and slavery, which had hitherto been an almost universal human institution, had behind it not only all the authority of force, but the unquestioned sanction of the highest civilisation which man had so far reached. The instincts which led men to prey on each other were scarcely more restrained than amongst the lower animals, and it must not be assumed that this was the result of the disorganised state of society ; for, following the example of the ancient empires, all associations of men with any definite pretensions to a national existence aspired as a legitimate object to prey on other peoples. The feudal lords, in like manner, preyed on their neighbours whenever their resources and following gave them hope of success, so that scarcely any district was long free from the horrors and outrage of war in one shape or another.

No glamour can hide the wretchedness of the masses of the people throughout the early stages of

the history of the present European peoples. Their
position was, at best, but one of slavery slightly
modified. The worse than animal conditions to
which they were subject, the unwholesome food on
which they fared, and the state of general destitution
in which they lived, must, in all probability, be held
to be associated with the general prevalence in
Europe late into the Middle Ages of widely prevalent diseases that have since become extinct.
The terrible "plague" epidemics periodically de-
vastated Europe on a scale and to an extent which
the modern world has no experience of, and which
we can only very imperfectly realise. After the
break-up of military feudalism the condition of
things was little better. The people were crushed
under the weight of rents, services, taxations, and
exactions of all kinds. Trade, commerce, industry,
and agriculture were harassed, restricted, and im-
poverished by the multitude of burthens imposed on
them—burthens which only during the last hundred
years have been eased or removed in most Western
countries. Many who now rightly recognise that we
have lived through the period of *laissez-faire*, but
who rail at the doctrine itself, have a very imperfect
conception of the time which produced it ; a time
when the power-holding classes—to use Carlyle's
forcible phrase—regarded "industry all noosed and
haltered, as if it were some beast of the chase for the
mighty hunters of this world to bait and cut slices
from," a time when it "cried passionately to its
well-paid guides and watchers, not *guide me ;* but
laissez-faire. Leave me alone of *your* guidance ! "[1]

[1] In the *Journal de la Société de Statistique de Paris*, March 1889,
Alfred Neymarck enumerates some of the burthens imposed on the

Slow though the improvement in material conditions has been, it has been, nevertheless, unmistakable as the people have gradually acquired a larger and larger share of political power; but it has, naturally, been greatest as we approach our own times. No careful student of history can ignore the significance of the improvement in the position of the masses of the people which has taken place in such countries as England and France during the nineteenth century. In England the progress, as we approach our own day, has been enormous. At the bottom of the scale we find, as Mr. Giffen showed a few years ago,[1] an almost continuous decrease in the proportion of paupers since 1855. The wages of almost all classes have greatly risen, and their purchasing power is greater. The savings bank deposits and depositors show a progressive increase which is most striking. The houses in which the masses of the people live are better, and continually increase in value; the conditions of life are more healthy and refined, and continually tend towards improve-

peasant in France one hundred years ago. "Without taking into account services to be paid for in kind, he was called upon to pay *dîmes, tailles, capitations, vingtièmes,* and *centièmes, corvées, aides, gabelles,* etc. If he was desirous of selling in the markets open to him the produce of his labour, he was forced to pay the dues on *mesurage, piquetage, minage, sterlage, palette, écuellée, pied fourchu, angayage, éprouvage,* and *étalage;* that is to say he was mulcted for each measure of grain sold; for each cow, pig, or sheep; for each load of wheat brought in by strangers; for each basket containing fowls, eggs, butter, and cheese, and for each horse examined and sold" (see translation of paper in *Journal of the Royal Statistical Society,* June 1889). See also Mill's *Political Economy,* Book v. chap. xi., for an account of the restrictions and burthens which the state formerly placed upon commerce and manufactures.

[1] Vide *Journal of the Royal Statistical Society,* December 1887; Presidential Address, Economic Section, British Association, Meeting December 1887.

ment. The hours of labour are much less, and tend towards further reduction ; the conditions of work have been greatly improved ; and education, amusement, and recreation are provided for the people on a greatly extended scale. Nay, at last, we have the rising school of orthodox political economists in England already beginning to question whether poverty itself may not be abolished, and whether it is necessarily any more a permanent human institution than was slavery.

It has been the same in France. It must be remembered that we have to compare the present condition of the mass of the population, not with their state under some ideal organisation of society, but with their actual condition in the past. In a very striking comparison of the present and the past in France by Alfred Neymarck, which appeared in the *Journal de la Société de Statistique de Paris* for March 1889, some interesting facts are recorded. " During the last centuries," says the author, " famine which we now only know by name, and of which we have no practical experience, was, in some sort, a permanent institution on the fertile soil of France. In the twelfth century it made its appearance over fifty times. Under Louis XIV. in 1663 and 1690, and in 1790, whole populations were absolutely dying of hunger." [1] A century ago the peasant in France suffered continual privation ; such a condition had become chronic. " White bread was a thing unknown ; once or twice a year, at Easter or at other high festivals, a piece of bacon was regarded as a luxury. Oil of rape-seed and beech-oil were used to render the most common vegetables palatable. The

[1] *Vide* Translation, *Journal Royal Statistical Society*, June 1889.

ordinary beverage was water; beer was dear, cider
not less so, and wine was a luxury exceedingly rare."

As against this the author contrasts the present
condition of the lower classes. "One has only to
glance at the labouring man when engaged at his
work, to see that the quality of his clothing has
improved, and that the shoe has replaced the sabot.
Instead of the tattered garments, veritable rags in
fact, formerly worn by women, has succeeded printed
calicoes, wool, and cloth; and in the poorest houses
it is a common thing to find linen, clean and white,
put away for use on Sundays and *fête* days, and it
is by no means unusual to find in a large number
of cottages both books and flowers. Wages have
increased three, four, five, and even tenfold in certain
industries. Formerly a workman barely gained, and
that with the hardest labour, from one to two francs
a day; he now receives from five, six, eight, and
sometimes ten francs."[1] The average duration of
life has, the author says, increased; the rate of
mortality is lower; the quality of food has improved;
house accommodation is better; clothing more healthy;
and temperance more extensively practised.

In whatever direction we look we find evidence
of this same tendency. Foreign economic writers
are already beginning to remark that one of the
most striking of recent economic phenomena in
England is the check which appears to have been
given to the growth of large fortunes, and the wider
and more even distribution of wealth which is taking
place. The same tendency is visible in France;
M. Claudio Jannet has recently stated that there are
not now in France more than 700 to 800 persons

[1] *Vide* Translation, *Journal Royal Statistical Society*, June 1889.

with £10,000 a year, and not more than 18,000 to 20,000 with £2000 and upwards.   He shows also that, whereas the national debt in that country has doubled from 1869 to 1881, the holders have quadrupled.   The number of small holders of bonds tends to greatly increase, and he mentions that one-half of the bonds of the city of Paris are owned by holders of a single bond.   Other figures quoted are also striking.   Out of 8,302,272 inhabited houses in France, he states that 5,460,355, or about 65 per cent, are occupied by their owners.[1]   Some years ago Mr. Goschen furnished us with an equally interesting set of facts exhibiting the tendency to the increase of moderate incomes in England.[2]

The conditions of life of the masses of the people show everywhere a progressive improvement—the improvement, so far, following the development by which the people have attained to a larger and larger share of political power.   This feature is sometimes dwelt upon by those who wished to draw conclusions

---

[1] See *Le Capital, la Spéculation et la Finance au xix* Siècle*, par Claudio Jannet, Paris, 1892. The author says (p. 30): "Le recensement des habitations auquel l'administration des contributions directes a procédé en 1888 pour évaluer la propriété bâtie, a mis ce fait en pleine évidence. Sur 8,302,272 maisons d'habitation (déduction faite de 612,251 non occupées), 5,460,355 sont habitées par leur propriétaire, ce qui fait plus de 65 p. 100, les deux tiers, pour la France entière."

His statement respecting the gradual increase in the number of holders of the public funds is as follows :—" Le nombre des inscriptions de rentes était, en 1886, de 3,861,280 pour 743 millions de rente 3 pour 100 et 4½ ; au 31 décembre 1889, il était de 4,708,348 pour 856 millions de rente.   Cela ne veut pas dire qu'il y ait un pareil nombre de rentiers, car le même personne possède souvent plusieurs inscriptions. M. Leroy-Beaulieu évaluait à environ un million le nombre des possesseurs de rente en 1881. Il est évidemment plus considérable aujourd'hui, car, au fur et à mesure que les grands emprunts se classent, la rente se dissémine davantage.   Tandis que, de 1869 à 1891, le chiffre total des rentes doublait, le nombre des inscriptions quadruplait " (p. 32).

[2] Vide *Journal of the Royal Statistical Society*, December 1887.

therefrom favourable to the continuance of the existing order of things.   But we must not on that
account ignore the facts altogether, as is sometimes
done by writers of extreme views on the other side.
In estimating the situation, our first duty clearly is
to take all its features fairly into account ; and when
this is done it must be frankly admitted that there is
no justification whatever for either thinking or speaking of the past century as a period of progressive
degeneration for the working classes.   All the facts
point unmistakably the other way.

If we look now in another quarter, the second
tendency of the developmental tendency which has
been, so far, in progress, is even more clearly dis-
cernible.   The movement which is thus slowly
raising the condition of the masses, and bringing
about more equal conditions of life amongst the
people, has not hitherto operated to suspend the
rivalry and competition of life.   On the contrary, the
more carefully we consider the whole process, the
more clearly does it appear that its tendency has
been in the opposite direction.   It is in countries
like England and the United States, where the
process has advanced farthest, that the rivalry
and competition have such well-marked features.
The conditions have tended to become freer, fairer,
more humanised.   But so also have the stress and
energy of life, developed thereby, tended to reach a
point distinctly higher than ever before attained in
human existence.   It is not that we are travelling
in the direction of that unregulated and anarchic state
of competition which the capitalist classes, with
obvious inaccuracy, often describe as " free " competition, but which the workers themselves more

correctly call " cut-throat " competition.   It is rather
that everywhere and always the competition is tending
towards higher *efficiency*.

The tendency amongst all the advanced peoples
appears to be unmistakable.   It is everywhere to
allow the fullest possible scope for the development
of the personality of the individual, and the widest
possible range of opportunity to follow wherever his
powers or abilities lead him.   We have, in a preceding chapter, dwelt upon the extent to which this
tendency is displayed in almost every department of
life amongst the leading Western peoples, and how
unmistakably it constitutes the characteristic feature
of the life of those sections of the race which are
obtaining the greatest ascendency in the world.

Looking back over the process of evolution which
has been unfolding in our civilisation, there can be
no mistaking its nature.   The slow break-up of the
military type of society out of which it arose ; the
abolition of slavery ;   the steady restriction of the
power retained over the people by those privileged
classes who obtained their rights and influence under
an earlier form of society ;   the disintegration of
military feudalism;   the slow and painfully achieved
steps in the emancipation (still incomplete) of agriculture, trade, and commerce, from the rights which
modified feudalism continued to retain over them ;
the hard-won stages in the political emancipation of
the masses (now approaching completion amongst
the Western peoples), accompanied by a gradual
improvement in the conditions of life amongst the
lower classes—these have all been the well-marked
stages in a single developmental process still pursuing
its onward course amongst us.   The inherent tendency

R

of the process from the beginning has been to ultimately bring all the excluded people into the rivalry
of life. But its significance has consisted in its
tendency to raise this rivalry to the highest level of
efficiency it has ever reached.

It would seem that there can be little doubt as
to the nature and the tendency of the development
so far. What then, it may be asked, is it destined
to accomplish in the future? The answer must
apparently be, that it must complete the process of
evolution in progress, by eventually bringing all the
people into the rivalry of life, not only on a footing
of political equality, *but on conditions of equal social
opportunities.* This is the end which the developmental forces at work in our civilisation are apparently
destined to achieve in the social life of those people
amongst whom it is allowed to follow its natural and
normal course uninterrupted by disturbing causes,—
an end, when its relationships are perceived, as
moving to the imagination, as vast and transforming
in character, as that which Marx anticipated. But
it is an end essentially and profoundly different in
character. Marx contemplated our Western civilisation culminating in a condition of society which it
was difficult, if not impossible, for any one who had
realised the essential unity and continuity under all
outward forms of the developmental forces at work
in human society, to imagine ; a state in which the
laws that had operated continuously from the beginning of life were to be suddenly interrupted and
finally suspended. But the state towards which we
are travelling is apparently not one in which these
laws will be suspended ; it will be only the highest
phase reached in human society of the same cosmic

process which has been in operation from the beginning. Great and transforming as the coming changes will in all probability be, no *bouleversement* of society is to be expected. We are moving, and shall merely continue to move, by orderly stages to the goal towards which the face of society has in reality been set from the beginning of our civilisation.

If we endeavour to present clearly to our minds the nature of this process as a whole, we shall find that we are now in a position to understand the meaning of that social development towards which our times are ripening, and with which the history of the twentieth century will undoubtedly be filled. Nay, more, we are enabled to distinguish, with some degree of clearness, the stages through which it must carry us in the immediate future. The period through which we are passing is perceived to be one of transition. A definite, long-drawn-out, and altogether remarkable era in the history of our civilisation is coming to a close amongst the more advanced peoples. We are entering on a new era. The *political* enfranchisement of the masses is well-nigh accomplished ; the process which will occupy the next period will be that of their *social* enfranchisement. The people have been, at last, admitted to equal political rights ; in the next stage they must apparently be admitted to equal social opportunities. When the nature of the transition is perceived, it becomes clear also that the questions around which the conflict of social forces must centre in the immediate future are just those questions the socialist movement has brought into such prominence, namely, those affecting the existing rights of capital and the present distribution of wealth.

In one of those frequent flashes wherewith Marx, for a moment, lights up the foundations of present-day society, he asserts that "the economic structure of (present) capitalist society has grown out of the economic structure of feudal society."[1] This is a fact which has not yet been fully realised by those progressive parties amongst us, who, having for the most part accepted the ideas of the older school of economists as to the relationships of labour, capital, and the state, have obtained therefrom a false sense of the continued normalcy and rigidity of these relationships. We have, however, only to watch closely the wave of change which is passing over economic science in England to learn in what a large measure the truth underlying Marx's statement is already being perceived and applied by the younger and rising school of economists.

There is a growing and highly significant tendency amongst this school to question whether the present "cruelty and waste of irresponsible competition, and the licentious use of wealth," do really form any essential feature of the institution of private capital, or any necessary accompaniment of "the services which competition renders to society, by tending to put the ablest men into the most important posts, the next ablest into the next most important, and so on, and by giving to those in each grade freedom for the full exercise of their faculties."[2] It is being questioned with growing confidence by this school

---

[1] *Capital*, vol. ii. chap. xxvi. English translation, Swan Sonnenschein & Co.

[2] *Vide* "Some Aspects of Competition," by Professor Alfred Marshall, *Journal of the Royal Statistical Society*, December 1890. Reprint of Address as President of Economic Section, British Association, 1890.

whether, allowing " that industrial progress depends
on our getting the right men into the right places
and giving them a free hand and sufficient incite-
ment to exert themselves to the utmost," it also
follows " that nothing less than the enormous fortunes
which successful men now make and retain would
suffice for that purpose." Professor Marshall goes
so far as to hold that this last position is untenable,
and that " the present extreme inequalities of wealth
tend in many ways to prevent human faculties from
being turned to their best account." And he continues : " All history shows that a man will exert
himself nearly as much to secure a small rise in
income as a large one, provided he knows before-
hand what he stands to gain, and is in no fear of
having the expected fruits of his exertions taken
away from him by arbitrary spoliation. If there
were any fear of that he would not do his best, but
if the conditions of the country were such that a
moderate income gave as good a social position as a
large one does now ; if to have earned a moderate
income were a strong presumptive proof that a man
had surpassed able rivals in the attempt to do a
difficult thing well, then the hope of earning such an
income would offer to all but the most sordid natures
inducements almost as strong as they are now, when
there is an equal hope of earning a large one." [1]

These are all indications of the direction in which
we are travelling—and indications of the utmost
significance at the present time as coming from the

[1] *Vide* " Some Aspects of Competition," by Professor Alfred
Marshall, *Journal of the Royal Statistical Society*, December 1890.
Reprint of Address as President of Economic Section, British Associa-
tion, 1890

younger orthodox school of economists in England.
The position occupied by this party is already clearly
defined. "They are most anxious to preserve the
freedom of the individual to try new paths on his
own responsibility. They regard this as the vital
service which free competition renders to progress ;
and desire, on scientific grounds, to disentangle the
case for it from the case for such institutions as tend
to maintain extreme inequalities of wealth ; to which
some of them are strongly opposed." [1]

The nature of the position which has been
reached amongst the advanced sections of the
Western peoples thus emerges more clearly into
view. Occupied as these peoples have been for a
prolonged period in winning and consolidating their
political freedom, they, as a consequence, have tended
—no less in the United States than in Germany,
France, and England—to magnify as the final end
the occupation of a merely preliminary position. We
have come to believe that the feudal system is
defunct. But the real fact, as Marx realised more
clearly than the older economists, is, that the dead
hand of feudalism still presses with crushing weight
upon the people through almost all the forms and
institutions of present-day society. A large part of
the existing unregulated and uncontrolled rights of
wealth and capital are in reality merely the surviving rights of feudalism adapted to new conditions.
Education must in time bring us to see that their
continued existence is incompatible with the attain-

[1] *Vide* "Some Aspects of Competition," by Professor Alfred
Marshall, *Journal of the Royal Statistical Society*, December 1890.
Reprint of Address as President of Economic Section, British Associa-
tion, 1890.

ment of the ideal which society will have set more
and more clearly before it in the stage of development
upon which we are entering.

How far we are at present from the realisation of
this ideal of equality of opportunity, we shall probably
perceive more clearly as the development continues.
Future generations may regard with some degree of
surprise, and may even smile at our conceptions of
present-day society as a condition in which we secure
the full benefits of competition ; in which we get the
right men into the right places and give them
sufficient inducements to exert themselves ; and in
which we have obtained for all members of the
community the necessary opportunity for the best
exercise of their faculties.   It requires but little
reflection to see how wide of the mark such a
conception really is.   A large proportion of the
population in the prevailing state of society take
part in the rivalry of life only under conditions
which absolutely preclude them, whatever their
natural merit or ability, from any real chance
therein.   They come into the world to find the best
positions not only already filled but practically
occupied in perpetuity.   For, under the great body
of rights which wealth has inherited from feudalism,
we to all intents and purposes allow the wealthy
classes to retain the control of these positions for
generation after generation, to the permanent exclusion of the rest of the people.   Even from that
large and growing class of positions for which high
acquirements or superior education is the only qualification, and of which we, consequently (with strange
inaccuracy), speak as if they were open to all comers,
it may be perceived that the larger proportion of the

people are excluded—almost as rigorously and as absolutely as in any past condition of society—by the simple fact that the ability to acquire such education or qualification is at present the exclusive privilege of wealth.

Before the rivalry of life can be raised to that state of efficiency as an instrument of progress towards which it appears to be the inherent tendency of our civilisation to continue to carry it, society will still have to undergo a transformation almost as marked as any through which it has passed in previous stages. We have evidence of the beginning of this transformation in that trend of present-day legislation which appears so puzzling to many of the old progressive school, who have not realised the nature of the process of development in progress. It may be noticed that the characteristic feature of this legislation is the increasing tendency to raise the position of the lower classes *at the expense of the wealthier classes.* All future progressive legislation must apparently have this tendency. It is almost a *conditio sine quâ non* of any measure that carries us a step forward in our social development.

This is the real meaning of a large class of proposed measures, amongst others that which aims at securing an eight hours day for adult labour enforced by law—measures, in the present transition period, loosely but inaccurately described as socialist, and still looked at askance by that radical party in England who have not yet clearly perceived that the principles of their faith carry them any farther than the mere political enfranchisement of the people. To shorten the hours of labour in such a manner is, at the present time, primarily and above everything else

to raise the conditions of life of the workers at the
expense of wealth ; and, consequently, ultimately to
place the workers more on a footing of equality in
the rivalry of life with those above them.   It is this
principle also that is behind various recent measures
in England—limited in character but tending to
gradually and greatly extend in scope—which aim
at bettering at the public expense the condition of
the lives of the lower classes of workers.   It underlies
the demand for graduated taxation, which may be
expected to increase in strength and importunity ;
and demands which may be expected to take
practical shape in the near future, for the revision of
the hereditary rights of wealth and the conditions
under which great fortunes are transmitted from
generation to generation.

The same principle will apparently underlie our
education legislation in future.   We must expect to
have to meet, before long, demands for a very considerable extension of the education provided by the
state and for state control in the interests of the
people of higher as well as of elementary education.
It may be remarked that over no other question is
the struggle between the old spirit and the new likely
to be more severe and prolonged than over this
question of education.   It is in reality one of the
last principal strongholds of the retreating party.   It
is not yet clearly perceived by the people that there
is not any more natural and lasting distinction
between the *educated* and the *uneducated* classes of
which we hear so much nowadays, than there has
been between the other classes in the past.   Citizen
and slave, patrician and plebeian, feudal lord and serf,
privileged classes and common people, leisured classes

and working masses, have been steps in a process of development. In the "educated classes" and the "uneducated classes" we have only the same distinction under a subtler and even less defensible form ; for the right to education in its highest forms now remains largely independent of any other qualification than the possession of mere riches to secure it ; it constitutes, in fact, one of the most exclusive, and at the same time one of the most influential, of the privileges of wealth.

There is also another aspect of the subject which we must be prepared to find coming into increasing prominence. It is a fact, the full significance of which has not yet been perceived by the masses, that the condition of society which renders the right of entry to the institutions for higher education the almost exclusive privilege of wealth, tends, from the close connection of these institutions with the intellectual life of society, to render them (however much they may, and do, from the highest motives endeavour to resist such tendency) influences retarding to a considerable degree the progress of the development which society is undergoing. We have, consequently, at the present day, in most of our advanced societies the remarkable phenomenon of the intellectual and educated classes, at first almost invariably condemning and resisting the successive steps in our social development, uttering the most gloomy warnings and forebodings as these steps have been taken—and then tardily justifying them when they have become matters of history ; that is to say, when approval or disapproval has long ceased to be of practical importance. It has to be confessed that in England during the nineteenth century the

educated classes, in almost all the great political
changes that have been effected, have taken the side
of the party afterwards admitted to have been in the
wrong,—they have almost invariably opposed at the
time the measures they have subsequently come to
defend and justify.   This is to be noticed alike of
measures which have extended education, which have
emancipated trade, which have extended the franchise.
The educated classes have even, it must be confessed,
opposed measures which have tended to secure
religious freedom and to abolish slavery.   The
motive force behind the long list of progressive
measures carried during this period has in scarcely
any appreciable measure come from the educated
classes ; it has come almost exclusively from the
middle and lower classes, who have in turn acted,
not under the stimulus of intellectual motives, but
under the influence of their altruistic feelings.

We have evidence of the same development
towards securing equality of opportunity in that
tendency towards the extension of the interference
of the state, which appears so revolutionary to
politicians of the old *laissez-faire* school.   The
progressive interference of the state (mostly in the
interests of the weaker classes, and at the expense of
wealth and privilege) in departments now looked
upon as quite outside the sphere of such action, is
apparently inevitable.   We do not yet fully realise
that with the completion of the political enfranchisement of the people, the state itself will have undergone
a profound transformation.   Its new relationship to
the people must be quite different from any that has
ever before prevailed in history.   The spirit which
produced the old *laissez-faire* doctrine has, in all

probability, still a great part to play in our social development ; but the doctrine itself is, in reality, what the party previously identified with it in England has for some time instinctively recognised it to be—the doctrine of a period beyond which we have progressed. It has served its end in the stage of evolution through which we have passed ; for the doctrine of the non-interference of the state was the natural political creed of a people who had won their political freedom through a process of slow, orderly, and hard-fought development, and to whom the state throughout this period represented the power-holding classes whose interests were not coincident with those of the masses of the people.

But the doctrine has no such part to play in the future. In the era upon which we are entering, the long uphill effort to secure equality of opportunity, as well as equality of political rights, will of necessity involve, not the restriction of the interference of the state, but the progressive extension of its sphere of action to almost every department of our social life. The movement in the direction of the regulation, control, and restriction of the rights of wealth and capital must be expected to continue, even to the extent of the state itself assuming these rights in cases where it is clearly proved that their retention in private hands must unduly interfere with the rights and opportunities of the body of the people. But the continuity of principle may be expected to remain evident under the new appearances. Even in such cases the state will, in reality, assume such functions in order to preserve or secure the advantages of competition rather than to suspend competition. *Hence the general tendency must be expected to be towards state interference and state control on a greatly extended scale rather than towards state management.*

It may, perhaps, be inferred from this that the development of society in the direction indicated will be itself a movement towards socialism. This is not so. The gulf between the state of society towards which it is the tendency of the process of evolution now in progress to carry us, and socialism is wide and deep. The avowed aim of socialism is to suspend that personal rivalry and competition of life which not only is now, but has been from the beginning of life, the fundamental impetus behind all progress. The inherent tendency of the process of social development now taking place amongst us is (as it has been from the beginning of our civilisation) to raise this rivalry to the very highest degree of efficiency as a condition of progress, by bringing all the people into it on a footing of equality, and by allowing the freest possible play of forces within the community, and the widest possible opportunities for the development of every individual's faculties and personality. This is the meaning of that evolutional process which has been slowly proceeding through the history of the Western peoples.

But in any consideration of the future tendency of our social progress, the overshadowing importance of that ethical development which has supplied the motive power behind the procession of events we call progress, must always be kept in mind. In the process of evolution through which we have passed, the main function of that ethical movement on which our civilisation is founded has been in the first place to provide the sanctions necessary to secure the continued subordination of the interests of the self-assertive individual to the larger interests of society. In the second place it has been to generate that great fund of altruistic feeling which, gradually saturating our entire social life, has slowly undermined the position of the power-holding classes, and so rendered possible the movement which is tending to ultimately bring all the people into the rivalry of life on conditions of equality.

The future progress of our social development continues to be indissolubly bound up with this movement. When the fundamental conditions of the problem which underlies human evolution are once clearly understood, it must be perceived that it is in the nature of things impossible for rationalism by itself to provide such sanctions or to generate, or even to keep up, this fund of altruistic feeling. We must regard it as a law that :—

The process which is proceeding in human society is always progressively developing two inherently antagonistic but complementary tendencies ; namely, (1) the tendency requiring the increasing subordination of the individual to society, and (2) the rationalistic tendency leading the individual at the same time to question, with increasing insistence, the authority of the claims requiring him to submit to a process of social order in which he has absolutely no interest, and which is operating largely in the interests of unborn generations. In a healthy and progressive society, the fundamental principle of its existence is, that the second tendency must be continually subordinated to the first. But the intellect has no power to effect this subordination.

With the decay of the ethical influences in question, we may imagine the cynical indifference, nay, the cultivated intellectual pride, with which a vigorous character would regard its emancipation from what it must, in such circumstances, regard as the mere vulgar thraldom of conventional standards of morality. If our conscious relationship to the universe is measured by the brief span of individual existence, then the intellect can know of only one duty in the individual, namely, his duty to himself to make the most of the few precious years of consciousness he can ever know. Every other consideration must appear dwarfed and ridiculous in comparison. Every pain avoided, every pleasure gained in these few years, is a consideration, beside which the intellect must count any aspiration to further a process of cosmic evolution in which the individual has no interest as mere dust in the balance. We must expect wealth and power, in such circumstances, to be grasped at with a fierce earnestness, not for what are called sordid motives, but for intellectual motives—for command of the pleasures and gratifications which they alone can secure. And it must be remembered that the universal experience of mankind has been, and is still, that wealth and culture divorced from the control of ethical influences of the kind in question have not sought to find satisfaction in what are called the higher altruistic pleasures, but that they have rather, as evolutionary science would have taught us, sought the satisfaction of those instincts which have their roots deepest in our natures. Voluptuousness and epicureanism in all their most refined and unmentionable forms have everywhere been, and everywhere continue to be, the accompaniments of irresponsible wealth and power, the corresponding mental habit being one of cultured contempt for the excluded and envious masses.

Nor must any weight be attached to the argument that would ask us to take note of the many exceptions to such a tendency to be found in present society, in individuals of the highest motives and purest lives, who are not in any way under the influence of the religious movement upon which our civilisation is founded. Such individuals are sometimes spoken of as if their example afforded disproof of the argument here developed. Their lives and teaching, it is urged, are themselves a worthy proof of that extraordinary development of the altruistic feelings which we have been regarding as the peculiar product of the religious development described. Yet the individuals themselves openly profess disbelief in the teaching which this movement inspires, and they would probably altogether disclaim its influence in ordering their lives or directing their conduct. How, it is asked, are we to reconcile these facts with the view of our civilisation as the product of this religious movement, and with our conception of the latter as the seat of those vital forces which are moving and reconstructing the modern world ?

The explanation is simple. It arises naturally when we come to regard the history of our civilisation as the record of a long process of social development, to the progress of which our interests as individuals are quite subordinate. It has been insisted throughout that the social development which is called Western civilisation is not the product of any particular race or people ; that it must be regarded as an organic growth, the key to the life-history of which is to be found in the study of the ethical movement which extends through it. If we look at the matter in this light, and then call

to mind what the histories of the nations and races
embraced within the life of this organic development
have been ; if we reflect how deeply these peoples have
been affected at every point by the movement in question ; if we consider how profoundly their laws, institutions, mental and moral training, ways of judging
conduct, and habits of thought have been influenced
for an immense number of generations in the course
of the development through which they have passed,
we shall at once realise that it would be irrational
and foolish to expect that any individuals, or classes,
or that the individuals of a single generation,
should have the power to free themselves from this
influence. We are, all of us, whatever our opinions
may be concerning this movement, unconsciously
influenced by it at every point of our careers, and in
every moment of our lives. We, like our times,
are mentally and morally the product of it ; we
simply have no power to help ourselves. There may
be amongst us those who profess to repudiate the
teaching in which the movement originated and by
which it is sustained, but, even if we do not go so
far as a recent writer and regard the ethical life of
such as absolutely parasitic, we are compelled to
admit of it that " it is sheltered by convictions which
belong, not to them, but to the society of which they
form part " ; and that it is " nourished by processes
in which they take no share." [1]   Should these convictions decay, and the processes to which they give rise
come to an end, the alien life which they have sustained would come to an end also. But while they
last no training, however rigorous and prolonged, no
intellectual effort, however consistent and concentrated,

[1] A. J. Balfour, *Foundations of Belief*, p. 83.

S

could ever entirely emancipate us from their influence.
As Dr. Martineau observes with force, in a society constituted as ours is, " the ethical action and reaction
of men upon each other will be infinite, and will so
far prevail over the solitary force of individual
nature, that no one, however exceptionally great,
will escape all relation to the general level of his
time. The dependence of the moral consciousness for its growth upon society is incident to its
very nature. But to suppose, on this account, that
if it were not there at all society could generate·it,
and, by skilful financing with the exchanges of
pleasure and pain, could turn a sentient world into
a moral one, will never cease to be an insolvent
theory which makes provision for no obligation."
In the life of the individual, the influence of habits
of thought or training once acquired can be escaped
from only with the greatest difficulty, and after the
lapse of a long interval of time. How much more
so in the immensely longer life of the social organism ? Once we have grasped the conception of our
civilisation as a developing organic growth, with a
life-history which must be studied as a whole, we
perceive that we are precluded from regarding any
of the units as independent of the influence of a
process which has operated upon society for so many
centuries. As well might we argue that because the
fruit survives for a time when removed from the tree,
and even mellows and ripens, that it was, therefore,
independent of the tree.

In this connection it should be remarked that the
relationship between true socialism and rationalism,
casually noticed by many observers, is not accidental
as it is often stated to be. It has its foundation

deep-seated in the very nature of things. The conflict between the forces shaping the course of the development we are at present undergoing, and the materialistic socialism of Marx, is but the present-day expression of that conflict in which we have seen man engaged against his own reason throughout the whole course of his social development. Socialism in reality aims at exploiting in the interests of the existing generation of individuals that humanitarian movement which is providing a developmental force operating largely in the interests of future generations. It would, in fact, exploit this movement while it cut off the springs of it. True socialism of the German type must be recognised to be ultimately as individualistic and as *anti*-social as individualism in its advanced forms. Scientifically, they are both to be considered as the extreme logical expression of rationalistic protest by the individual against the subordination of his interests to the process of progressive development society is undergoing from generation to generation. But though we have thus to identify socialism with political materialism, no greater mistake can be made than to suppose that the ultimate triumph of materialism in our Western civilisation would imply the realisation of the ideals of socialism. The state to which we should probably attain long before reaching this stage would be one in which the power-holding classes, recognising the position, would with cynical frankness proceed to utilise the inherent strength of their own position. Instead of slowly yielding their position as they are now doing, under the softening influence upon general character of an ethical movement—which by undermining their faith in their own cause has deprived them of the power of making effective resistance — they might be expected to become once more agressive in the open profession of class selfishness and contempt for the people. History presents a melancholy record of the helplessness of the latter when society has reached this stage. The deliberate effectiveness with which the power-holding classes in ancient Rome dealt with the rights of the people in such circumstances in the long downward stage under the Empire is instructive, and bears its moral on the surface. In such a state of society the classes who have obtained wealth and power, and all other classes in turn, instead of acting, as they now do, under the influence of an evolutionary force operating largely in the future interests of society, come to hold it as a duty to themselves to serve their own present interests by such direct means as may be available. In vague popular phraseology, society in this stage is said to be irremediably corrupt ; speaking in more exact terms, the social organism has exhausted its physiological capital, and has, therefore, entered on the downward stage towards disintegration.

CHAPTER IX

HUMAN EVOLUTION IS NOT PRIMARILY INTELLECTUAL

THE biologist who has attempted to carry the methods of his science thus far into the consideration of the phenomena presented in human society, now finds himself approaching a conclusion of a remarkable kind. If the inferences it has been the object of the preceding chapters to establish are justified, it must be evident that they have a very wide significance of a kind not yet considered.

It is not improbable that the reader, as he has advanced through the last three chapters, may have felt that one idea has assumed increasing prominence in his mind. Admitting, he may say, that our civilisation is to be viewed as a single organic growth, the significance whereof consists in the fact that the developmental process proceeding therein tends to raise the rivalry of life to the highest degree of efficiency by bringing all the people into it on a footing of equality ; that the motive force which has been behind this development has its seat in that fund of altruistic feeling with which our civilisation has become equipped ; and that this fund of altruistic feeling has been the characteristic product of the religious system associated with our civilisation—whither does this lead us ? What guarantee have we that the development which has been proceeding is to continue ? Do not the signs of the times indicate a decline in the strength and vitality of those feelings and ideas upon which our religious systems have been founded ?

It is to be feared that the rationalistic school which has been in the ascendant during the greater part of the nineteenth century, and which has raised such unstinted pæans in honour of the intellect, regarding it as the triumphant factor of progress in the splendid ages to come, is destined to undergo disillusionment in many respects. Sooner or later it must become clear to all the more far-seeing thinkers amongst this party that, in so far as the Western peoples have to depend solely on their intellectual capacity, and the results of their intellectual development, to maintain the supremacy they have obtained over what are called the lower races, they are leaning on a false hope. As time goes on, it must be realised that the promise of the intellect in this respect is a delusive one. All the conquests of mind, all the arts and inventions of life, will be open to the rest of the world as well as to these peoples, and not only may be equally shared in by others, but may be utilised with effect against the Western races themselves in the competition of life. As the process of development proceeds it must become increasingly evident that the advanced races will have no power, in virtue of their intellectual characteristics alone, to continue to retain the position of ascendency they have hitherto enjoyed throughout the world, and that if they have no other secret of rule than this, the sceptre is destined eventually to pass from them.

But is this, then, the message of evolutionary science? Has the development which has been in progress throughout the centuries no other meaning than that the social progress of the Western peoples has been, after all, but a passing sport of life? Do we only see therein humanity condemned to an aimless Sisyphean labour, breasting the long slope upwards, to find when the top has been reached that our civilisation must slide backwards again through a period of squalid ruin and decay, leaving nothing gained or won for the race in the process of the strenuous centuries through which we have passed?

The answer to these questions, which it appears that evolutionary science must give to the biologist, who has endeavoured without prepossession or prejudice to carry the methods of his science thus far into the midst of the phenomena of human existence, is very remarkable. It would appear that the evolution which is slowly proceeding in human society is not primarily intellectual; but that since man became a social creature the expansion of his intellect has become a subordinate phase in the development in progress. In short it would appear that :—

The process at work in society is evolving religious character as a first product, and intellectual capacity only so far as it can be associated with this quality.

In other words, the conclusion which Darwinian science would appear to establish is that :—

The most distinctive feature of human evolution as a whole is, that through the operation of the law of natural selection the race must continue to grow ever more and more religious.

Our progress, it must be remembered, is, over and above everything else, social progress. It is always tending to secure, in an increasing degree, the subordination of the present interests of the self-assertive individual to the future interests of society, his expanding intellect notwithstanding. The manner in which apparently this result is being attained in human society is by the slow evolution in the race of that type of individual character through which this subordination can be most effectively secured. This type appears to be that which would be described in popular language as the religious character. The winning races have been those in which, other things being equal, this character has been most fully developed. Amongst these again the races that have acquired an ever-increasing ascendency have been those which have possessed the best ethical systems; that is to say, ethical systems which, having secured this subordination of the present interests of the individual to the larger interests of an indefinitely longer-lived social organism, have then allowed the fullest possible development of the powers and faculties of all the individuals concerned. We appear to have, throughout human history, two well-marked developments, proceeding simultaneously—a development of religious character in the individual on the one hand, and an evolution in the character of religious beliefs on the other.

It would appear also that we must regard many of the estimates which have been made and the opinions which have been formed in the past as to the decay of religious influences and tendencies as altogether untrustworthy. The subject must be

approached from a much higher and wider standpoint than any hitherto attempted. When the
nature of the process of evolution we are undergoing
is understood, it must be recognised that we have
been estimating the vitality of religious influences on
a wrong principle. They do not derive their strength
from the support given to them by the intellect.
Any form of belief which could claim to influence
conduct solely because of its sanction from individual
reason would, in fact, from the nature of things, be
incapable of exercising the functions of a religion in
the evolution of society. The two forces are inherently antagonistic. The intellect has, accordingly,
always mistaken the nature of religious forces, and
regarded as beneath notice movements which have
had within them the power to control the course of
human development for hundreds and even thousands
of years. Again, the plasticity of religious systems
has not been realised. These systems are themselves
—under the outward appearances of rigidity, and
while always preserving their essential characteristics
—undergoing profound modifications. They are in
a continuous state of evolution. Lastly, it has not
been understood or taken into account that the great
deep-seated evolutionary forces at work in society
are not operating against religious influences and in
favour of the uncontrolled sway of the intellect. On
the contrary, it seems to be clear that these religious
influences have been always and everywhere triumphant in the past, and that it is a first principle of
our social development that they must continue to
be in the ascendant to the end, whatever the future
may have in store for us.

In short, the law of natural selection would appear

to be operating in human society under conditions, a fuller knowledge of which is likely to necessitate a very considerable readjustment of the standpoint from which the subject of our progress has been hitherto regarded. Let us now see whether history and anthropology furnish any evidence in support of this inference that the progress the race has been making has not been primarily progress in intellectual development. For if the inference be correct it is evident (1) that our intellectual progress must be far smaller, less significant, and more irregular than has been generally supposed ; (2) that the wide interval between the peoples who have attained the highest social development and the lowest races is not mainly the result of a difference in intellectual, but of a difference in ethical development ; (3) that there is not that direct connection between high social development and high intellectual development which has been hitherto almost universally assumed to exist.

Now any one who has been closely interested in that department of higher thought, which for the past fifty years has been concerned with the subject of human progress as a whole, must have become conscious at times of a peculiar undercurrent of opinion, which seems to set in an opposite direction to the ordinary and larger current of thought on this subject of progress. Nothing can be less doubtful, in the first place, than the tendency of general opinion on the subject. By the world at large, and by most of those to whom it looks for information and guidance, our progress has long been accepted as mainly a matter of intellectual development. The almost universal tendency has been to regard the intellectual factor as the ruling and dominant one in the advance we have made.   The facts upon which this general opinion is founded are, indeed, regarded as being so prominent, and their import as being so clear, that the conclusion is usually accepted as beyond dispute ; so much so that it is scarcely ever felt necessary nowadays to subject it to any general and detailed scrutiny.

The principal links in the chain of evidence seem to stand out clearly, and to have all the appearance of strength and stability.   One of the unquestioned facts of biology is the progressive increase in brain development as we rise in the scale of life.   The increase is steady and continuous, and the rule is almost without exception.   This, too, is apparently only what we should have to expect if we accept the Darwinian hypothesis ; for of all the successful variations which it is the part of natural selection to accumulate, none can have been more profitable in the struggle for existence than those which increased the intelligence of the forms of life engaged therein. The increase of brain development, therefore, continues throughout life until it finally culminates in man, whom we find standing in unquestioned supremacy at the head of creation, and holding his high position in virtue of the exceptional intellectual development to which he has attained.

When the anthropologist, restricting himself to human progress, now takes up the tale, it may be observed that he proceeds, almost as a matter of course, to marshal his facts so as to bring out the same developmental law.   Ethnological treatises are filled with facts intended to exemplify the great mental gulf which exists between the members of the higher and those of the lower races of the human family, and with others intended to establish the close connection which is assumed to exist between high social development and high intellectual development. Popular imagination has, in like manner, its own evidences in view; for what more conclusive argument, it is asked, can we have as to the direct connection between mental and social development than the visible difference in the world to-day between the position of the lower and the higher races, and the characteristics that accompany this difference? On the one side we have to witness the higher races with their complex civilisations, high state of culture, and advanced knowledge of the arts and sciences, and all that this implies; and on the other side we have to note the inferior races, existing almost in a state of nature, possessing and desiring only the bare necessities of an animal existence, unacquainted with the higher arts and sciences, often without knowledge of metals or agriculture, and not infrequently with no words in their language to express numbers higher in the scale than five.

All this appears, at first sight, striking and impressive. Nevertheless, strange to say, a tendency is undoubtedly to be observed in certain quarters to question whether the assumption which underlies all arguments of this kind has ever been proved, and whether it is even capable of proof. If the attention of the observer is arrested, and if he proceeds to analyse for himself the facts upon which the prevailing view as to the dominance of the intellectual factor in human progress is founded, he soon becomes conscious of such peculiar discrepancies and such extraordinary and unexplained contradictions that he finds himself driven to the conclusion that the

question must be much more difficult and complex
than this prevailing view would have led him to
suppose.

A class of facts which, not improbably, will attract
attention at the outset is that respecting the ancient
civilisations.   Since the revival of learning in Europe,
there may be traced very clearly a tendency in the
minds of those who have devoted attention to the
subject to compare the average intellectual development in the old civilisations, and more particularly
in that of the Greeks, with the average mental
development under our own civilisation, and always
to the disparagement of the latter.   This tendency
is more remarkable in recent times, as it is quite unaffected by the prevailing disposition (for which
there is probably every justification) to regard our
own civilisation as being, nevertheless, the very
highest, both in kind and degree, the human race
has so far reached.

That the intellectual development reached by the
ancients should have excited attention in the period
of the Renaissance was only natural.   The civilisations of the Greek and Roman peoples represented,
at the time of the reawakening of the European
mind, the highest efforts of the race in almost every
department of intellectual activity, and it was inevitable that the mental qualities of these peoples,
and of the Greeks in particular, should excite the
wonder and admiration of men after the long period
of intellectual stagnation through which the world
had passed.   But the point to which attention is
more particularly directed is that, although a new
age has since arisen, although our Western civilisation has developed a strength, a magnificence, and

an undoubted promise which overshadows the fame
and the achievements of these former civilisations,
the fuller knowledge and the more accurate methods
of research and examination of our own time have
only tended to confirm the view, that in average
mental development we are not the superiors, but the
inferiors, of these ancient peoples who have so completely dropped out of the human struggle for
existence.   Judged by the standard of intellectual
development alone, we of the modern European
races who seem to have been so unmistakably marked
out by the operation of the law of natural selection
to play a commanding part in the history of the
world, have, in fact, no claim to consider ourselves
as in advance of the ancient Greeks, all the extraordinary progress and promise of the modern world
notwithstanding.

During the nineteenth century the opening up of
many widely different branches of research has
brought a crowd of workers in various departments
into close contact with the intellectual life of the
Greeks.   The unanimity of testimony which comes
from these representatives of different spheres of
thought as to the high average standard of intellectual development reached by this remarkable
people, is very striking.   It is not only that the
mental calibre of isolated minds like Socrates,
Aristotle, Plato, or Phidias, appears so great when
carefully measured, and the state of knowledge and
the circumstances of the time taken into account.
It is rather that the mental average of the whole of
the people should have been so unmistakably high.
In both respects the Greeks seemed to have surpassed us.

Mr. Lecky regards it as one of the anomalies of history which we can only imperfectly explain, " that within the narrow limits and scanty population of the Greek States should have arisen men who, in almost every conceivable form of genius, in philosophy, in epic, dramatic, and lyric poetry, in written and spoken eloquence, in statesmanship, in sculpture, in painting, and probably also in music, should have attained almost or altogether the highest limits of human perfection." [1]   Similar views expressed forcibly, though withal temperately, and in well-weighed words, may be found scattered up and down throughout European literature at the present time.   Yet it is not from what may be called the literary and philosophical section of the workers who have attempted to estimate the capacity of the Greek intellect that the most striking testimony comes. Those who may fairly claim to speak with authority in the name of science, do so with even more emphasis and directness.   Mr. Galton, whose anthropological investigations, and statistical and other measurements of human faculties, physical and mental, under a wide range of circumstances, give him a peculiar right to be heard, is of opinion that "the ablest race of whom history bears record is unquestionably the ancient Greeks, partly because their masterpieces in the principal departments of intellectual activity are still unsurpassed, and partly because the population which gave birth to the creators of those masterpieces was very small." [2]   He asserts that we have no men to put by the side of Socrates and Phidias, and that "the millions of all

[1] *History of European Morals*, vol. i. p. 418.
[2] *Hereditary Genius*, p. 329.

Europe, breeding as they have done for the subsequent two thousand years, have never produced
their equals." He also considers that our average
intellectual development is far below that of the
Greeks as a people. Summarising a very striking
argument, he continues—" It follows from all this,
that the average ability of the Athenian race is, on
the lowest possible estimate, very nearly two grades
higher than our own ; that is, about as much as our
race is above that of the African negro. This
estimate, which may seem prodigious to some, is
confirmed by the quick intelligence and high culture
of the Athenian commonalty, before whom literary
works were recited, and works of art exhibited, of a far
more severe character than could possibly be appreci-
ated by the average of our race, the calibre of whose
intellect is easily gauged by a glance at the contents
of a railway bookstall." [1]

This is a very remarkable expression of opinion,
allowing for all possible considerations which may
be taken to detract from its significance. If the
average mental development reached by the Greeks
was so superior to ours as this, we have here a fact,
the import of which in human evolution has not yet
been clearly perceived. If the intellectual ability of
the people who developed this extinct civilisation is
to be taken as being, not only in excess of that of
those modern European races whose civilisation is
winning such an ascendency in the world to-day, but
as being as far above it as the mental ability of
these latter is above that of some of the lowest of
the peoples whom they have displaced through the
operation of natural selection, then it seems extremely

[1] *Hereditary Genius*, p. 331.

difficult to reconcile this fact with an unshaken belief in any theory according to which intellectual development must be taken as the dominant factor in human evolution.   We may be prepared to accept Sir Henry Maine's view that in an intellectual sense nothing moves in this Western world that is not Greek in its origin ; but no homage of this kind to the Greek intellect, however well it may be deserved, can blind our eyes to the fact that the Greek peoples themselves, like the ancient Romans, have absolutely disappeared in the human struggle for existence. Even their blood cannot be distinguished in the populations of large tracts of Eastern and Southern Europe, and Western Asia, where these ruling races were once predominant both in numbers and influence.   Judged from the standpoint of the evolutionist, the ancient Greek races were as far below the European peoples of to-day in the qualities that have won for the latter the ascendency they have obtained in the greater part of the world, as these latter are held to be below the Greeks in intellectual development.   The human race has, beyond possibility of doubt, advanced in some direction in the interval.   But if we are to accept the opinions of high authorities, the development has not apparently been an intellectual development.

If we continue our examination, the difficulties in the way of the theory as to the direct connection between intellectual development and social progress do not tend to disappear, but rather to crowd in upon us.   Not only is it probable that the average intellectual development of the races which are winning in the struggle for existence to-day is below that of some of the peoples which have long

T

ago disappeared from the rivalry of life, but there seems every reason to suppose that the average intellectual development of successive generations amongst ourselves does not show any tendency to rise above that of the generations immediately preceding them.

There may be noticed in the literature of the time indications that a conclusion of this kind is already forcing itself on the minds of students of social phenomena who are specialists in their own departments. It may be observed, before we deal with the evidence to this effect, that even the general mind is not quite at ease as regards the position which is usually taken up on this question. A proportion of the indications come, doubtless, from those who by training and temperament are inclined to distrust modern progressive tendencies in general ; but others proceeding from authorities who regard our development as tending undoubtedly upwards, but who still speak with doubt and hesitation of our intellectual progress, are more significant. Few men, for instance, have had a more extensive and prolonged personal acquaintance with the English people and with English public and intellectual life generally than Mr. Gladstone ; and from the position he has occupied as leader of the progressive party for a period of exceptional duration, few would probably be less likely to speak disparagingly of the amount and nature of the progress which we have made and are still making. Yet he is reported to have said recently : " I sometimes say that I do not see that progress in the development of the brain power which we ought to expect. . . . Development, no doubt, is a slow process, but I do not see it at all. I do not think we are stronger, but weaker than men of the Middle Ages... I would take it as low down as the men of the sixteenth century. The men of the sixteenth century were strong men, stronger in brain power than our men." [1]

Opinions of this kind are justified by our social and vital statistics to a greater extent than might be readily expected. The inquirer will find it increasingly difficult, the farther he proceeds, to assent to the view so commonly held that the rivalry of life prevailing amongst the advanced European peoples has tended in the past, and is tending now, to produce an increase of that kind of intellectual development which is transmitted from generation to generation by inheritance, and accumulated by natural selection. The facts seem to point to a different conclusion. While it appears to be beyond question that our progress towards a state of free rivalry and equality of opportunity has been favourable to the development of certain vigorous and virile qualities that have given the leading races the ascendency they have come to enjoy in the world, it is at the same time in the highest degree doubtful whether it has been favourable to an increased intellectual development of the kind in question. One of the most marked and characteristic features of the evolutionary process which has been in progress in our Western civilisation appears to be its tendency to restrain intellectual development.

To understand how such a result can be possible in modern society it is desirable to carry the mind back a stage. It has lately become well known that

[1] *Review of Reviews*, April 1892.   Interview with Mr. W. T. Stead.

the attempts which have been made in the past by
the nobles and power-holding classes in almost every
country to perpetuate the stock of the privileged
classes to which they have belonged have invariably
failed.   The most favourable conditions for rendering
the attempt successful have in many cases prevailed ;
and every device that human ingenuity could invent
to attain the end in view has been tried by these
classes in order to secure success.   But the result
has always been the same.   After a limited number
of generations the stock has become extinct, and the
privileged classes have been able to maintain themselves only by the continual infusion of new blood and
by intermarriage with the classes below them.   We
had, for instance, amongst the Romans, in the Patricians and the Plebeians, what Gibbon calls "the
proudest and most perfect separation which can be
found in any age or country between the nobles and
the people."   Intermarriages were prohibited by the
laws of the XII. Tables.   Wealth and honours, the
offices of the state, and the ceremonies of religion,
were almost exclusively possessed by the Patricians ;
and the most jealous pride of birth reinforced the
barriers which had been erected in law, sentiment,
and religion with the object of preserving the purity
of their blood.   Yet Gibbon records that the Patrician
families, "whose original number was never recruited
till the end of the Commonwealth, either failed in
the ordinary course of nature, or were extinguished
in so many foreign or domestic wars, or, through a
want of merit or fortune, insensibly mingled with
the mass of the people.   Very few remained who
could derive their pure and genuine origin from the
infancy of the city or even from that of the Republic

when Cæsar and Augustus, Claudius and Vespasian, created from the body of the senate a competent number of new Patrician families in the hope of perpetuating an order which was still considered as honourable and sacred." [1]   But these new artificial supplies soon went the way of the others, until, in the reign of Constantine, we find it recorded that little more was left than "a vague and imperfect tradition that the Patricians had once been the first of the Romans."

The existing aristocratic families amongst the modern European peoples are continually undergoing the same process of decay.   The manner in which the English aristocracy (which has been, to a large extent, recruited from those who, in the first instance, attained to the position by force of character or intellect) is continually dying out, has become a commonplace of knowledge since the investigations of Galton, Evelyn Shirley, and others threw light on the subject.   Only five out of over five hundred of the oldest aristocratic families in England, at the present time, can trace direct descent through the male line to the fifteenth century.   Despite the innumerable safeguards with which they have been able to surround themselves, such classes seem to be quite unable to keep up the stock for more than a limited number of generations ; they are continually dying out at the top and being recruited from below.   A similar state of things has been found to exist in France by M. Lageneau, and by others who have investigated the records of the noble families of that country, and it is known to prevail also in nearly all countries where an aristocratic class exists.

[1] *Decline and Fall of the Roman Empire,* vol. i. chap. xvii.

Now, a great number of reasons have been given
from time to time to account for this tendency of
aristocratic families to die out ; and, while some
weight must be attached to most of them, there can
be no doubt that the true cause is a very simple one
with no mystery whatever about it. One of the
deepest instincts implanted in human nature, as the
result of the long rivalry through which we have
come, is the desire always to go forward. Man is
never satisfied with his position. Having attained a
competency, he is no more content than when the
bare necessities of existence were hardly secured to
him. Nor is he usually more content with luxury
than with competency. He must, if possible, always
go onwards ; he is never willing to go backwards.
In a very effective passage Mr. Henry George has
noted how characteristic this feature is of man ; and
it becomes progressively more marked as we ascend
from the lower to the higher races.[1] A certain rest-

[1] Mr. George says of man, "He is the only animal whose desires
increase as they are fed ; the only animal that is never satisfied. The
wants of every other living thing are uniform and fixed. The ox of
to-day aspires to no more than did the ox when man first yoked him.
The sea-gull of the English Channel who poises himself above the swift
steamer, wants no better food or lodging than the gulls who circled
round as the keels of Cæsar's galleys first grated on a British beach.
Of all that nature offers them, be it ever so abundant, all living things
save man can only take, and only care for, enough to supply wants
which are definite and fixed. The only use they can make of additional supplies or additional opportunities is to multiply. But not so
with man. No sooner are his animal wants satisfied, than new wants
arise. Food he wants first, as does the beast ; shelter next, as does
the beast ; and these given, his reproductive instincts assert their sway,
as do those of the beast. But here man and beast part company. The
beast never goes farther ; the man has but set his feet on the first step
of an infinite progression—a progression upon which the beast never
enters ; a progression away from and above the beast. The demand
for quantity once satisfied, he seeks quality. The very desires that he
has in common with the beast become extended, refined, exalted. It

less energy, an always unsatisfied ambition to go forward, is one of the most pronounced of the individual and racial characteristics of the winning sections of the human family.

Now, one of the most common of all forms in which this instinct expresses itself is the unwillingness of men, in a state of civilisation such as that in which we are living, to marry and bring up families in a state of life lower than that into which they were themselves born. As we rise beyond the middle classes the endeavour of the individual to maintain himself, in this respect, at what he considers his natural level involves, however, more and more effort the higher we go; until amongst the highest aristocratic families the attempt can be successful only on a very restricted scale. While we have, therefore, on the one hand, the constant tendency of aspiring ability to rise into the highest class, we have, on the other hand, within the class itself, the equally constant tendency towards restriction of numbers, towards celibacy, and towards reversion to the classes below. This is the largest operating cause constantly tending to the decay and extinction of aristocratic families.

But while this cause has been already, to a con-

is not merely hunger, but taste, that seeks gratification in food ; in clothes, he seeks not merely comfort, but adornment ; the rude shelter becomes a house ; the undiscriminating sexual attraction begins to transmute itself into subtle influences, and the hard and common stock of animal life to blossom and to bloom into shapes of delicate beauty. As power to gratify his wants increases, so does aspiration grow. Held down to lower levels of desire, Lucullus will sup with Lucullus ; twelve boars turn on spits that Antony's mouthful of meat may be done to a turn ; every kingdom of Nature be ransacked to add to Cleopatra's charms, and marble colonnades and hanging gardens and pyramids that rival the hills arise."—*Progress and Poverty*.

siderable extent, recognised in the limited application here noticed, its vital connection with a much wider natural law, operating throughout society at large, and upon the race in general, has scarcely received any attention. Not only do the aristocratic classes die out, but it would appear that the members of the classes, into which it is always the tendency of a very prevalent type of intellectual ability to rise, are being continually weeded out by a process of natural selection, which it appears to have been the effect of our own civilisation to foster to a peculiar degree. This natural law was clearly brought out in a remarkable paper read by Dr. Ogle before the Statistical Society of London in March 1890.[1] The professional and independent classes (to the level of which the intellectual ability of all the classes below continually tends to rise) marry, says the author, considerably later, and have far fewer children per marriage than the classes below them. For instance, he shows that the mean age at marriage in the professional and independent classes is seven years more advanced for men and four years more advanced for women than amongst miners ; and, further, " *that the lower the station in life the earlier the age at which marriage is contracted, and that the difference, in this respect, between the upper and lower classes is very great indeed.*" In addition to this it was also found that the professional and independent classes possessed a proportion of permanent bachelors far above the rest.

We have here apparently the same tendency extending downwards through the community, and continually operating to prevent the intellectual average of one generation from rising above the

[1] *Journal of the Royal Statistical Society,* June 1890.

level of that preceding it.   The same law of population has been noticed in France, where it is found that the agricultural population have more children than the industrial, and that still fewer children are born to families where the fathers follow a liberal profession.   It operates also in other countries, and it does not at all tend to be restricted, but rather the reverse, by that social development taking place amongst us which is ever tending to lighten the burthens of existence for the lower classes of the community at the general expense.

The full meaning of these facts is not, indeed, immediately perceived.   Mr. Galton, in a striking passage, has dealt with what he described as the heavy doom of any subsection of a prolific people, which in this manner multiplied less rapidly than the rest of the community ; and the example which he takes may be profitably quoted at length.   He says, " Suppose two men M and N about 22 years old, each of them having, therefore, the expectation of living to the age of 55, or 33 years longer ; and suppose that M marries at once, and that his descendants, when they arrive at the same age, do the same ; but that N delays until he has laid by money, and does not marry before he is 33 years old, that is to say, 11 years later than M, and his descendants also follow his example.   Let us further make the two very moderate suppositions that the early marriages of race M result in an increase of $1\frac{1}{2}$ in the next generation, and also in the production of $3\frac{3}{4}$ generations in a century ; while the late marriages of race N result in an increase of only $1\frac{1}{4}$ in the next generation, and in $2\frac{1}{2}$ generations in one century.   It will be found that an increase of $1\frac{1}{2}$

in each generation accumulating on the principle of compound interest during $3\frac{3}{4}$ generations becomes rather more than $\frac{18}{4}$ times the original amount, while an increase of $1\frac{1}{4}$ for $2\frac{1}{2}$ generations is barely as much as $\frac{7}{4}$ times the original amount. Consequently the increase of the race of M at the end of a century will be greater than that of N, in the ratio of 18 to 7, that is to say, it will be rather more than $2\frac{1}{2}$ times as great. *In two centuries the progeny of M will be more than 6 times, and in three centuries more than 15 times as numerous as those of N.*" [1]

These are noteworthy conclusions. It is evident that our society must be considered as an organism which is continually renewing itself from the base, and dying away in those upper strata into which it is the tendency of a large class of intellectual ability to rise ; the strata which possess the reproductive capacity most fully being probably the lower sections of the middle class. Taken in connection with the probable higher intellectual development of past races now extinct, such facts must be held as tending to establish the view that our intellectual development is a far slower and more complex process than we have hitherto imagined it to be. They render it still more difficult for us to adhere to the view according to which human progress is to be regarded as being mainly a matter of intellectual development. This latter development seems to be subject to larger evolutionary forces which, so far from furthering it, tend, in the conditions we have been discussing, to check and restrain it in a most marked manner.

[1] *Hereditary Genius*, p. 340.

If the examination is continued, and we now carry forward into other departments our scrutiny of the facts upon which the prevailing opinion which identifies social progress with intellectual progress is founded, it is only to discover that difficulties and discrepancies of the most striking kind continue to present themselves even in quarters where they might be least expected.   A great quantity of data as to the relative cranial development of different races, existing and extinct, has been collected by anthropologists, but the conclusions to which many leading authorities have come as the result of a comparison of these data are not a little interesting.   It may be observed that in nearly all anthropological literature of this kind the position which is assumed, almost as a matter of course, at the outset, and from which all the argument proceeds is, that the attainment by any people of a state of high social development should imply a corresponding state of high intellectual development.   But having started with these premises, it will be noticed what difficulties present themselves. Criticising a widely quoted table of the cranial capacity of various races, published by M. Topinard in his *Anthropologie*, De Quatrefages says that its chief value is to show into what serious errors an estimation of the development of a race from its cranial capacity would lead us.   " By such an estimation the troglodytes of the Cavern of L'Homme-Mort would be superior to all races enumerated in the table, including contemporary Parisians." [1]

Farther on, from a criticism of these and other features of the same table, De Quatrefages reaches

[1] *The Human Species*, by A. De Quatrefages, chap. xxx.

the conclusion that " there can be no real relation between the dimensions of the cranial capacity and social development.[1] But as social development is taken by the author to imply a corresponding intellectual development, the two being often used as interconvertible terms by anthropologists, he finds himself, therefore, driven to the remarkable conclusion that the evidence generally seems to " establish beyond a doubt the fact, which already clearly results from the comparison of different races, namely, that the development of the intellectual faculties of man is to a great extent independent of the capacity of the cranium, and the volume of the brain." [2]

If, however, we come to examine for ourselves that large class of facts drawn from contemporary life, upon which this popular opinion as to the intimate connection between the high social development and the high intellectual development of a people is founded, it is only to find other difficulties in the way of this view confronting us. The evidence upon which the general opinion as to the existence of an immeasurable intellectual gulf between the higher and the lower races is based is certainly of a very marked kind. The well-known achievements of our civilisation in all the arts of life are pointed to, and we are asked to compare these with the results obtained by races lower in the scale than ourselves. The greatest confusion of mind prevails, however, as to the lessons to be drawn from such a state of things. Conclusions utterly unwarrantable and unjustifiable as to the nature of the interval which separates us from

[1] *The Human Species*, by A. De Quatrefages, chap. xxx.
[2] *Ibid.*

what are called the lower races are constantly drawn from these facts.

It may of course be fully admitted, at the outset, that the achievements of the human mind, in our present civilisation, are calculated to impress the mind in the highest degree, and more especially when they are compared with the absence of any such imposing results amongst the lower races. To communicate instantaneously, and to speak with each other when separated by great distances; to compute years in advance, and accurately to a fraction of time, the movements of heavenly bodies distant from us by many millions of miles; to take a mechanical impression of spoken words, and to reproduce them after the lapse of an indefinite period; to describe with absolute knowledge the composition of fixed stars, through analysis, with delicate instruments, of light which left its source before the dawn of our history—all appear stupendous achievements of the human intellect. In like manner the complexity of our civilised life, our trades and manufactures, and the implements and machinery with which they are carried on, as well as the stored-up knowledge from which they all result, would appear to separate us by an immense gulf from the lower races.

But to take, as is often done, such results to be the measure of the intellectual difference separating us from the lower races, is clearly a most short-sighted and altogether unjustifiable procedure. It only needs a little reflection to enable us to perceive that the marvellous accomplishments of modern civilisation are primarily the measure of the social stability and social efficiency, and not of the intel-

lectual pre-eminence, of the peoples who have produced them.   They do not necessarily imply any
extraordinary intellectual development in ourselves
at all.   They are not the colossal products of individual minds amongst us ; they are all the results
of small accumulations of knowledge slowly and
painfully made and added to by many minds
through an indefinite number of generations in the
past, every addition to this store of knowledge
affording still greater facilities for further additions.
It must not be assumed, even of the minds that
have from time to time made considerable additions
to this common stock of accumulated knowledge,
that they have been separated from the general
average, or from the minds of other races of men of
lower social development, by the immense intellectual
interval which each achievement standing by itself
would seem to imply.

For it must be remembered that even the ablest
men amongst us, whose names go down to history
connected with great discoveries and inventions,
have each in reality advanced the sum of knowledge
by a comparatively small addition.   In the fulness
of time, and when the ground has been slowly and
laboriously prepared for it by a vast army of
workers, the great idea fructifies and the discovery
is made.   It is, in fact, not the work of one, but of
a great number of persons whose previous work has
led up to it.   How true it is that all the great ideas
have been the products of the time rather than of
individuals, may be the more readily realised when
it is remembered that, as regards a large number of
them, there have been rival claims for the honour of
authorship put forward by persons who, working

quite independently, have arrived at like results almost simultaneously.   Thus, rival and independent claims have been made for the discovery of the Differential Calculus, the doctrine of the Conservation of Energy, the Evolution theory, the interpretation of Egyptian Hieroglyphics, the Undulatory theory of Light; for the invention of the Steam Engine, the method of Spectrum Analysis, the Telegraph and the Telephone, as well as many other of the discoveries and inventions which have been epoch-making in the history of the world.   No great idea can, in truth, be said to have been the product of a single mind.   As a recent socialist writer very aptly and truthfully remarks, " All that man produces to-day more than did his cave-dwelling ancestors, he produces by virtue of the accumulated achievements, inventions, and improvements of the intervening generations, together with the social and industrial machinery which is their legacy," and further, " Nine hundred and ninety-nine parts out of the thousand of every man's produce are the result of his social inheritance and environment." [1]   This is so ; and it is, if possible, even more true of the work of our brains than of the work of our hands.

When, however, we turn now to that great body of literature which deals with the comparative development of the inferior races, it is not a little surprising to find that one of its features is the tendency almost invariably displayed therein, even by high authorities, to quite lose sight of and ignore the foregoing considerations.   Thus, one of the

----

[1] E. Bellamy, *Contemporary Review*, July 1890, " What Nationalism means."

commonest assumptions to be met with in anthropological literature is that that kind of development
which is the result, almost exclusively, of social
inheritance, and which must, therefore, be regarded
only as the true mark and evidence of the high
social qualities of a race, is to be taken as evidence
of the high intellectual development of that race.
And as a consequence we find the converse assumption equally common. If a race is without qualities
contributing to social efficiency, and has consequently
advanced little towards social development, its
members have hitherto been relegated (equally
unhesitatingly and as a matter of course) to a
corresponding grade of intellectual impotency.

We have, accordingly, presented to us the strange
sight of those who make comparisons between ourselves and the lower races, taking as the measure of
our individual mental stature the whole of that vast
intellectual accumulation which belongs to society
and past generations, and which is, strictly speaking,
the true measure of our social efficiency. The result
is of course highly flattering to our intellectual pride
when we are compared in this way with races of low
social efficiency, and, therefore, of no social history.
It is to some extent as if one standing on the dome
of St. Paul's should forget for a moment the vast
structure beneath him and triumphantly call the
world to witness the immense difference between his
physical stature and that of the persons below him
in the street.

Let us examine in detail the evidence generally
accepted as tending to exhibit the great intellectual
difference between the members of the higher and
the lower races, and see what conclusions we are

warranted in drawing therefrom. It will be noticed that there is a class of facts usually accepted as evidence of this mental interval which attracts attention before any other. The lower races have, as a rule, no words in their languages to express many of the more complex ideas and relationships that have been familiar to members of the higher races from childhood, and a knowledge of which has become almost second nature to these latter. For instance, savage races are nearly always without any but the most elementary conception of numbers. They are generally unable to count, and not infrequently they are without words in their language to express numbers higher than five or even three. This last-mentioned fact has been very generally noticed ; scarcely any other peculiarity seems to make so much impression upon members of the higher races when first brought into contact with uncivilised men. Yet the peoples who are in this state often possess flocks and herds, and each owner knows when he has got all his own cattle and will instantly detect the loss of one ; not, however, because he can tell how many he possesses, but only because he remembers each one individually.

. Mr. Francis Galton relates, in this connection, incidents in his experience with the Damaras which have become classical in anthropological literature. They have been universally quoted as exhibiting the great mental interval between the higher and the lower races. He states : "When bartering is going on each sheep must be paid for separately. Thus, suppose two sticks of tobacco to be the rate of exchange for one sheep, it would sorely puzzle a Damara to take two sheep and to give him four

U

sticks." [1]   He relates having attempted a transaction
of this kind, and the resulting confusion of the
Damara is described.   It continued " till two sticks
were put into his hand and one sheep driven away,
and then the other two sticks given him and the
second sheep driven away." [2]   When a heifer was
bought for ten sticks of tobacco, the large hands of
the native were spread out on the ground and a stick
had to be placed on each finger.

The effect of experiences of this kind—and they
are quoted at great length by most travellers and
explorers who have come into contact with uncivilised races—is nearly always the same on
European observers.   The impression produced
thereby on Mr. Galton's mind is, indeed, made quite
clear.   He forms, in consequence, a very low estimate
of the mental capacity of the Damaras ; so much so,
that a little farther on he relates that while he watched
a Damara floundering hopelessly in a calculation on
one side, he observed his spaniel equally embarrassed
on the other.   She had half a dozen new-born puppies,
and two or three had been removed, but she could
not make out if all were present.   She evidently had
a vague notion of counting, but the figures were too
large for her ; and Mr. Galton draws the conclusion
that, taking the two, the dog and the Damara,
" the comparison reflected no great honour on the
man." [3]

The fallacy which underlies the reasoning based
on facts of this kind, by which the mental inferiority
of uncivilised races is supposed to be proved, is not
immediately apparent ; but an undoubted and extra-

[1] *Narrative of an Explorer in Tropical South Africa,* p. 133.
[2] *Ibid.*   [3] *Ibid.*

ordinary fallacy exists nevertheless. It is one of the commonest examples of that prevailing tendency to confuse the mental equipment which we receive from the civilisation to which we belong, with the mental capacity with which nature has endowed us. Mr. Galton might, by a very simple experiment, have convinced himself at any time that most of us—proud inheritors of "the supreme Caucasian brain" though we be—possess as individuals only much the same natural grasp of numbers as the Damara of whom he had so low an opinion. Any one who doubts this may try the experiment for himself. Let him, next time he makes a purchase and receives a number of coins in change, say whether or not he has received the correct number *without counting*, and he will probably discover that above a very low number he has no natural power of telling the exact number of coins he is looking at.

But he can count them, it will be said. Very true; it is here that the fallacy begins. We make the mistake of reckoning this power of counting as part of the intellectual equipment that we individuals of the civilised races have received from nature. We have only to reflect to perceive that it is nothing of the kind. Our scale of numbers is nothing more than a kind of mental tape-measure, with which we are provided ready-made by the society to which we belong, and which we apply to aggregates of numbers just as we should an ordinary tape-measure to aggregates of units of length to determine how many there are. But this mental scale is certainly not born with us. It has been the slowly perfected product of an immense number of generations stretching back into the dim obscurity of the past; and we obtain the power which it gives us over uncivilised man, not as a gift direct from nature to ourselves, but as part of the accumulated stock of knowledge of the civilisation to which we belong. Without this scale we should, in fact, have . to resort to the method of uncivilised man with his cattle—we should have to identify and remember each unit individually. When we count we are really performing no higher intellectual operation than the Damara who told his tobacco sticks against his fingers. The mechanical scale with which we are provided by society in our system of numeration is, of course, a far superior one. But that is all ; for, when we count, we only tell off the units against it one by one in exactly the same manner that the savage tells them off against his fingers.

The true lesson of this, and of the large class of similar experiences, commonly supposed to prove the low mental development of uncivilised man, is not that he is so inferior to ourselves, intellectually, as to be almost on a level with Mr. Galton's dog, but that he is almost always the representative of a race of low social efficiency with consequently no social history. On the other hand, the individuals of civilised races with whom he is contrasted are the members of a community with a long record of social stability and continuity, which is, therefore, in possession of a vast accumulated store of knowledge inherited from past generations. That is to say, we are the representatives of peoples necessarily possessing high social qualities, but not by any means, and to the same degree, these high intellectual qualities we so readily assume.

It will be found, if we continue our examination in other directions, that this exaggerated conception of our intellectual superiority to races of lower social development rests to a great extent on the same precarious foundations.   Facts which seem to be difficult, if not impossible, to reconcile with the prevailing views as to our intellectual superiority over the peoples known as the lower races, continue to be encountered on every side.   The European races in India, if judged by those qualities which win for a race ascendency in the world, have some claim to consider themselves the superiors of the natives over whom they rule.   Yet, since the development of an efficient system of higher education in India, these natives have proved themselves the rivals of Europeans in European branches of learning.   Indian and Burmese students, who have come to England to be trained for the legal and other professions, have proved themselves to be not the inferiors of their European colleagues ; and they have, from time to time, equalled and even surpassed the best English students against whom they have been matched.

Even those races which are melting away at the mere contact of European civilisation supply evidence which appears to be quite irreconcilable with the prevailing view as to their great intellectual inferiority.   The Maoris in New Zealand, though they are slowly disappearing before the race of higher social efficiency with which they have come into contact, do not appear to show any *intellectual* incapacity for assimilating European ideas, or for acquiring proficiency and distinction in any branch of European learning.   Although they have, within fifty years, dwindled from 80,000 to 40,000, and still continue to make rapid strides on the down- ward path, the Registrar-General of New Zealand, in a recent report on the condition of the colony, says of them that they possess fine characteristics, both mental and physical, and readily adopt the manners and customs of their civilised neighbours. He asserts that in mental qualifications they can hardly be deemed naturally an inferior race, and that the native members of both the Legislative Council and the House of Representatives take a dignified, active, and intelligent part in the debates, especially in those having any reference to Maori interests.[1]

Even the Australian aborigines seem to provide us with facts strangely at variance with the prevailing theories. The Australian native has been, by the common consent of the civilised world, placed intellectually almost at the bottom of the list of the existing races comprising the human family. He has been the zero from which anthropologists and ethnologists have long reckoned our intellectual progress upwards. His mental capacity is universally accepted as being of a very low order. Yet this despised member of the race, possessing usually no words in his native languages for numbers above three, whose mental capacity is reckoned degrees lower than that of the Damara whom Mr. Galton compared disparagingly with his dog, exhibits under our eyes powers of mind that should cause us seriously to reflect before committing ourselves hastily to current theories as to the immense mental gulf between him and ourselves. It is somewhat startling, for instance, to read that in the state schools in the Australian colonies it has been observed that

[1] Report from the Registrar-General of New Zealand on the Condition of the Colony. Vide *Nature*, 24th October 1889.

aboriginal children learn quite as easily and rapidly
as children of European parents ; and, lately, that
" for three consecutive years the aboriginal school at
Remahyack, in Victoria, stood highest of all the
state schools of the colony in examination results,
obtaining 100 per cent of marks." [1]   The same facts
present themselves in the United States.   The
children of the large negro population in that country
are on just the same footing as children of the white
population in the public elementary schools.   Yet
the negro children exhibit no intellectual inferiority ;
they make just the same progress in the subjects
taught as do the children of white parents, and the
deficiency they exhibit later in life is of quite a
different kind.

Lastly, if we closely examine the statements of
those who, while acknowledging that the lower races
show this ability to learn easily and rapidly in suitable circumstances, nevertheless maintain that they
do not make progress beyond a certain point, we
find that the causes to which this result is attributed
by discriminating observers throw a flood of light on
the whole subject.   Members of the inferior races, it
is pointed out, scarcely ever possess those qualities of
intense application and of prolonged preserving effort,
without which it is absolutely impossible to obtain
high proficiency in any branch of learning.   Exactly
so ; it is here that we have the true cause of the
deficiency displayed by the lower races.   But such a
deficiency is not to be described as profound intellectual inferiority.   The lacking qualities are not

---

[1] Rev. John Mathew on the Australian Aborigines.   *Proceedings of
the Royal Society of New South Wales*, vol. xxii. part ii.   Quoted
from summary in *Nature*, 25th December 1890.

intellectual qualities at all ; they are precisely those which contribute in so high a degree to social efficiency and racial ascendency, and they are, consequently, as might be expected, the invariable inheritance of those races which have reached a state of high social development, and of those races only.[1]

Again, these considerations acquire a certain significance, which must not be passed unnoticed, from the current history of the peoples comprised in our Western civilisation. In view of the profound intermixture of races that has taken place in almost every European country, and that is taking place on a large scale in America at the present day, it is, strictly speaking, inadmissible to speak of any particular nationality as representing any particular race. National types of character, in so far as they have had a racial origin, probably result from blends in varying degrees of the mental characteristics of the races which have gone to make up the nations.

[1] Soon after the publication of the first edition of this book the *Westminster Gazette* quoted, in support of the argument here developed, the example of the rapid progress in the acquirement and use of European knowledge made by the natives of British Central Africa. The Blantyre Mission Station was founded in 1876. In 1891 the European population was only eighteen. Speaking in 1894 Mr. H. H. Johnston, British Commissioner for Central Africa, is reported to have said, in an interview with a representative of the *London Daily Chronicle*, "The Yaos are very intelligent people. An interesting fact is that the entire printing of the Government administration and of the *British Central African Gazette* is done by native printers, trained either at Blantyre or the Universities' Mission Stations. They work even without the supervision of a white man, and very few mistakes are made in setting up copy. Surely this is wonderful work for utter savages. Only the last issue of the *British Central African Gazette*, printed before my departure, contained a notice inserted at the request of the German authorities, dealing with the regulation and use of firearms in German territory. This notice, written in German, was simply handed to the Yao head printer, and it was set up with scarcely a single mistake, although the printers had never seen German before."

Nevertheless we may still, within limitations, draw certain conclusions as to the racial characteristics of some of the peoples who have become ingredients in our modern nationalities. Certain characteristics of two such well-defined groups as the Celtic and Teutonic peoples may still be clearly distinguished.

Now there can be little doubt that, as regards the peoples of the Celtic stock, they must be classed high intellectually. We must recognise this, both from a review of the history of individuals and from an examination of the history of the countries in which the characteristics of these peoples have found the fullest and truest expression they have obtained in our civilisation. If we take France, which of the three leading countries of Western Europe probably possesses the largest leaven of Celtic blood, any impartial person, who had fairly considered the evidence, would probably find himself compelled to admit that a very strong if not a conclusive case could be made out for placing the French people a degree higher as regards certain intellectual characteristics than any other of the Western peoples. When all due allowance is made for national jealousies, the extent to which this general obligation to the French intellect is acknowledged by discriminating observers in various countries is remarkable. The influence of the French intellect is, in fact, felt throughout the whole fabric of our Western civilisation; in the entire region of politics, in nearly every branch of art, and in every department of higher thought.

Even where the intellect of the Teutonic peoples obtains the highest possible results, it may be noticed that there is a certain distinction in kind to be made between the two qualities of intellect. The Teutonic peoples tend, as a rule, to obtain the most striking intellectual results where profound research, painstaking, conscientious endeavour, and the laborious piecing together and building up of the fabric of knowledge go to produce the highest effects.   But the idealism of the French mind is largely wanting. That light, yet agile and athletic grasp of principles and ideas which is characteristic of the French mind is to some extent missing.   Certain qualities, too, peculiar to the ancient Greek mind, seem to find a truer expression amongst the French people than they do elsewhere in our civilisation.   Even in the art of the Teutonic peoples we seem to miss some of the highest qualities—a deficiency which has been sometimes defined as that of a people in whom the ethical sense overshadows the æsthetic.   Any conscientious observer, when first brought into close contact with the French mind, must feel that there is an indefinite something in it of a distinctly high intellectual order which is not native to either the German or the English peoples.   It is felt in the current literature and the current art of the time no less than in the highest products of the national genius in the past.   In the streets of the capital and the provincial towns, in the public buildings, in the churches, temples, and art galleries, even in the bookstalls, one encounters at every turn something of that noble intellectual sense of the ideal and the appropriate which was characteristic of the Greek mind.[1]

But while all this must be acknowledged, the

---

[1] It is interesting to notice, in this connection, that Mr. Grant Allen has recently asserted ("The Celt in English Art," *Fortnightly Review*, part i. 1891) that, while in our complex English nationality

fact, nevertheless, remains that the Teutonic peoples undoubtedly possess certain equally characteristic qualities, not in themselves intellectual, which contribute in a higher degree to social efficiency, and which—having in view the manner in which natural selection is operating and the direction in which the evolution of the race is proceeding—must apparently be pronounced to be greatly more important than these merely intellectual qualities. At a future time, when the history of the nineteenth century comes to be written, with that sense of proportion which distance alone can give, it will be perceived that there are two great features of this century which give a distinctive character to its history, and by the side of which all other developments and events will appear dwarfed and insignificant. The first is the complete and absolute triumph throughout our Western civilisation of the principles of that political idealism which found expression in the French Revolution. The second is the equally triumphant and overwhelming expansion of the peoples of Teutonic stock, and the definite and final worsting by them in the struggle for existence, at nearly every point of contact throughout the world, of that other branch of the Western peoples whose intellectual capacity has so distinctly left its mark upon the century.

By the middle of the eighteenth century England and France had closed in what—when all the issues dependent on the struggle are taken into account——

the Celt's place in literature is unquestionable, in art it only needs pointing out. He maintains also that the idealism which exists in English art and literature, and even in English religion and politics, is largely a Celtic product.

is undoubtedly one of the most stupendous duels that history records. Before it came to a close the shock had been felt throughout the civilised world. The contest was waged in Europe, in India, in Africa, over the North American continent, and on the high seas. Judged by all those appearances which impress the imagination, everything was in favour of the more brilliant race. In armaments, in resources, in population, they were the superior people. In 1789 the population of Great Britain was only 9,600,000,[1] the population of France was 26,300,000.[2] The annual revenue of France was £24,000,000,[3] that of Great Britain was only £15,650,000.[4] At the beginning of the nineteenth century the French people numbered some 27,000,000,[5] while the whole English-speaking peoples, including the Irish and the population of the North American states and colonies, did not exceed 20,000,000.[6]

By the beginning of the last decade of the nineteenth century the English-speaking peoples, not including subject peoples, aboriginal races, or the coloured population of the United States,

---

[1] *Political Geography. Statistical Tables of the States of Europe,* 1789. Lowdnes, London.
[2] Estimated by E. Levasseur. Vide *La Population Française.*
[3] *Political Geography. Statistical Tables of the States of Europe,* 1789. Lowdnes, London.   [4] *Ibid.*
[5] *Le premier dénombrement de la Population de la France, celui de* 1801, 27,445,297. E. Levasseur.
[6] *The Statistical Tables of Europe,* by J. G. Boetticher, dated 1800, and said to be correct to 1799, gives the figures as follows :—

England	.	.	.	8,400,000
Scotland	.	.	.	1,600,000
Ireland	.	.	.	4,000,000

In the Report on 10th census of the United States, the population of that country in 1800 is estimated at 5,308,000.

had, however, expanded to the enormous total of 101,000,000, while the French people scarcely numbered 40,000,000.   Looking back it will be seen that the former peoples have been successful at almost every point throughout the world at which the conflict has been waged.   In nearly the whole of the North American and Australian continents, and in those parts of Southern Africa most suitable for European races, the English-speaking peoples are in possession.   No other peoples have so firmly and permanently established their position.   No limits can be set to the expansion they are likely to undergo even in the next century, and it would seem almost inevitable that they must in future exercise a preponderating influence in the world.

As against this the record of the capable French race stands out in strong contrast.   One of the principal features of the last half of the nineteenth century has been the further humiliation it has undergone at the hands of another branch of the Teutonic peoples ; and here also the historian will probably have to distinguish that the result has been in no way accidental, but due to causes which had their roots deep in the general causes which are shaping the evolution we are undergoing.   But remarkable as have been the developments of the past 150 years, none of them has more clearly contributed to the decadence of the people who, at the beginning of the century, probably represented the highest development of the intellect of the Western peoples, than a cause which is in operation within their own borders.   No more striking history of racial self-effacement has ever been witnessed than that which is revealed by the French population

statistics.   The rate of increase of the French population has been for years growing less and less, until
it has at length reached the vanishing point; and
France stands now, a solitary example amongst
European peoples, with a population showing an
actual tendency to decrease.   The excess of births
over deaths, which is 13 per thousand in England,
and 10 per thousand in Germany, oscillates in France
between an excess of only 1 per thousand and an
actual deficiency.   Nay more, the only section of
the community amongst whom the births show a
decided tendency to outnumber the deaths are the
foreigners domiciled in France; and it is only this
increase, and the continual influx of foreigners, which
prevent a considerable decrease of population year by
year in France.[1]

[1] The following table shows the movement of population in France
in the period between 1881 and 1890. It is summarised from a paper
by V. Turquan, which appeared in the *Economiste Français*, 31st
October 1891 :—

Year.	Births.	Deaths.	Excess or Deficiency of Births.
1881	937,057	822,828	+ 114,229
1882	935,566	838,539	+ 97,027
1883	937,944	841,141	+ 96,803
1884	937,758	858,784	+ 78,974
1885	924,558	836,897	+ 87,661
1886	912,838	860,222	+ 52,616
1887	899,333	842,797	+ 56,536
1888	882,639	837,967	+ 44,672
1889	880,579	794,933	+ 85,646
1890	838,059	876,505	− 38,446

The facts for a wider period are given by P. Leroy-Beaulieu in a
paper that appeared in the *Economiste Français*, 20th and 27th
September 1890, of which a translation will be found in Appendix
III.

Viewed from the standpoint from which the evolution of the human race as a whole is to be regarded, the record of the past 150 years must be pronounced to have been almost exclusively disastrous to the French people.   Not only have they withdrawn worsted at almost every point from that great rivalry of races which filled the world in the eighteenth century, but their decadence continues within their borders.   Even on the soil of France they do not appear to hold their own with the stranger that is within their gates ; so that we have an economic writer, of the standing of M. Leroy-Beaulieu, actually proposing as the most efficacious remedy, for a country like France which has many attractions for foreigners, to obtain the naturalisation of from 50,000 to 100,000 aliens annually.[1]   M. Lageneau points out that the present tendency of population must be to place France within the next half-century in a very disadvantageous position compared with other great nations.   Within a century, said *La France* recently, there will be ten men speaking English for every one speaking French.   *L'Univers* has expressed the opinion that within half a century " France will have fallen below Italy and Spain to the rank of a second-rate power.   There is no denying the figures.   If this continues in addition to other causes of decadence, we are a lost nation."

It will thus be seen that we have, proceeding under our eyes, and in our own time, a rivalry of races tending, when its results are understood, to confirm the general conclusion at which we have already arrived.   It can hardly be held that intellectual capacity has been the determining factor on

[1] *Vide* Appendix III.

the side of the peoples who have made most headway in this rivalry, or that, in the result, natural
selection has exhibited any tendency to develop this
quality. On the contrary, we would appear to have
evidence of the same tendency that has been distinguished elsewhere in the history of social progress.
It is not intellectual capacity that natural selection
appears to be developing in the first instance, but
other qualities contributing more directly to social
efficiency, and, therefore, of immensely more importance and potency in the social evolution which
mankind is undergoing. There can be little doubt
that the ascendency which the Teutonic peoples have
won, and are winning in the world, is mainly due
to the higher and fuller development these last-
mentioned qualities have attained amongst them.
There can also, apparently, be as little room for
question that the possession of even the highest
intellectual capacity in no way tends to compensate
for the lack of these qualities. We may even go
farther and say that its possession without these
qualities distinctly tends to further lower the social
efficiency of a people.

The causes of the more recent decadence of the
French nation are well known. The decline in the
population is almost entirely due to voluntary causes.
On the average, out of every thousand men over
twenty years of age in the whole of France, only 609
are married.[1] Out of every thousand families, as many
as 640 have only two children or under [2] (and 200 of

[1] Statement by M. Lageneau at a meeting of the Académie des
Sciences, July 1890.

[2] *Vide* Return presented to the Chamber by the Minister of
Finance summarised in the *Times*, 23rd June 1890.   *Vide* also *La
Population Française*, by E. Levasseur.

these families have no children at all).   The voluntary
limitation of offspring M. Lageneau attributes to " the
desire of the parents to make ample provision for
the children they do have."   P. Leroy-Beaulieu,
while recognising this cause, finds it "associated still
more with a lessening of religious belief on the part
of the people, and a modification of the old ideas of
resignation and submission to their lot."   We have,
in fact, in the circumstance only one of the simplest
instances of that enlightened selfishness in the individual which must always lead him to rank his own
interests, or those of his immediate belongings, in the
actual present before the wider and entirely different
interests of the longer-lived social organism to which
he belongs.   It is but a phase of that central
problem underlying our development in society
which we have been discussing throughout.   It is
one of the commonest examples of the disintegrating
influence of that self-assertive rationalism in the
individual, towards the control of which the forces
at work in the evolution of human society have
been from the beginning slowly but unceasingly
operating.

If we now review the ground over which we have
travelled, we find that we have got a remarkable
series of facts which must appear perplexing and
inexplicable if we are to accept the view that the
evolution the race is undergoing in society, and by
which certain sections of it acquire ascendency over
others, is mainly an intellectual evolution.   We
have seen that a people like the Greeks, who developed a civilisation anterior to our own, and long
since extinct, are held by high authorities to have
been considerably our mental superiors.   We have

X

seen that, despite the ascendency our own civilisation is winning in the world at the present time, it is not certain that intellectual development is proceeding *pari passu* with social development therein, and that it is even probable that the tendency of our civilisation has been to restrain intellectual development. We have also seen that anthropologists are unable to establish that clear connection between social development and cranial capacity that we might have expected ; that science apparently often directs our attention to instances of large brain capacity in peoples of low social development. We have seen that current conceptions of an immense intellectual interval between ourselves and races of lower social development are greatly exaggerated, and even to a large extent fallacious ; that they are not borne out by the facts as we find them ; and that they must be held to have originated in the erroneous tendency to take as the measure of the mental development of individuals belonging to the civilised races that intellectual inheritance of civilisation which has been accumulated during a long series of generations in the past, and which is, strictly speaking, only to be taken as evidence of the social efficiency of the races which have accumulated it.

Lastly, we have seen that in the rivalry of nationalities which is actually proceeding in our civilisation, existing facts do not appear to point to the conclusion that high intellectual development is the most potent factor in determining success. We have seen that certain qualities, not in themselves intellectual, but which contribute directly to social efficiency, are apparently of greater importance ; and that in the absence of these qualities high intel-

lectual development may even lower social efficiency
to a dangerous degree, and so contribute to the
decided worsting, in the evolution which is proceeding,
of the people possessing it.

When all these facts are now taken together, they
undoubtedly tend to support, with a very striking
class of evidence, a conclusion towards which we
have been advancing in the preceding chapters. It
would appear that when man became a social
creature his progress ceased to be *primarily* in the
direction of the development of his intellect. Thenceforward, in the conditions under which natural selection has operated, his interests as an individual were
no longer paramount ; they became subordinate to
the distinct and widely-different interests of the
longer-lived social organism to which he for the time
being belonged. The intellect, of course, continues to
be a most important factor in enabling the system to
which the individual belongs to maintain its place in
the rivalry of life ; but it is no longer the prime
factor. And it continually tends to come into conflict
with those large evolutionary forces which, through the
instrumentality of religious systems, are securing the
progressive subordination of the present interests of
the self-assertive individual to the future interests of
society. The lesson of human history appears to
be that it is these larger forces which are always
triumphant. Natural selection seems, in short, to be
steadily evolving in the race that type of character
upon which these forces act most readily and
efficiently ; that is to say, it is evolving religious
character in the first instance, and intellectual character only as a secondary product in association with
it. It is not that the nature of man is to be regarded

as a house divided against itself. It is rather that
the willingness to submit reason to the control of
sanctions beyond the reach of reason is the most
important and characteristic product of the process
of evolution at work in human society. The race
would, in fact, appear to be growing more and more
religious, the winning sections being those in which,
cæteris paribus, this type of character is most fully
developed.

But, like all movements of the kind, the evolution
is proceeding very slowly. One after another, races
and civilisations appear to be used up in the process
as it proceeds. When the intellectual development
of any section of the race has, for the time being,
outrun its ethical development, natural selection has
apparently weeded that section out like any other unsuitable product. Regarding our social systems as
organic growths, there appears to be a close analogy
between their life-history and that of forms of organic
life in general. We have, on the one side, in the ethical
systems upon which they are founded, the developmental force which sets in motion that life-continuing,
constructive process which physiologists call ana-
bolism. On the other side, and in conflict with it,
we have in the self-assertive rationalism of the
individual, the tendency—by itself disintegrating and
destructive—known as katabolism. In a social
system, as in any other organism, the downward
stage towards decay is probably commenced when
the katabolic tendency begins to progressively over-
balance the anabolic tendency.

A preponderating element in the type of character
which the evolutionary forces at work in human
society are slowly developing, would appear to be

the sense of reverence. The qualities with which it
is tending to be closely allied are, great mental
energy, resolution, enterprise, powers of prolonged
and concentrated application, and a sense of simple-
minded and single-minded devotion to conceptions
of duty.

CHAPTER X

CONCLUDING REMARKS

IT seems likely, when the application of the principles of evolutionary science to history comes to be fully understood, that we shall have to witness almost as great a revolution in those departments of knowledge which deal with man in society as we have already seen taking place in the entire realm of the lower organic sciences through the development and general application, during the latter half of the nineteenth century, of the biological theories enunciated by Darwin. It is evident that we are approaching a period when we shall no longer have the same justification, as in the past, for regarding human history as a bewildering exception to the reign of universal law—a kind of solitary and mysterious island in the midst of the cosmos given over to a strife of forces without clue or meaning Despite the complexity of the problems encountered in history, we seem to have everywhere presented to us systematic development underlying apparent confusion. In all the phases and incidents of our social annals we are apparently regarding only the intimately related phenomena of a single, vast, orderly process of evolution.

If the explanation of the principles governing the evolution of society which has been given in the preceding chapters is in the main correct, these principles must have an application far too wide to be adequately discussed within the limits to which it is proposed to confine this book.   It has been no part of the aim of the writer, in the task he has here undertaken, to treat the subject in its relations to that wider domain of philosophical inquiry of which it forms a province.   It only remains now to deal with a few matters directly arising out of the argument so far as it has proceeded.

Emphasis has been laid throughout the preceding pages on the necessity for a clear and early recognition of the inherent and inevitable antagonism existing in human society between the interests of the individual, necessarily concerned with his own welfare, and the interest of the social organism, largely bound up with the welfare of generations yet unborn.   The fundamental conception underlying the reasoning of that hitherto predominant school of thought which has sought to establish in the nature of things a rationalistic sanction for individual conduct, has always been that the interests of the individual either already are, or are immediately tending to become, coincident with the interests of society as a whole.   The principles of this *Utilitarian* school have come down to us through Hobbes and Locke, and have been developed by a large and distinguished group of philosophical writers, amongst the more influential of whom must be counted Hume, Jeremy Bentham, and the two Mills.   They will, in the future, not improbably be recognised to have received their truest scientific expression in the Synthetic Philo-

sophy of Mr. Herbert Spencer.   There can be no
mistaking the central conception of this school.   The
idea of the identification of the interests of the individual with those of society, as a whole, has been
brought into ever-increasing prominence.   The key
to the political system of Bentham was expressed in
a single phrase of Priestley's—" the greatest happiness
of the greatest number "—long a prominent doctrine
in English politics.   In John Stuart Mill's writings
again, this conception of the identity of the two
classes of interests found constant and clear expression.   He insisted, as a means of making the
nearest approach to the perfection of Utilitarian
morality, that " utility would enjoin that laws and
social arrangements should place the happiness or
(as speaking practically it may be called) the
interests of every individual as nearly as possible
in harmony with the interest of the whole." [1]   Mr.
Herbert Spencer has attempted to develop the
position a stage farther, and to establish it on a
scientific foundation.   In his *Data of Ethics* he
professes to see, in the process of social evolution
going on around us, a conciliation taking place
" between the interests of each citizen and the
interest of citizens at large, tending ever towards a
state in which the two become merged in one, and
in which the feelings answering to them respectively
fall into complete concord." [2]

It would appear that we must reject this conception as being inconsistent with the teaching of
evolutionary science.   The forces which are at work
in the evolution of society are certainly, on the

[1] *Utilitarianism*, by J. S. Mill, p. 25.
[2] *Data of Ethics*, by Herbert Spencer, p. 243.

whole, working out the greatest good of the greatest number in a progressive community. But the earlier utilitarian conception of the greatest number has always related merely to the majority of the existing members of society at any time. The greatest good which the evolutionary forces, operating in society, are working out, is the good of the social organism as a whole. *The greatest number in this sense is comprised of the members of generations yet unborn or unthought of, to whose interests the existing individuals are absolutely indifferent.* And, in the process of social evolution which the race is undergoing, it is these latter interests which are always in the ascendant.

There cannot, it would appear, be found in Darwinian science, as it is now understood, any warrant for anticipating the arrival of that state of society contemplated by Mr. Herbert Spencer. The author of the Synthetic Philosophy had in view a state of things in which the antagonism between societies having entirely ceased on the one hand, and the conciliation between the interests of the individual and those of the social organism having been perfectly attained to on the other, the individual also will have reached a stage of development in which it will afford him the highest pleasure to act in a manner conducive to the good of the social organism, and this even where such conduct is, to all appearance, directly antagonistic to his own material interests—just as at present the highest happiness is often obtained in parental sacrifice. This altruistic instinct may, in fact, according to Mr. Spencer, " be expected to attain a level at which it will be like parental altruism in

spontaneity," and so lead the individual to obtain
the highest of all satisfactions in voluntary sacrificing
himself in the interests of the social organism.[1]

By this conception of an ideal social state, Mr.
Herbert Spencer must mean one of two things. Let
us take each separately. If he imagined, as the
older utilitarians apparently did imagine, a conciliation of the interests of the individual and those of
society taking place with human nature exactly as it
is, but under a different organisation of society to
that now prevailing, then he is at one with certain
socialist reformers of the time. Nothing more is
necessary to bring about such a state of society than
to draw a ring fence round our borders, to suspend the
competitive forces, to organise society on a socialist
basis, and in future to regulate the population
strictly according to the conditions of existence for
the time being. Conduct contributing to the present
welfare of society in such a community would be but
that dictated by " enlightened self-interest " in the individuals ; and the conciliation of interests would be,
as far as possible, complete. We have already dealt
with the difficulties in the way of such a society
in the chapter on socialism. But the evolutionist
who has perceived the application of that development which the Darwinian law of Natural Selection
has undergone in the hands of Weismann, is precluded at the outset from contemplating the continued
success of such a society. The evolutionist who has
once realised the significance of the supreme fact
up to which biology has slowly advanced,—namely,
that every quality of life can be kept in a state of
efficiency and prevented from retrograding only by

[1] Vide *Data of Ethics*, chap. xiv.

the continued and never-relaxed stress of selection —simply finds it impossible to conceive a society permanently existing in this state. He can only think of it existing at all on one condition—in the first stage of a period of progressive degeneration.

But it may be replied on behalf of Mr. Herbert Spencer that he has advanced beyond this position, that such an argument, however applicable to the views of some of the older utilitarians, and to some of the prevailing socialist theories of society, does not reach his position. For he *does*, it may be said, contemplate the necessary sacrifice of the interests of the individual to those of the social organism which the conditions of evolution require. Only the individual will be so constituted that this sacrifice will be made spontaneously. He will obtain the highest satisfaction and happiness in making it. His character will, in fact, have undergone so profound a modification that this social altruism " may be expected to attain a level at which it will be like parental altruism in spontaneity." Let us deal with this modified view.

The deficiency in Mr. Spencer's reasoning here is the same deficiency which to a large extent pervades the whole of his synthetic philosophy in its application to our social phenomena. He has never realised the nature of the essential difference which distinguishes human evolution from all other evolution whatsoever : namely, the existence therein of the factor of individual reason. He has, therefore, not perceived that, while our evolution is in the first place pre-eminently a social evolution, the most profoundly individualistic, anti-social, and anti-evolutionary of all human qualities, when uncontrolled, is one which tends to be progressively developed in the race, namely, reason. He has, accordingly, never realised that the central feature of our evolution has always been the supreme struggle in which the control of this disintegrating influence is being continually affected in the interest of society first, and of the race in the next place ; and that the function of the immense and characteristic class of social phenomena which we have in our religious systems is to secure this necessary subordination of the present interests of the self-assertive individual to the general interests of the process of evolution which is in progress. To expect the subordination —in the manner contemplated by Mr. Spencer—of that feeling in the individual which prompts him to consider his own interests first, to a feeling leading him to sacrifice these interests to further a process of evolution with which he has no concern, is to ignore facts and conditions around us, the meaning of which is unmistakable.

For it would be impossible to conceive any altruistic feeling of this kind which could exceed in strength the parental instinct. Yet one of the plainest facts of our time and of past history is the perversion of this instinct under the influence of rationalism, and the suspension of its operation in furthering the evolution the race is undergoing. We have discussions proceeding in the literature of the time in which rationalism, with reiterated emphasis, points out, to use the phrase already quoted, that " there is something pathetically absurd in this sacrifice to their children of generation after generation of grown people." No observant person who has watched the signs of the times can have the least doubt that, in a state of unrestricted rationalism, the institution of marriage and the family would undergo modifications incompatible with the continuance of that process of simple self-sacrifice with which the interests of the race are bound up. We have unmistakable evidence of the perversion of the parental feelings amongst the Greeks and Romans under such rationalistic influences. Speaking of the decay of the Athenian people, Mr. Francis Galton says, "We know, and may guess something more, of the reason why this marvellously gifted race declined. Social morality grew exceedingly lax ; marriage became unfashionable and was avoided ; many of the more ambitious and accomplished women were avowed courtesans, and consequently infertile, and the mothers of the incoming population were of a heterogeneous class." [1] The same state of popular feeling with respect to marriage prevailed during the decline of the Roman Empire. "The courtesans," says Mr. Lecky, "were raised in popular estimation to an unexampled elevation, and aversion to marriage became very general." And we have at the present day that striking example, referred to in the last chapter, of the perversion, under similar circumstances, of the parental feelings amongst the most brilliant and able race amongst the European peoples, and the consequent failure of that race to maintain its place amongst others in the evolution which is proceeding under our eyes in the civilisation in which we are living.

Yet these parental instincts which give way thus before rationalism have an accumulated strength

---

[1] *Hereditary Genius*, p. 331.

behind them dating back to the beginning of life, developed, as they have been, through all those countless æons of time through which we rise from the lowest organisms upwards to man. To anticipate, as Mr. Herbert Spencer has done, the development, during the infinitesimal length of any period of human evolution that can be taken in comparison, of a feeling or instinct of a similar kind, but of sufficient strength to do what the parental feelings already fail to do, is to altogether misunderstand the nature of the characteristic problem human evolution presents, and consequently to misinterpret some of the plainest facts of the times in which we are living, and of the history of the race in the past.

It would appear that the teaching of evolutionary science as applied to society is that there is only one way in which the rationalistic factor in human evolution can be controlled ; namely, through the instrumentality of religious systems. These systems constitute the absolutely characteristic feature of our evolution, the necessary and inevitable complement of our reason. It is under the influence of these systems that the evolution of the race is proceeding ; it is in connection with these systems that we must study the laws which regulate the character, growth, and decay of societies and civilisations. It is along the ever-advancing or retreating frontiers where they encounter each other that we have some of the most striking effects that natural selection is producing on the race. It is within their borders that we witness the process by which the eternal forces that are working out the destiny of the race are continually effecting the subordination of the interests of suc- cessive generations of men to those larger interests to which the individual is indifferent, and of which he has only very feeble power to realise either the nature or the magnitude.

We have seen, in the previous chapters, that the process of evolution enfolding itself in our civilisation has consisted essentially in the slow disintegration of that military type of society which attained its highest development in a social stage in which the greater part of the people were excluded from participating in the rivalry of existence on terms of equality, and in which their lives were continuously exploited for the exclusive benefit of a comparatively small privileged and power - holding class. The history of the modern world we have observed to be simply the history of the process of development that, having undermined the position of these power-holding classes, emancipated the individual, and enfranchised the people, is now tending to bring, for the first time in the history of the race, all the members of the community into the rivalry of life on a footing of equality of opportunity. This is the movement which has raised our Western civilisation to the place it now occupies in the world, and all the social and political movements in progress in every country where it prevails are but aspects of it.

Now, while the import in this process of development of the movement known as the Reformation has been already referred to, the exact manner in which this movement has influenced and is still influencing our social and political development is seldom clearly perceived. That the effects on national character of the religious movement of the sixteenth century have been important is already fully recognised by students of social phenomena. Thus we find Professor Marshall, in his *Principles of Economics*, recently laying stress on the economic significance of the change which it produced in the English character. Its doctrines, he says, deepened the character of the people, "reacted on their habits of life, and gave a tone to their industry." Family life was intensified, so much so, that "the family relations of those races which have adopted the reformed religion are the richest and fullest of earthly feeling ; there never has been before any material of texture at once so strong and so fine with which to build up a noble fabric of social life."[1]

The character of the people had, in fact, not only been deepened and strengthened, it had been softened to an extent hitherto unknown. It is probable that the changes in doctrine which had principally contributed to produce this result were those which had tended to bring the individual into more intimate contact with the actual life and example of the Founder of Christianity, and therefore with the essential spirit that underlay our religious system and served to distinguish it from all other systems. As has been frequently correctly pointed out, the characteristic feature of Latin Christianity was different. This form has always tended, as it still tends, to treat as of the first importance, not the resulting change in character in the individual, but rather his belief in the authority of the Church and of an order of men, and in the supreme efficacy of sacramental ordinances which the Church has decreed itself alone competent to dispense. On the other hand, the central idea of the Reformation was the necessity for a spiritual change in the individual, and

[1] Vide *Principles of Economics*, vol. i. pp. 34, 35.

the recognition, in virtue thereof, of the priesthood
in his own person.   As Professor Marshall states,
" Man was, as it were, ushered straight into the
presence of his Creator with no human intermediary;
life became intense and full of awe, and now for the
first time large numbers of rude and uncultured
people yearned towards the mysteries of absolute
spiritual freedom.   The isolation of each person's
religious responsibility from that of his fellows rightly
understood was a necessary condition for the highest
spiritual progress." [1]   Thus, on the one hand, individual character tended to be greatly strengthened
by the isolation of individual responsibility, and, on
the other, to be deepened and softened by being
brought into close and intimate contact with those
wonderfully moving and impressive altruistic ideals
which we have in the simple story of the life and
acts of the Founder of Christianity.

The resulting difference in character, which may
mean much or little in theological controversy according to the standpoint of the observer, assumes, however, profound importance in the eyes of the student
of our social evolution.   The fact must be kept in
view, which has been throughout insisted on, that it
is this softening and deepening of character, with
the accompanying release in our social life of an
immense and all-pervading fund of altruistic feeling,
which has provided the real motive force behind the
whole onward movement with which our age is
identified.   It may be noticed, consequently, how
much farther the development of the humanitarian
feelings has progressed in those parts of our civilisation most affected by the movement of the sixteenth

---

[1] *Principles of Economics*, vol. i. p. 34.

Y

century, and more particularly amongst the Anglo-Saxon peoples. The great wave of altruistic feeling which caused the crusade against slavery to attain such remarkable development amongst these peoples has progressed onward, carrying on its crest the multitude of philanthropic and humanitarian undertakings which are so characteristic a feature of all English-speaking communities, and such little-understood movements as anti-vivisection, vegetarianism, the enfranchisement of women, the prevention of cruelty to animals, and the abolition of state regulation of vice. It is in these that we have the outward appearances which mark the nature of the larger impetus which, amongst these peoples, is behind that social and political movement which has gradually enfranchised and uplifted the people, and which is now steadily tending to bring them all into the rivalry of life on conditions of equality.

Now, Mr. Lecky has recently said that there is probably no better test of the political genius of a nation than the power it possesses of adapting old institutions to new wants, and he finds the English people pre-eminent in this characteristic.[1] There can be little doubt, however, that the quality here called political genius, which is undoubtedly, on the whole, characteristic of the Anglo-Saxon peoples, has its roots, in this instance, in causes intimately and directly associated with the exceptional development which the altruistic feelings have attained amongst these peoples as the result of the causes mentioned. We have, therein, one of the clearest examples of how profoundly the social development of particular peoples has been influenced by the

[1] *The Political Value of History*, 1892.

course which the ethical movement on which our civilisation is founded has taken amongst them.

In England, where the religious movement of the sixteenth century proceeded with little interruption, it has been noticed that the most significant feature of the process of social development in which the power-holding classes are in full conscious retreat before the incoming people is, that these classes are themselves deeply affected by the softening influences of the time. *All* classes of society have become sensitive in a high degree to the sight of suffering or wrong of any kind. The effect on the power-holding classes is to take away their faith in their own cause. With all the enormous latent strength of their position these classes do not make, and either consciously or unconsciously realise that they cannot make, any effective resistance to the onward movement which is gradually uplifting the people at their expense. The best of them are, in fact, either openly or in their hearts, on the side of the people, and the only fighting policy of the party is consequently one of temporising defence.

The practical consequence is of great significance. It is that the development in which the excluded masses of the people are being brought into the competition of life on a footing of equality of opportunity is proceeding, and will apparently continue to proceed in Great Britain, not by the violent stages of revolution, but as a gradual and orderly process of social change. The power-holding classes are in retreat before the people ; but the retreat on the one side is orderly and unbroken, while the advance on the other is the steady, unhastening, onward movement of a party conscious of the strength and rectitude of its cause, and in no doubt as to the final issue. There is, consequently, no deep-seated bitterness on either side. Both opponents, still respecting each other, recognise as it were the ultimate issue of the battle. *The great process is proceeding as a natural and orderly development*—we are adapting the old institutions to the new wants. This is the real secret of that political genius the Anglo-Saxon peoples are now displaying, and there is scarcely any other quality which promises to stand them in such good stead in that great social revolution with which the history of the twentieth century will be filled.

But when we turn to those peoples amongst whom the religious movement of the sixteenth century was interrupted or suppressed, and amongst whom the Latin form of Christianity prevails, we find that the situation is not exactly the same. Amongst these people the idea of the innate equality of all men, with the consequent conception of the fundamental right of all to equal opportunities which is the peculiar product of the ethical system on which our civilisation is founded, has practically reached the same development as elsewhere. But the profound change *in social character* which has accompanied this development, amongst the Anglo-Saxon peoples for instance, has not proceeded so far. The deepening of individual character, resulting in a certain inbred sense of integrity which has rendered the sense of wrong intolerable, and the softening process which has made the Anglo-Saxon peoples so sensitive to the sight of misery or suffering, have not progressed to the same extent.

In practice this is a difference of great importance. The two great opposing parties in the process of social development that is proceeding,—namely, the Power-holding classes and the People, the Haves and the Have-nots,—confront each other in a different spirit. The struggle, amongst the peoples who have not been so deeply affected by the humanitarian movement, tends to become more a selfish trial of strength in which each party is determinedly and bitterly fighting for its own material interests, and in which the issue swings, according to the relative strength of the opponents, between successful resistance on the one hand and successful revolution on the other. Either result is almost equally dangerous. With successful resistance on the part of the power-holding classes we have stagnation and interrupted development; with successful revolution on the part of the people we have irregular and uncertain progress. We have examples of either one or the other of these results amongst the European nations that have not been affected by the religious development of the sixteenth century. The victory naturally tends to be with the people; but the cost of successful revolution in such conditions is great. For, as has been recently pointed out with truth and insight, "few greater calamities can befall a nation than to cut herself off, as France (in these circumstances) has done in her great revolution, from all vital connection with her own past."[1] As our civilisation, as a whole, must be regarded as the unfolding of a process of life, so—as will not improbably be recognised with growing clearness in the future—those sections of it which have remained unaffected by the great natural development which the ethical system upon which it is founded underwent in the sixteenth century—

[1] W. E. H. Lecky, *The Political Value of History.*

wherein, beyond doubt, a profound social instinct found expression—will lack certain well-marked characteristics, possessing a high value in the process of social evolution which is still proceeding. It is to be doubted whether the peoples who, in suppressing the religious development of the sixteenth century, succeeded in preserving the outward forms of ecclesiastical unity, will be so successful in ultimately preserving the essential spirit of Christianity as those amongst whom the development was allowed to pursue its natural course. Amongst the former peoples the subsequent movements of opinion have unmistakably been direct to rationalism. It is apparently amongst the latter peoples that the social transformation, which our civilisation is destined to accomplish, will reach its most successful expression and proceed thereto by the most regular and orderly stages.

In any forecast of the future of our civilisation, one of the most important of the questions presenting themselves for consideration, is that of the future relationship of the European peoples to what are called the lower races. Probably one of the most remarkable features of the world-wide expansion the European peoples are undergoing will be the change that this relationship is destined to undergo in the near future. In estimates which have been hitherto made of our coming relations to the coloured races, a factor which will in all probability completely dominate the situation in the future has received scarcely any attention.

The relationships of the Western peoples to the inferior races, with which they have come into contact in the course of the expansion they have under-

gone, is one of the most interesting subjects in
history. Confused though these relationships may
appear, it may be distinguished that they have passed
through certain well-marked stages of development.
We must set aside, as being outside our present field
of vision, those races which have inhabited countries
suitable for European colonisation. The fate of all
races occupying territories of this kind has been
identical. Whether wars of extermination have been
waged against them, or whether they have been well
treated and admitted to citizenship, they have always
tended to disappear before the more vigorous incoming race. It is with the inhabitants of regions unsuitable for European settlement, and mostly outside
the temperate zone, that we are concerned.

The alteration observable in our relations to these
races since the sixteenth and seventeenth centuries
has been very gradual, but its general character is
unmistakable. During the sixteenth, seventeenth,
and eighteenth centuries, a great part of the richest
regions in the tropical countries of the earth passed
under the dominion of the four great sea powers
of Western Europe. Spain, Holland, France, and
England have successively engaged in the keenest
rivalry for the possession of vast regions of this kind,
unsuitable for permanent colonisation, but possessing
rich natural resources. The general idea which lay
behind this extension of dominion was in the main
that of military conquest. The territories of the
weaker peoples were invaded, taken possession of, and
exploited for the benefit of the more vigorous invader.
The interests of the original occupiers were little, if
at all, regarded. The main end in view was the
immediate profit and advantage of the conquerors.

In the West India Islands the native population was worked in the mines and the plantations until it became in great part extinct, and the Spaniards began to introduce negroes from Africa. Operations were conducted on so great a scale that in the 20 years before the opening of the eighteenth century 300,000 slaves were exported from Africa by the English, and in the 80 years which followed, over 600,000 slaves were landed in the Island of Jamaica alone. Slave labour was employed to an enormous extent in most of the countries of which possession was obtained. The natural resources of the territories occupied were, however, developed to a considerable degree. The enormous wealth which Spain drew from her conquests and undertakings in tropical America was long a very powerful factor in the wars and politics of Europe : Holland, France, and England also enriched themselves both directly and indirectly. In the Spanish, Dutch, and English settlements and plantations in the Eastern Hemisphere, and in those in the West Indies and South America, under Spanish, Dutch, French, and English rule, great enterprises in trade, agriculture, and mining were successfully undertaken. Order and government were introduced, and large cities sprung up rivalling European cities in size and magnificence. This first period was one of feverish activity, and of universal desire on the part of the invaders to quickly enrich themselves. There was much cruelty to weaker races, and although all the powers were not equally guilty in this respect, none, at least, were innocent. But looking at the period as a whole, and regarding the enterprises undertaken in their true light—namely, as an attempt to develop, by forced coloured labour under European supervision, the resources of countries not suitable for European settlement—a certain degree of success must be admitted to have been attained, and the enterprises undoubtedly contributed to increase, for the time being, the material wealth and resources of the powers concerned.

Towards the end of the eighteenth century the tendency of the change that was taking place began to be visible. It had become clear that the European peoples could not hope to settle permanently in the tropical lands they had occupied, and that, if the resources were to be developed, it must be by native labour under their supervision. Already, however, the effects of the altruistic development which had been so long in progress were becoming generally evident, and before the opening of the nineteenth century men had glimpses of the nature of the social revolution it was eventually to accomplish in our civilisation. The institution of slavery in tropical lands under European auspices was clearly doomed. So also, to the more far-reaching minds, seemed another institution upon which depended, to all appearance, the continued maintenance of European enterprise and European authority in lands not suitable for the permanent settlement of the Western races.

The right of occupation and government in virtue of conquest or force tended, it was felt, to become an anachronism ; it was antagonistic to, and it involved a denial of, the spirit which constituted the mainspring of that onward movement which was taking place in our civilisation, and which was slowly bringing the people into the rivalry of life on conditions of equality. Although almost every European people, that had attained to any consciousness of national strength, .iad in the past endeavoured to imitate the military ideals of the ancient empires, and to extend their rule by conquest over other peoples of equal civilisation, they had done so with ever-diminishing success. The growth of influences and conditions tending to render the realisation of such aims more and more difficult was unmistakable.   Any nation which would embark upon such an enterprise, on a great scale and against a European people, would, it was felt, find in the near future forces arrayed against it of which the ancient world had no experience, and which no military skill, however great, and no national strength and resolution, however concentrated and prolonged, could entirely subdue.   To keep in subjection, therefore, by purely military force a people of even greatly lower development must, it was felt, become correspondingly difficult ; and this, not so much because of the fear of effective resistance in a military sense, but because of the lack of moral force on the part of the stronger peoples to initiate an effort involving a principle antagonistic to the spirit governing the development which these peoples were themselves undergoing.

Throughout the early and middle decades of the nineteenth century we have, therefore, to watch the development of this spirit and the effects it produced. Before the close of the eighteenth century the agitation against the slave-trade in the colonies had assumed large proportions.   In England a motion was carried in the House of Commons in 1792, providing for the gradual abolition of the traffic.   In 1794 the French Convention decreed that all slaves throughout the French colonies should be admitted to the rights of French citizens; and, although slavery did not cease in the French dominions for some fifty years after, the Convention in this as in other matters only anticipated the future. The agitation in England against the slave-trade having been largely successful, the feeling against the employment of slaves continued to grow in strength until an Act was at length obtained in 1834, finally abolishing slavery in the British settlements, the slave-owners being awarded £20,000,000 as indemnification. The negroes in the French settlements were emancipated in 1848, those in the Dutch colonies in 1863; while the slaves in the Southern states of the American Union obtained their freedom as the result of the Civil War of 1862-65.

Meanwhile the growth of the other influence tending to undermine the position of the European races in the tropical countries they had occupied had continued. By the end of the eighteenth century the coloured races of Hayti, under the influence of the ideas of the French Revolution, had thrown off the rule of France. Before the first quarter of the nineteenth century had passed away the Spanish territories of Central and South America—often still spoken of as if they were inhabited by Europeans, although in most of which, it must be remembered, the vast bulk of the population consists of native Indians, imported negroes, and mixed races—had, one after another, declared their independence of European rule. It came to be looked upon as only natural and inevitable that it should be so; and it was held to be only a question of time for the Dutch possessions and the remaining Spanish settlements to follow suit. The English settlements in the West

Indies, it was supposed, would become independent too.   They came to be regarded as being as good as gone.   We have Mr. Froude's word for it that he had it on high official authority, about 1860, that all preparations for the transition had been already made. " A decision had been irrevocably taken.   The troops were to be withdrawn from the Islands, and Jamaica, Trinidad, and the English Antilles were to be masters of their own destiny."[1]   The withdrawal did not take place, but the general feelings in the minds of politicians in England at the time was undoubtedly such as might have prompted such a decision.

If we turn now to the condition of affairs accompanying these events in the countries in question we have presented to us what is probably one of the most extraordinary spectacles the world has beheld. The enterprise that once attempted to develop the resources of the countries concerned has been to a large extent interrupted.   Regarding the West Indies first, we have to note that their former prosperity has waned.   The black races under the new order of things have multiplied exceedingly.   Where left to themselves under British rule, whether with or without the political institutions of the advanced European peoples, they have not developed the natural resources of the rich and fertile lands they have inherited.   Nor do they show any desire to undertake the task.   The descriptions we have had presented to us for many years past by writers and politicians of some of the West India Islands, read like accounts of a former civilisation.   Decaying harbours, once crowded with shipping ; ruined wharves, once busy with commerce ; roofless warehouses ; stately buildings falling to ruins

[1] *The English in the West Indies,* p. 6.

and overgrown with tropical creepers ; deserted mines and advancing forests,—these are some of the signs of the change. In Hayti, where the blacks have been independent of European control for the greater part of a century, we have even a more gloomy picture. Revolution has succeeded revolution, often accompanied by revolting crime ; under the outward forms of European government every form of corruption and licence has prevailed ; its commerce has been more than once almost extinguished by its political revolutions ; the resources of the country remain undeveloped ; intercourse with white races is not encouraged, and the Black Republic, instead of advancing, is said to be drifting slowly backwards.

Turning to the mainland of Central America and the vast territories embraced in tropical South America, once under the rule of the Spaniards and Portuguese, the spectacle is in some respects more noteworthy. In this expanse, which includes over three-fourths of the entire continental area south of the United States, we have one of the richest regions of the earth. Under the outward forms of European government it appears, however, to be slowly drifting out of our civilisation. The habit has largely obtained amongst us of thinking of these countries as inhabited by European races and as included in our Western civilisation,—a habit doubtless due to the tendency to regard them as colonies of European powers which have become independent after the manner of the United States. As a matter of fact this view has little to justify it. In the twenty-two republics comprising the territory in question, considerably over three-fourths of the population are descendants of the original Indian inhabitants, or imported negroes, or mixed races. The pure-white population appears to be unable to maintain itself for more than a limited number of generations without recruiting itself from the outside. It is a gradually diminishing element, tending to ally itself to an increasing degree with " colour." Both for climatic reasons, and in obedience to the general law of population already noticed, by which the upper strata of society (to which the white population for the most part belongs) are unable to maintain themselves apart for any considerable period, we must, apparently, look forward to the time when these territories will be almost exclusively peopled by the Black and Indian races.

Meanwhile the resources of this large region remain almost undeveloped or run to waste. During the past fifty years the European powers may be said to have endeavoured to develop them in a manner that apparently promised to be advantageous to both parties, and not inconsistent with the spirit of the new altruistic ideas which have come to govern men's minds. Since the period of their independence, immense sums have been borrowed by the republics of Central and South America, with the object of developing their resources, and large amounts have also been invested by private persons in public enterprises undertaken by Europeans in these countries. But the general prevalence of those qualities which distinguish peoples of low social efficiency has been like a blight over the whole region. In nearly all the republics in question the history of government has been the same. Under the outward forms of written laws and constitutions of the most exemplary character, they have displayed

a general absence of that sense of public and private
duty which has always distinguished peoples who
have reached a state of high social development.
Corruption in all departments of the government,
insolvency, bankruptcy, and political revolutions
succeeding each other at short intervals, have become
almost the normal incidents of public life — the
accompanying features being a permanent state of
uncertainty, lack of energy and enterprise amongst
the people, and general commercial stagnation.
Much of the territory occupied by these states is
amongst the richest in the world in natural resources.
Yet we seem to have reached a stage in which the
enterprise of the Western races is almost as effectively excluded therefrom, or circumscribed therein,
as in the case of China.   Not, however, through any
spirit of exclusiveness in the people or desire to
develop these resources themselves, but by, on the
one hand, the lack, in the inhabitants, of qualities
contributing to social efficiency, and, on the other,
by the ascendency in the minds of the Western
peoples of that altruistic spirit which, except in a
clear case of duty or necessity, deprives any attempt
to assume by force the government and administration of the resources of other peoples of the moral
force necessary to ensure its success.

Now it would appear probable that we have, in
the present peculiar relationship of the Western
peoples to the coloured races, the features of a transition of great interest and importance, the nature of
which is, as yet, hardly understood.   It is evident
that, despite the greater consideration now shown for
the rights of the lower races, there can be no question as to the absolute ascendency in ·the world

to-day of the Western peoples and of Western civilisation. There has been no period in history when this ascendency has been so unquestionable and so complete as in the time in which we are living. No one can doubt that it is within the power of the leading European peoples of to-day— should they so desire—to parcel out the entire equatorial regions of the earth into a series of satrapies, and to administer their resources, not, as in the past, by a permanently resident population, but from the temperate regions, and under the direction of a relatively small European official population. And this without any fear of effective resistance from the inhabitants. *Always, however, assuming that there existed a clear call of duty or necessity to provide the moral force necessary for such action.*

It is this last stipulation which it is all-important to remember in any attempt which is made to estimate the probable course of events in the future. For it removes at once the centre of interest and observation to the lands occupied by the European peoples themselves. It is, in short, in the development in progress amongst these peoples, and not in the events taking place to-day in lands occupied by the black and coloured races, that we must seek for the controlling factor in the immediate future of the tropical regions of the world.[1]

[1] Mr. C. H. Pearson, in a prediction which has recently attracted attention, has, it appears to the writer, made the serious mistake of estimating the future by watching the course of events outside the temperate regions, rather than by following the clue to those events which we have in the development in progress amongst the Western peoples. He accordingly ventures to foretell that "The day will come, and perhaps is not far distant, when the European observer will look round to see the globe girdled with a continuous zone of the black and yellow races, no longer too weak for aggression or under tutelage, but

Now, stress has been laid in the preceding chapters on the fact that we have in the altruistic
development that has been slowly taking place
amongst the European peoples the clue to the efficiency of our civilisation. It is this development
which—by its influence in breaking down an earlier
organisation of society, and by its tendency to bring,
for the first time in the history of the race, all the
people into the rivalry of life on a footing of equality
of opportunity—has raised our Western civilisation
to its present position of ascendency in the world.
It must be always remembered, however, that a
principal cause operating in producing it has been
the doctrine peculiar to the ethical system upon which
our civilisation is founded—the doctrine, steadfastly
and uncompromisingly held, of the native equality
of all men. So great has been the resistance to be
overcome, so exceptional in the history of the race
has been the nature of the process of expansion
through which we have passed, that only a doctrine

independent, or practically so, in government, monopolising the trade
of their own regions, and circumscribing the industry of the European;
when Chinamen and the nations of Hindostan, the States of South
America, by that time predominantly Indian, and it may be African
nations of the Congo and the Zambesi, under a dominant caste of
foreign rulers, are represented by fleets in the European seas, invited
to international conferences, and welcomed as allies in the quarrels of
the civilised world. The citizens of these countries will then be taken
up into the social relations of the white races, will throng the English
turf, or the salons of Paris, and will be admitted to intermarriage.
It is idle to say that, if all this should come to pass, our pride of place
will not be humiliated. We were struggling amongst ourselves for
supremacy in a world which we thought of as destined to belong to the
Aryan and to the Christian faith, to the letters and arts and charm of
social manners which we have inherited from the best times in the
past. We shall wake to find ourselves elbowed and hustled, and
perhaps even thrust aside, by peoples whom we looked down upon as
servile and thought of as bound always to minister to our needs."—
National Life and Character, chap. i.

held as this has been, and supported by the tremendous sanctions behind it, could have effected so great a social transformation. Of such importance has been the character of this process, and so strong has been the social instinct that has recognised its vital significance to the Western peoples themselves, that everything has gone down before the doctrine which produced it. It is this doctrine which has raised the negro in the Southern States of North America to the rank of citizen of the United States, despite the incongruous position which he now occupies in that country. It is before this doctrine *because of its predominant importance to ourselves*, and not before the coloured races, that the European peoples have retreated in those tropical lands which, being unsuitable for colonisation, could have been ruled and developed only under a system of military occupation.

We must, therefore, in any attempt to estimate our future relationship to the coloured races outside the temperate regions, keep clearly in mind the hitherto supreme importance to the Western peoples of this altruistic development, and, therefore, of the doctrine of the native equality of men which has accompanied it.

Now, there are two great events which will in all probability fill a great part in the history of the twentieth century. The first will be the accomplishment amongst the Western peoples of the last stage of that process of social development which tends to bring all the people into the rivalry of life on conditions of social equality. The other will be the final filling up by these peoples of all those tracts in the temperate regions of the earth suitable for permanent occupation. As both these processes tend towards completion, it would appear that we must expect our present relationship towards the coloured races occupying territories outside the temperate zones to undergo further development. With the completion of that process of social evolution in which the doctrine of the native equality of men has played so important a part—and, therefore, with the probable modification of that instinct which has hitherto recognised the vital necessity to ourselves of maintaining this doctrine in its most uncompromising form—it seems probable that there must arise a tendency to scrutinise more closely the existing differences between ourselves and the coloured races as regards the qualities contributing to social efficiency ; this tendency being accompanied by a disposition to relax our hitherto prevalent opinion that the doctrine of equality requires us to shut our eyes to those differences where political relations are concerned.

As the growth of this feeling will be coincident with the filling up to the full limit of the remaining territories suitable for European occupation and the growing pressure of population therein, it may be expected that the inexpediency of allowing a great extent of territory in the richest region of the globe —that comprised within the tropics—to remain undeveloped, with its resources running largely to waste under the management of races of low social efficiency, will be brought home with ever-growing force to the minds of the Western peoples. The day is probably not far distant when, with the advance science is making, we shall recognise that it is in the tropics, and not in the temperate zones that

we have the greatest food-producing and material-
producing regions of the earth ; that the natural
highways of commerce in the world are. those
which run north and south ; and that we have the
highest possible interest in the proper development
and efficient administration of the tropical regions,
and in an exchange of products therewith on a
far larger scale than has been yet attempted or
imagined.

The question that will, therefore, present itself
for solution will be : How is the development and
efficient administration of these regions to be
secured ?   The ethical development that has taken
place in our civilisation has rendered the experiment
once made to develop their resources by forced
native labour no longer possible, or permissible even
if possible.   We have already abandoned, under
pressure of experience, the idea which at one time
prevailed that the tropical regions might be occupied
and permanently colonised by European races as
vast regions in the temperate climes have been.
Within a measurable period in the future, and under
pressure of experience, we shall probably also have
to abandon the idea which has in like manner prevailed for a time, that the coloured races left to
themselves possess the qualities necessary to the
development of the rich resources of the lands they
have inherited.   For a clearer insight into the laws
that have shaped the course of human evolution
must bring us to see that the process which has
gradually developed the energy, enterprise, and
social efficiency of the race northwards, and which
has left less richly endowed in this respect the
peoples inhabiting the regions where the conditions

of life are easiest, is no passing accident or the
result of circumstances changeable at will, but part
of the cosmic order of things which we have no
power to alter.

It would seem that the solution which must
develop itself under pressure of circumstances in
the future is, that the European races will gradually
come to realise that the tropics must be adminis-
tered from the temperate regions. There is no
insurmountable difficulty in the task. Even now
all that is required to ensure its success is a clearly
defined conception of moral necessity. This, it
would seem, must come under the conditions referred to, when the energetic races of the world,
having completed the colonisation of the temperate
regions, are met with the spectacle of the resources
of the richest regions of the earth still running
largely to waste under inefficient management.

In discussing the present condition of the tropical
regions of America no reference was made to the
experiment which, in the corresponding regions of
the Eastern Hemisphere, has been taking place
under British rule in India. For the past half-
century the relationship existing between England
and India has been the cause of considerable heart-
searching and conflict of opinion amongst politicians
of the more advanced school in England. The
means whereby a footing was at first obtained in
that country had little to distinguish them from
those already mentioned which led the European
races at one time to occupy vast territories in
tropical regions. In the altruistic development of
the nineteenth century which has so profoundly
affected the relationships of the European peoples

to other races, it has come to be felt by many politicians that the position of Great Britain in India
involved a denial of the spirit actuating the advanced peoples, and that it tended to become in
consequence morally indefensible.   This was undoubtedly the feeling in the minds of a considerable
section of persons in England at no distant date in
the past.

Nevertheless, as time has gone by, other features
of the position have pressed themselves with growing force upon the minds of the British people.
Exceptionally influenced as the British nation has
been by the altruistic spirit underlying our civilisation, its administration of the Indian peninsula has
never been marked by those features which distinguished Spanish rule in the American continent.
English rule has tended more and more to involve
the conscientious discharge of the duties of our
position towards the native races.   We have respected their rights, their ideas, their religions, and
even their independence to the utmost extent compatible with the efficient administration of the government of the country.

The result has been remarkable.   There has been
for long in progress in India a steady development
of the resources of the country which cannot be
paralleled in any other tropical region of the world.
Public works on the most extensive scale and of the
most permanent character have been undertaken
and completed ; roads and bridges have been built ;
mining and agriculture have been developed ; irrigation works, which have added considerably to the
fertility and resources of large tracts of country,
have been constructed ; even sanitary reform is

beginning to make considerable progress. European enterprise too, attracted by security and integrity in the government, has been active. Railways have been gradually extended over the Peninsula. Indian tea, almost unknown a short time ago, has, through the planting and cultivation of suitable districts under European supervision, already come into serious competition with the Chinese article in the markets of the world. The cotton industry of India has already entered on friendly rivalry with that of Lancashire. Other industries, suited to the conditions of the country, are in like manner rising into prominence, without any kind of artificial protection or encouragement ; the only contribution of the ruling powers to their welfare being the guarantee of social order and the maintenance of the conditions of efficiency and integrity in the administration of the departments of government.

The commerce of the country has expanded in a still more striking manner. In the largest open market in the world, that which Great Britain provides, India now stands third on the list as contributor of produce, ranking only below the United States and France, and above Germany and all the Australian colonies of Great Britain together. She takes, too, as much as she gives, for her exports to and imports from the United Kingdom nearly balance each other. In the character of importer she is, indeed, the largest of all the customers of Great Britain, the Australasian colonies and the United States coming after her on the list. This exchange of products has all the appearance of being as profitable as it is creditable to both parties concerned.

Very different, too, is the spirit animating both sides in this development of the resources of India as compared with that which prevailed in past times. There is no question now of the ruling race merely exploiting India to their own selfish advantage. Great Britain desires to share in the prosperity she has assisted in creating, it is true ; but, for the most part, she shares indirectly and in participation with the rest of the world.   India sends her products to British markets, but she is equally free to send them elsewhere.   As her development proceeds she offers a larger market for the products of British industries ; but England has reserved to herself no exclusive advantages in Indian markets.   Under the principle of free trade all the rest of the world may compete with her on equal terms in those markets. The gain of England tends to be a gain, not only to India, but to civilisation in general.

The object-lesson that all this has afforded has not been without its effect on English public opinion — an effect which deepens as the true nature of the relationship existing between the two countries is more generally understood.   Nor is there lack of similar experiences elsewhere.   The work undertaken by France in Algeria and Tunis, although it has differed in many important respects from that performed by Great Britain in India, and although it has been undoubtedly more directly inspired by the thought of immediate benefit to French interests,[1] has been on the whole, it must

[1] For instance, the *Times* prints the following dispatch from its correspondent at Dunkirk, dated 4th August 1893 : " From 1st October the carrying trade between Algeria and France will be exclusively confined to French vessels, all foreign Powers, including Great Britain, having given up their right to participate in it.   This

be frankly confessed, work done in the cause of civilisation in general. Within the past decade we have had a more striking lesson still in the case of Egypt. Some seventeen years ago that country, although within sight of, and in actual contact with, European civilisation, had reached a condition of disaster through misgovernment, extravagance, and oppression without example, as a recent writer, who speaks with authority, has insisted, " in the financial history of any country from the remotest ages to the present time." [1] Within thirteen years the public debt of a country of only 6 millions of inhabitants had been increased from 3 millions to 89 millions, or nearly thirty-fold.[2] With a submissive population, a corrupt bureaucracy, and a reckless, ambitious, and voluptuous ruler, surrounded by adventurers of every kind, we had all the elements of national bankruptcy and ruin. Things drifted from bad to worse, but it was felt that nothing could be more at variance, theoretically, with the principles of the Liberal party then in power in England than active interference by the English people in the affairs of that country. Yet within a few years circumstances had proved stronger than prevailing views, and England found herself most unwillingly compelled to interfere by force in the government of Egypt ;

measure will chiefly affect British ships which held the bulk of the trade. At this port alone the British tonnage employed in trading with Algeria amounted in 1891 to 34,507 tons net register, and in 1892 to 31,103 tons. Had any European Power withheld its sanction the trade must, in virtue of existing treaties, have remained open to all flags. None save England, however, were sufficiently interested in it to oppose this new concession to protection."

[1] *England in Egypt*, by Alfred Milner, late Under-Secretary for Finance in Egypt. London, 1893.

[2] *Ibid,*

and obliged to attempt, in the administration of its affairs, what, in the peculiar conditions prevailing, appeared to be one of the most hopeless, difficult, and thankless tasks ever undertaken by a nation.

Yet the results have been most striking. Within a few years the country had emerged from a condition of chronic and apparently hopeless bankruptcy, and attained to a position of solvency, with a revenue tending to outrun expenditure. Great improvements in the administration of the state departments had been effected. Public works which have greatly contributed to the prosperity of the country had been completed. The Kurbash had been suppressed ; the Corvée had been reduced ; the Barrage had been repaired ; the native administration of justice had been improved. Under an improved system of irrigation the area of land won from the desert for cultivation was enormously increased. The cotton crop, representing one-third of the entire agricultural wealth of the country, had increased 50 per cent in a few years. The foreign trade increased to the highest point it had ever attained ; and the credit of the country so far improved that within nine years the price of its Unified stock had risen from 59 to 98.

All these results were attained by simple means ; by the exercise of qualities which are not usually counted either brilliant or intellectual, but which nevertheless are, above all others, characteristic of peoples capable of attaining a high degree of social efficiency, and of those peoples only. British influence in Egypt, Mr. Milner maintains, " is not exercised to impose an uncongenial foreign system upon a reluctant people. It is a force making for the triumph of the simplest ideas of honesty, humanity, and justice, to the value of which Egyptians are just as much alive as any one else." [1]

Nor can it be said that Great Britain has exploited Egypt in her own interest, or obtained any exclusive advantage by the development of the resources of the country. It is true that she does benefit, and benefit considerably, by the improvement which has followed. But it is in the same manner as in India. For, says Mr. Milner, " the improvement of Egyptian administration leads directly to the revival of Egyptian trade, and in that increase, England, who has more than half the trade of Egypt in her hands, possesses a direct interest of the most unmistakable kind. Our own country does thus, after all, obtain a recompense, and a recompense at once most substantial and most honourable for any sacrifices she may make for Egypt. She gains, not at the expense of others, but along with others. If she is the greatest gainer, it is simply because she is the largest partner in the business." [2] But " neither directly nor indirectly has Great Britain drawn from her predominant position any profit at the expense of other nations." [3] Her gain is there also the gain of civilisation.

It is to be expected that as time goes on, and an approach is made to the conditions before mentioned, such object-lessons as these will not be without their effect on the minds of the European races. It will probably come to be recognised that experiments in developing the resources of regions unsuitable for European colonisation, such as that now in progress

[1] *Op. cit.*   [2] *Ibid.*   [3] *Ibid.*

in India, differ essentially both in character and in spirit from all past attempts. It will probably be made clear, and that at no distant date, that the last thing our civilisation is likely to permanently tolerate is the wasting of the resources of the richest regions of the earth through the lack of the element- ary qualities of social efficiency in the races possess- ing them. The right of those races to remain in possession will be recognised ; but it will, in all probability, be no part of the future conditions of such recognition that they shall be allowed to prevent the utilisation of the immense natural resources which they have in charge. At no re- mote date, with the means at the disposal of our civilisation, the development of these resources must become one of the most pressing and vital questions engaging the attention of the Western races. The advanced societies have, to some extent, already intuitively perceived the nature of the coming change. We have evidence of a general feeling, which recognises the immense future importance of the tropical regions of the earth to the energetic races, in that partition of Africa amongst the European powers which forms one of the most remarkable signs of the times at the end of the nineteenth century. The same feeling may be per- ceived even in the United States, where the necessity for the future predominance of the influence of the English-speaking peoples over the American Con- tinents is already recognised by a kind of national instinct that may be expected to find clearer ex- pression as time goes on.

Lastly, it will materially help towards the solution of ,this and other difficult problems, if we are in a position, as it appears we shall be, to say with greater clearness in the future, than we have been able to do in the past, what it is that constitutes superiority and inferiority of race. We shall probably have to set aside many of our old ideas on the subject. Neither in respect alone of colour, nor of descent, nor even of the possession of high intellectual capacity, can science give us any warrant for speaking of one race as superior to another. The evolution which man is undergoing is, over and above everything else, a social evolution. There is, therefore, but one absolute test of superiority. It is only the race possessing in the highest degree the qualities contributing to social efficiency that can be recognised as having any claim to superiority.

But these qualities are not as a rule of the brilliant order, nor such as strike the imagination. Occupying a high place amongst them are such characteristics as strength and energy of character, humanity, probity and integrity, and simple-minded devotion to conceptions of duty in such circumstances as may arise. Those who incline to attribute the very wide influence which the English-speaking peoples have come to exercise in the world to the Machiavelian schemes of their rulers are often very wide of the truth. This influence is, to a large extent, due to qualities not at all of a showy character. It is, for instance, a fact of more than superficial significance, and one worth remembering, that in the South American Republics, where the British peoples move amongst a mixed crowd of many nationalities, the quality which has come to be accepted as distinctive of them is simply " the word of an Englishman." In like manner it is qualities such as humanity, strength, and uprightness of character, and devotion to the immediate calls of duty without thought of brilliant ends and ideal results, which have largely contributed to render English rule in India successful when similar experiments elsewhere have been disastrous. It is to the exercise of qualities of this class that we must also chiefly attribute the success which has so far attended the political experiment of extraordinary difficulty which England has undertaken in Egypt. And it is upon just the same qualities, and not upon any ideal schemes for solving the social problem, that we must depend to carry us safely through the social revolution which will be upon us in the twentieth century, and which will put to the most severe test which it has yet had to endure, the social efficiency of the various sections of the Western peoples.

It must be noticed that the conclusion here emphasised is the same towards which the historian, with the methods hitherto at his command, has been already slowly feeling his way. Said Mr. Lecky recently, speaking of the prosperity of nations, and the causes thereof as indicated by history: "Its foundation is laid in pure domestic life, in commercial integrity, in a high standard of moral worth and of public spirit, in simple habits, in courage, uprightness, and a certain soundness and moderation of judgment which springs quite as much from character as from intellect. If you would form a wise judgment of the future of a nation, observe carefully whether these qualities are increasing or decaying. Observe especially what qualities count for most in public life. . Is character becoming of greater or less importance? Are the men who obtain the highest posts in the nation men of whom in private life and irrespective of party competent judges speak with genuine respect? Are they of sincere convictions, consistent lives, indisputable integrity? . . . It is by observing this moral current that you can best cast the horoscope of a nation." [1]

This is the utterance of that department of knowledge which, sooner or later, when its true foundations are perceived, must become the greatest of all the sciences. It is but the still small voice which anticipates the verdict which will be pronounced with larger knowledge, and in more emphatic terms, by evolutionary science, when at no distant date it must enable us, as we have never been enabled before, " to look beyond the smoke and turmoil of our petty quarrels, and to detect, in the slow developments of the past, the great permanent forces that are steadily bearing nations onward to improvement or decay."

The fuller light in which we are thus able to view the great fundamental problems of human society cannot be without a certain strengthening and steadying influence on character. We see that, under all the complex appearances our Western civilisation presents, the central process working itself out in our midst is one which is ever tending to bring, for the first time in the history of the race, all the people into the competition of life on a footing of equality of opportunity. In this process the problem, with which society and legislators will be concerned for long into the future, will be how to secure to the

[1] *The Political Value of History*, by W. E. H. Lecky.

fullest degree these conditions of equality, while at the same time retaining that degree of inequality which must result from offering prizes sufficiently attractive to keep up within the community that state of stress and exertion, without which no people can long continue in a high state of social efficiency. For in the vast process of change in progress it is always the conditions of social efficiency, and not those which individuals or classes may desire for themselves, that the unseen evolutionary forces at work amongst us are engaged in developing. It is by the standard of social efficiency that we as individuals are ever being tested. It is in this quality of social efficiency that nations and peoples are being continually, and for the most part unconsciously, pitted against each other in the complex rivalry of life. And it is in those sections of the race where, for the time being, this quality obtains the highest development, that we have present all the conditions favourable to success and ascendency.

Nor is there any reason why the great social development proceeding in our civilisation which has been but feebly and inadequately described in the preceding chapters, should be viewed with distrust by those of more conservative instincts amongst us who profess to have at heart the highest interests of humanity. The movement which is uplifting the people—necessarily to a large extent at the expense of those above them—is but the final result of a long process of organic development. All anticipations and forebodings as to the future of the incoming democracy, founded upon comparisons with the past, are unreliable or worthless. For the world has never before witnessed a democracy of the kind that is now slowly assuming supreme power amongst the Western peoples. To compare it with democracies which held power under the ancient empires is to altogether misunderstand both the nature of our civilisation and the character of the forces that have produced it. Neither in form nor in spirit have we anything in common with the democracies of the past. Great as has been the progress in outward forms, the more important difference lies far deeper. The gradual emancipation of the people and their rise to supreme power has been in our case the product of a slow ethical development in which character has been profoundly influenced, and in which conceptions of equality and of responsibility to each other have obtained a hold on the general mind hitherto un-paralleled. The fact of our time which overshadows all others is the arrival of Democracy. But the perception of the fact is of relatively little importance if we do not also realise that it is a new Democracy. There are many who speak of the new ruler of nations as if he were the same idle Demos whose ears the dishonest courtiers have tickled from time immemorial. It is not so. Even those who attempt to lead him do not yet quite understand him. Those who think that he is about to bring chaos instead of order, do not rightly apprehend the nature of his strength. They do not perceive that his arrival is the crowning result of an ethical movement in which qualities and attributes which we have been all taught to regard as the very highest of which human nature is capable, find the completest expression they have ever reached in the history of the race.

APPENDIX I

THE following is an extract (by permission of the Author and of the Royal Statistical Society) from a paper on Marriage-Rates and Marriages-Ages by Dr. William Ogle, M.A., F.R.C.P., etc., read before the Royal Statistical Society of London, March 1890, and printed in the Society's Journal, June 1890.

. . . . . .

But if the average age at marriage varies but little from year to year, it is not so with the marriage-ages in different classes, as is very clearly to be seen in the two following tables (Tables F and G), in the former of which are given the mean ages at marriage of bachelors and spinsters in different occupational groups, while the other gives the age-distribution of bachelors and spinsters in the several groups at the time of marriage.

TABLE F.—*Average Ages at Marriage*, 1884-85.[1]

Occupations.	Bachelors.	Spinsters.
Miners	24.06	22.46
Textile hands	24.38	23.43
Shoemakers, tailors . . .	24.92	24.31
Artisans	25.35	23.70
Labourers	25.56	23.66
Commercial clerks . . .	26.25	24.43
Shopkeepers, shopmen . .	26.67	24.22
Farmers and sons . . .	29.23	26.91
Professional and independent class	31.22	26.40

[1] The age distribution of the men employed in the different occupations differs much; and this would, if uncorrected, of course cause some difference in the mean

TABLE G.—*Age-Distribution per* 1000, *of Bachelors in different Occupations, and of their Wives, at time of Marriage.*

Ages.	Miners.		Textile Factory Hands.		Labourers.		Artisans.		Shoemakers and Tailors.	
	Men.	Women.	Men.	Women.	Men.	Women.	Men.	Women.	Men.	Women.
Under age	169	439	144	337	121	318	109	282	172	276
21–25	535	388	558	432	455	408	489	448	477	412
25–30	228	123	205	149	277	184	278	192	232	183
30–35	47	30	58	49	88	54	73	48	76	79
35–40	14	11	16	18	29	20	25	16	23	30
40–45	6	4	12	7	18	9	17	8	6	10
45–50	..	4	5	4	7	5	4	4	8	4
50 and upwards	} 1	1	2	4	5	2	5	2	6	6

Ages.	Shopkeepers and Shopmen.		Commercial Clerks.		Farmers and Farmers' Sons.		Professional and Independent Class.	
	Men.	Women.	Men.	Women.	Men.	Women.	Men.	Women.
Under age	55	226	27	197	31	111	7	127
21–25	412	449	432	450	253	396	144	402
25–30	323	232	379	262	349	262	376	278
30–35	128	62	130	61	217	115	272	107
35–40	53	18	13	17	75	65	98	34
40–45	19	7	11	7	47	20	43	24
45–50	6	6	6	3	14	20	26	11
50 and upwards	} 4	..	2	3	14	11	34	17

These tables are based upon samples taken by me from the marriage registers of 1884-85. The samples were of considerable size; still it is quite possible that had they been larger, and had they extended over a greater number of years, the figures might have been somewhat different, though it is scarcely possible that they would have been materially altered. They show, at any rate, with sufficient clearness, that the ordinary belief that the lower the station in life, the earlier the age at which marriage is contracted, is true, and that the difference in this respect between the upper and the lower classes is very great indeed. It will be enough if we take a single example, and compare miners, for instance, with the professional class. Of the miners who marry, 704 in 1000 are under 25 years of

marriage-ages of the groups. To meet this difficulty, so far as possible, in the professional and independent group were included students of law, medicine, theology, etc., as also all men described simply as gentlemen; so also with shopkeepers were included shopmen, and with farmers their sons or other near relatives living with them.

age ; of the professional and independent class only 151 ;
while the miners' wives, 827, and of the upper classes only
529, per 1000 are under that age.   The average marriage-age
of the miners is 24, and of their wives 22½ years ; while the
ages for the professional and independent class are respectively
31 and 26½ years ; a difference of seven years for the husbands
and four years for the wives.

The table of mean ages has already appeared in the forty-
ninth Annual Report of the Registrar-General, and has been
often quoted since ; but, whenever I have chanced to see it
cited, I have been somewhat surprised to find that the ages for
the men were alone given, and no notice taken of the respective
ages of the wives.   It appears, however, to me that the ages
of the men at marriage are, so far as concerns the growth of
population, of comparatively small importance.   For there is
no reason whatsoever, so far as I am aware, to suppose
the retardation of marriage in case of men, of course
within reasonable limits, will materially affect the number of
their offspring, excepting that the older a man is when he
marries the older will also be probably his wife, and further,
that the older he and she are at marriage, the greater somewhat will be the chance that either he or she will die before
the child-bearing period is fully completed.   But independently
of these considerations, there is, as I say, no reason to believe
that a man who marries at 30 will have a smaller family than
a man who marries at 20, so long as the two wives are of one
and the same age.   Doubtlessly in the long-run the wives in
the two cases will not be of one and the same age, for, as
Table H shows, though older men usually marry older wives,
they do not marry wives older in proportion to their own
greater age.   So far then as increase in population goes, the
matter of importance is the age of the wife, not of the husband ;
and any material diminution in the growth of the people that
is to be looked for from retarded marriage, must be obtained
by retarding the marriages of women, not those of men.   If
greater age on the part of the husband were to have this effect,
the ancient writers whom I have already quoted, who desired
above all things the rapid growth of the population, would
have been in serious error in proposing that the age of the
husband should be 30 or 37 years ; but as a matter of observation they were well aware that the age of the man had
but little to do with the number of the progeny, while the age

of the wife was of considerable importance, and this, as we
have seen, was put by them at 18 or 19.

As regards men, it is not the age at which they marry that
is of importance, but the question whether they marry at all,
and I have consequently tried to make some estimate of the
relative proportions in which men in different classes of life
altogether abstain from matrimony. The method I employed
was to go through a large number of the census enumeration
books, and ascertain what proportions of labourers and artisans,
of shopkeepers, and of professional and independent men, in
1881, were still bachelors when they had reached the mature
age of 50 years. I expected to find that the proportion would
be smallest among the artisans and labourers, and highest in
the professional and independent class; but, as a matter of
fact, it turned out that it was among the shopkeepers that the
proportion of confirmed bachelors was far the lowest, as
probably, with more thought given to the subject, might have
been anticipated, seeing that to a shopkeeper a wife is often
almost a business necessity. Next to the shopkeepers, but a
good way from them, came the artisans and labourers; while
far ahead of all were the professional and independent class,
with a proportion of permanent bachelors far above the rest.
What is true of the men in these several groups is probably
also true of the women, but I have no statistical evidence of
this. I find, however, testimony to that effect given by those
who are conversant with the habits of working women. Thus
Miss Collett, writing [1] of the east end of London, says, " Every
girl in the lowest classes can get married, and with hardly any
exceptions every girl does marry. This is not true of the
middle classes." It thus appears that in the upper classes not
only do a larger proportion of persons remain throughout life
unmarried, but those who do marry, marry at a much more
advanced age than is the case with the rest of the population.

[1] *Labour and Life of the People*, p. 472.

APPENDIX II

THE WHITE AND COLOURED POPULATION OF THE SOUTHERN UNITED STATES, 1890

(Reprinted from the *Census Bulletin* No. 48, dated 27th March 1891)

THE relative rate of increase of the white and coloured population of the Southern States during the last decade is a matter of such general importance and interest as to demand special attention. What is termed the race-count has, therefore, been made for the South Atlantic and South Central States, and for Missouri and Kansas, in advance of the main work of tabulation. As will be seen from the accompanying tables, the total population embraced in this count is 23,875,259, of which 16,868,205 were white, 6,996,166 coloured, and 10,888 Chinese, Japanese, and Indians. In the States herewith included were found in 1890 fifteen-sixteenths of the entire coloured population of the United States, so that for the purpose of immediately ascertaining the percentage of increase the returns of these States are adequate and not likely to be materially affected by the returns of the other States and territories, where the coloured population is small.

The abnormal increase of the coloured population in what is known as the Black Belt during the decade ending 1880 led to the popular belief that the negroes were increasing at a much greater rate than the white population. This error was a natural one, and arose from the difficulty of ascertaining how much of the increase shown by the Tenth Census was real, and how much was due to the omissions of the census of 1870. This question has been fully discussed in *Bulletin* No. 16, and it is now merely necessary to add that the tabulations herewith given sustain the theory already advanced, that the high rate of increase in the growth of the coloured population as shown in 1880 was apparent, not real, and was due to imperfect enumeration in the Southern States in 1870.

Attention is first called to Table I., showing the white and coloured population of the States under discussion at each census since 1790, together with the number of coloured to each 100,000 white, and the percentage of increase respectively of white and coloured for the several decades.

The table summarises the entire case. In 1890 there were in the States under discussion 6,996,166 coloured inhabitants, and in 1880, 6,142,360. The coloured element increased during the decade at the rate of 13.90 per cent. The white population of these States in 1890 numbered 16,868,205, and in 1880 13,530,408. They increased during the decade at the rate of 24.67 per cent, or nearly twice as rapidly as the coloured element.

In 1880 the proportion of white to persons of colour in these States was in the relation of 100,000 to 45,397. In 1890 the proportion of the latter class had diminished, being then as 100,000 to 41,475.

During the past decade the coloured race has not held its own against the white in a region where the climate and conditions are, of all those which the country affords, the best suited to its development.

TABLE I.

Years.	Population.		Number of Coloured to 100,000 White.	Per Cent of Increase.	
	White.	Coloured.		White.	Coloured.
1790	1,271,488	689,884	54,258	..	..
1800	1,702,980	918,336	53,925	33.94	33.11
1810	2,208,785	1,272,119	57,594	29.70	38.52
1820	2,831,560	1,653,240	58,386	28.20	29.96
1830	3,660,758	2,187,545	59,757	29.28	32.32
1840	4,632,530	2,701,901	58,325	26.55	23.51
1850	6,222,418	3,442,238	55,320	34.32	27.40
1860	8,203,852	4,216,241	51,393	31.84	22.49
1870	9,812,732	4,555,990	46,429	19.61	8.06
1880	13,530,408	6,142,360	45,397	37.89	34.82
1890	16,868,205	6,996,166	41,475	24.67	13.90

Referring again to this table it is seen that in but three decades, that is, from 1800 to 1830, during a part of which time the slave-trade was in progress, has the coloured race increased more rapidly than the white. Since 1830 the white people have steadily increased at a more rapid rate than the coloured. This increase has not been affected by the aid of immigration, for with the exception of Kansas and Missouri these States have received comparatively few immigrants either from foreign countries or from the Northern States.

Similarly the proportion of the coloured inhabitants to the white increased somewhat between 1800 and 1830, but since that time it has steadily diminished. In 1830, when this proportion was at its maximum, there were nearly 6 coloured inhabitants to 10 white, but this proportion has been reduced to a trifle more than 4 at the present date, or by nearly one-third of its amount.

The deficiencies of the ninth census are so apparent in this table that any extended reference to them is wholly unnecessary.

Table II. shows for each of the States under discussion the number of white, coloured, Chinese, Japanese, and Indian inhabitants according to the census of 1890 :—

TABLE II.

States.	Total Population.	White.	Coloured.	Chinese.	Japanese.	Indians.
Total	23,875,259	16,868,205	6,996,166	2581	100	8207
Alabama	1,513,017	830,796	681,431	40	..	750
Arkansas	1,128,179	816,517	311,227	131	..	3`4
Delaware	168,493	139,429	29,022	38	..	4
District of Columbia .	230,392	154,352	75,927	86	8	19
Florida	391,422	224,461	166,678	101	14	168
Georgia	1,837,353	973,462	863,716	110	1	64
Kansas	1,427,096	1,374,882	51,251	107	..	855
Kentucky	1,858,635	1,585,526	272,981	29	1	98
Louisiana. . .	1,118,587	554,712	562,893	315	39	628
Maryland	1,042,390	824,149	218,004	197	6	34
Mississippi	1,289,600	539,703	747,720	122	1	2054
Missouri	2,679,184	2,524,468	154,131	413	4	168
North Carolina. .	1,617,947	1,049,191	567,170	15	..	1571
South Carolina . .	1,151,149	458,454	692,503	20	..	172
Tennessee	1,767,518	1,332,971	434,300	64	10	173
Texas	2,235,523	1,741,190	492,837	727	3	766
Virginia	1,655,980	1,014,680	640,867	50	13	370
West Virginia . . .	762,794	729,262	33,508	16	..	8

[Tables III. IV. and V. are not printed.]

TABLE VI.

States.	Increase of White.				Increase of Coloured.			
	1880-90.	1870-80.	1860-70.	1350-60.	1880-90.	1870-80.	1860-70.	1850-60.
	Per cent.	Per cent.	Per cent.	Per cent.	Per cent.	Per cent.	Per cent.	Per cent.
Alabama . .	25.46	27.01	0.93*	23.39	13.55	26.20	8.62	26.85
Arkansas . .	38.03	63.35	11.71	99.86	47.73	72.44	9.81	133.21
Delaware . .	16.04	17.55	12.84	27.29	9.76	16.00	5.40	6.21
District of Columbia .	30.80	33.68	45.28	60.15	27.40	37.31	203.19	4.15
Florida . .	57.40	48.46	23.55	64.71	31.56	38.17	46.29	55.75
Georgia . . .	19.16	27.86	8.01	13.42	19.11	33.02	17.06	21.08
Kansas . . .	44.40	174.89	225.57	..	18.89	151.97	2,628.55*	..
Kentucky . .	15.13	25.35	19.49	20.76	0.56	22.16	5.91	6.87
Louisiana . .	21.93	25.66	1.29	39.91	16.38	32.80	3.95	33.59
Maryland . .	13.72	19.69	17.36	23.44	3.70	19.86	2.49	3.66
Mississippi . .	12.58	25.20	8.19	19.67	14.98	46.40	1.55	40.73
Missouri . .	24.80	26.18	50.74	79.64	6.04	23.10	0.36*	31.61
North Carolina	20.98	27.82	7.70	13.91	6.76	35.65	8.33	14.40
South Carolina	17.22	35.02	0.56*	6.10	14.59	45.34	0.85	4.66
Tennessee . .	17.05	21.65	13.23	9.23	7.73	25.07	13.89	15.10
Texas . . .	45.43	112.01	34.17	173.25	25.28	55.20	38.57	212.38
Virginia . . .	15.19	23.70	8.48†	17.04†	1.46	23.16	†3.23*	4.18†
West Virginia .	23.07	39.74	..	..	29.44	43.97	..	..

* Decrease.   † Including West Virginia.

Table VII. shows the number of coloured inhabitants in each of the States under discussion at each census from 1850 to 1890 inclusive, under the supposition that the total number of white was 100,000 :—

TABLE VII.

States.	Number of Coloured to 100,000 Whites.				
	1890.	1880.	1870.	1860.	1850.
Alabama	82,021	90,625	91,201	83,183	80,914
Arkansas	38,116	35,614	33,738	34,324	29,415
Delaware	20,815	22,005	22,299	23,874	28,612
District of Columbia . .	49,191	50,502	49,167	23,560	36,230
Florida	74,257	88,840	95,453	80,618	85,253
Georgia	88,726	88,766	85,322	78,725	73,741
Kansas	3,728	4,527	4,939	589	..
Kentucky	17,217	19,711	20,225	25,685	29,024
Louisiana	101,475	106,309	100,592	98,018	102,654
Maryland	26,452	29,010	28,966	33,170	39,501
Mississippi	138,543	135,647	126,328	123,596	105,103
Missouri	6,105	7,185	7,365	11,143	15,209
North Carolina	54,058	61,261	57,725	57,390	57,142
South Carolina	151,052	154,519	143,549	141,545	143,480
Tennessee.	32,581	35,400	34,433	34,234	32,488
Texas	28,305	32,858	44,887	43,460	38,016
Virginia	63,160	71,705	72,019	52,412	58,880
West Virginia	4,595	4,369	4,240	..	..

The last two tables are of special interest, as they illustrate the movements of the coloured element during the past half-century.   An inspection of them makes it evident that there has been no extended northward movement of this element since the time of the civil war.   Indeed, with the exception of the District of Columbia, the border States appear to have lost rather than gained, and during the last decade there becomes perceptible a southward movement of the coloured element from the border States into those bordering the Gulf, particularly into Mississippi and Arkansas, where they have increased proportionately to the white.   Let the States under consideration be divided into two groups, the first comprising Delaware, Maryland, District of Columbia, Virginia, West Virginia, North Carolina, Kentucky, Tennessee, Missouri, and Kansas, and the second South Carolina, Georgia, Florida, Alabama, Mississippi, Louisiana, Texas, and Arkansas.   In the first of these groups the increase of the white population from 1880 to 1890 was at the rate of 22 per cent, while that of the coloured element was but 5.50 per cent.   In the second group the rate of increase of the white was 29.63 per cent, while that of the coloured was but 19.10 per cent.   In the first group the number of coloured to 100,000 white diminished between 1880 and 1890 from 26,700 to 23,089, or 13.52 per cent, while in the second it diminished from 80,116 to 73,608 or only 8.12 per cent.   There is, therefore, a perceptible tendency southward of the coloured people, which, while by no means powerful, has resulted in drawing a notable proportion of that element from the border States and in producing in two of the far southern States a more rapid increase of the coloured element than of the white.

Of the States under discussion, three, namely, South Carolina, Mississippi, and Louisiana, contained in 1890 a larger number of coloured people than of white.   Of the population of South Carolina more than three-fifths are coloured. Five other States, namely, Alabama, Florida, Georgia, North Carolina, and Virginia, contained a coloured element ranging from one-third to one-half of the population.

California by Race—1890 and 1880.

A special count by race was also made by this office for the State of California in order to separate the Chinese and Indians from the rest of the population, as required by the laws of that

State, for purposes of State apportionment. For the State as a whole the white population has increased from 767,181 in 1880 to 1,111,558 in 1890, an increase of 344,377, or 44.89 per cent. The coloured population in the State shows an increase during the decade of 5419, or 90.05 per cent, while there has been a decrease in the Chinese of 3451, or 4.59 per cent. The whole number of Indians in the State is less in 1890 than in 1880 by 3922, or a decrease of 24.10 per cent. The number of Japanese in 1890 as compared with 1880 is large, although relatively small as compared with the whole population. The number of Japanese returned in 1890 is 1099, as against 86 in 1880. The total population of the State for 1890 is 1,208,130, as compared with 864,694 for 1880, the increase being 343,436, and the per cent of increase 39.72.

California.

	White.		Coloured.		Chinese.		Japanese.		Indians.	
	1890.	1880.	1890.	1880.	1890.	1880.	1890.	1880.	1890.	1880.
The State	1,111,558	767,181	11,437	6018	71,681	75,132	1099	86	12,355	16,277

APPENDIX III

The Influence of Civilisation upon the Movement of the Population. By P. LEROY - BEAULIEU. (Translation from the *Economiste Français*, 20th and 27th September 1890, published in the *Journal of the Royal Statistical Society of London*, June 1891.)

(Reprinted by permission of M. Leroy-Beaulieu and the Royal Statistical Society.)

$\bullet$ $\bullet$ $\bullet$ $\bullet$ $\bullet$ $\bullet$

The following are the facts in so far as regards France: From 1801 to 1810 the number of births was in the proportion of 32.3 per 1000; from 1811 to 1820 it was 31.6; while from 1820 to 1830 it was 30.8. This proportion, which by reason of its lowness is much to be regretted, had not, however, anything very extraordinary in itself. It is true that it was lower than the actual birth-rate in Prussia, Bavaria, Italy, Austria, Hungary, and Switzerland, but it nevertheless assured to us an annual excess of nearly 200,000 births over deaths. From 1830 until 1850 the diminution in the birth-rate became accentuated. From 1831 to 1840 the proportion of births was in the ratio of 29 per 1000 inhabitants, and from 1841 to 1850, of 27.4 per 1000. Under the second empire there was another slight falling off. From 1851 to 1860 the average rate was 26.3 per 1000; and it remained absolutely stationary during the period 1860-70. Since then the falling off has become more marked, as from 1870 to 1880 the mean rate was no higher than 25.4 per 1000, and this proportion fell to 24.6 during the period 1881-85; it fell still lower in 1886, until in 1887 it reached 23.5, while in 1888 it was only 23.4. Since the commencement of this century, therefore, the procreative power of the nation has fallen from 32.3 per 1000 to

23.4, or a loss of about one-fourth, and since 1870 alone this power has diminished from the proportion of 26.3 to 23.4 per 1000.

In face of this systematic sterility which characterises the French race, we can only derive consolation from the fact that all other civilised nations appear to be tending in the same direction. Up to the present this tendency, it is true, has not been particularly marked, but soon, probably in a quarter or half a century, it will become more and more accentuated. According to M. de Foville, it was only in Austria and Hungary that the birth-rate was the same in 1882 or 1883 as it was in 1865. In Italy during this short interval the proportion of births to every 1000 of the population fell from 38.3 to 36.9; in Prussia it fell from 39.1 to 36.3; in Bavaria from 36.9 to 36.2; in the Netherlands from 35.9 to 35.1; in Switzerland from 35.5 to 32.5; in Belgium from 31.4 to 30.5; in England from 35.5 to 33.7; in Scotland and Ireland the birth-rate fell to the same level as the French, namely, from 24.9 to 23.6 per 1000. Moreover, in England and Wales the number of births in 1888 was the smallest on record since 1876, and the report of the Registrar-General for the first quarter of 1890 showed that the English birth-rate had fallen to 30 per 1000, a proportion higher than the French rate, it is true, but much lower than that shown for all the preceding years.

Belgium offers a similar example. Here the birth-rate was only 29.4 per 1000 in 1888, as compared with 30.3 in 1885 and 32.1 in the period comprised between 1871 and 1880. In 1840 it was 34.2, and the fact is worthy of some remark that it is particularly in the Walloon provinces, which contain the largest proportion of educated persons and those who are in easy and comfortable circumstances, that the birth-rate is low, while it remains comparatively high in the Flemish provinces, which are not characterised by the same degree of material ease and well-being.

In France the only departments in which a high birth-rate is observable are the poorest, namely, Morbihan, Finistère, Côtes du Nord, Lozère, Corsica, Aveyron, La Vendée, Landes and the Nord, and the Pas de Calais, where a large number of Belgians are to be found.

A German newspaper, the *Frankfurter Zeitung*, which did us the honour of criticising an article we wrote on this important question in the *Journal des Débats*, affirmed that we had failed to furnish a shadow of proof in support of our theory that the development of the general well-being, and the democratic condition of society tend to bring about a diminution in the birth-rate. It would appear that our German *confrère* is hard to convince, as we should have thought that an enumeration of the departments is in itself a proof of our assertion. The generality of these departments is signalised by moderate rates of wages, in many cases very low, by a somewhat low standard of education, and a very moderate school attendance. If we compare two maps, one showing the departments classified according to the number of married couples who have received a certain education, and the other the departments classified according to the birth - rate, we should find that these two maps would be almost the reverse one of the other. We do not for a moment assert that there are not certain exceptions, although there is not a single one of what we may term the educated department appearing in those characterised by a high birth-rate ; while, on the other hand, the greater part of the latter, as for example Brittany, Haute Vienne, Aveyron, and Corsica, figure among the less-educated departments. Neither do we affirm that education is the sole factor which reduces the birth-rate, as this is only one of the factors which, combined with material ease, less fervid religious sentiments, and an ardent desire to attain a higher and better material standard, form an aggregation of intellectual and moral qualities which are little favourable to a high birth-rate.

It is the same in Belgium. We have already called attention to the fact that in the Walloon provinces the birth-rate is infinitely weaker than in the Flemish provinces, while in the former there is a higher standard of education ; and, moreover, wages are also higher. The subjoined tabular statement will show this very clearly :—

	Number of Persons able to Read and Write per 100 of the Population.	Average Daily Wages of Agricultural Labourers (Men) without Board.		Number of Births per 100 of the Population.
		s.	d.	
Flemish Provinces—				
Antwerp . .	59.41	I	2	3.52
Flanders, West .	52.67	I	5½	3.17
,, East .	51.68	I	4	3.12
Limbourg . .	57.68	I	3½	2.95
Mixed Province—				
Brabant . .	58.47	I	4½	2.98
Walloon Provinces—				
Hainault	54.88	I	11	2.43
Liège . . .	61.88	I	11½	2.76
Luxembourg .	73.42	I	11½	2.54
Namur . . .	70.21	2	1½	2.34

The above table has been prepared from the data supplied by the *Annuaire de Statistique de la Belgique* for 1889 ; the figures relating to education and wages refer to the year 1880, no later data being available, while the birth-rates are for the year 1888.   It shows that in all the Flemish provinces the birth-rate is high, education little advanced, and wages low, similar conditions being observable in Brabant ; while, on the other hand, in the Walloon provinces the birth-rate is very low, wages are much higher, and, with the exception of Hainault, where there are a large number of coal mines, education is much more advanced.   Thus we may take it that in general (but we are not prepared to say that it is an absolute rule without exception) a low birth-rate goes hand in hand with high wages and the spread of education.   It also appears to be particularly associated with democratic aspirations, and still more with a lessening of religious belief on the part of the people, and a modification of the old ideas of resignation and submission to their lot.

Thus what it has been agreed to call civilisation, which is really the development of material ease, of education, of equality, and of aspirations to rise and to succeed in life, has undoubtedly conduced to a diminution of the birth-rate.

It cannot be said that this falling off in the number of births, if it only brings in its train a smaller increase and not a diminution of the population in the old countries, is an actual misfortune, for the human race cannot go on indefinitely increasing on a planet which itself does not increase. But in the present condition of the world, now that so many lands are insufficiently populated, and that nations have established a forced military service, and are ready at any moment to declare war one with the other, this reduction of births, particularly when it manifests itself in a country like France for example, must certainly be regarded as a relative misfortune. In one respect it is particularly unfortunate. This is that in the case of a family consisting of one or two children, the excessive tenderness of the parents, their perpetual fears of misfortune happening to their offspring, and the manner in which the latter are frequently indulged, have the effect of depriving the male children of any spirit of boldness and enterprise and of any power of endurance. From this evil France is suffering at the present day.

This is no reason why a nation with a medium density of population, such as France, should consider the stagnation of its population as a circumstance in itself wholly insignificant, and one not calling for any special notice. This stagnation, for reasons to which we have already called attention at the commencement of this review, is sufficiently regrettable. But the question arises, how is it to be remedied ? The cause of it lies in the new mental condition of the population, and it is very difficult to change by laws or regulations the mental condition of a people.

Certain suggestions have been made which are absolutely ludicrous in themselves—such for example as the special taxation of the unmarried. This was tried under the Romans, but without effect. Moreover, when the law presumes to punish persons for acts which are in themselves morally lawful, then it strikes at the liberty of the subject. It would soon be found that the generality of the persons unmarried had very good reasons for remaining so, either infirmity, weakness of constitution, want of position, poverty, and sometimes they would be actuated by moral considerations of the highest order. A government, therefore, which would be ill-advised enough to adopt such an absurd system of taxation, would

2 B

very speedily be swept from power by the force of public indignation.

And, moreover, it is not in the insufficiency of marriages that the evil lies. In France there are almost as many marriages as elsewhere—at the present time the proportion is in the ratio of 7.4 to every 1000 of the population—as compared with 7.8 in the period comprised between 1821 and 1830. The French marriage-rate is higher therefore than the Belgian, where there are 7.1 marriages only per 1000 inhabitants—but in the latter country the infant population is much greater.

The evil consists in the small number of children to each family—the number in France being one, two, or three, where foreigners have four, five, and six. Does it therefore follow that it is necessary to give a bounty to those persons in France who have six or seven children ? This is another very doubtful remedy. In the first place it is not the sixth or seventh child whose birth it is desirable to encourage, it is rather the third or fourth. Families consisting of six or seven children are so very rare that if they had an additional one or two it would result in but an insignificant increase to the population, and to give bounties to the third or fourth child it would be necessary, in order that the rewards should be efficacious, that an addition of hundreds of millions of francs should be made to the budget. We are, however, very far from saying that it would not be possible by judicious and inexpensive measures, by a good use of scholarships, of dispensations from military service and other expedients, to reduce to some extent the burdens of large families.

We are by no means disposed to recommend the re-establishment of so-called *tours*, that is official foundling receptacles, as we regard these as both immoral and in-efficacious, but we are at the same time quite prepared to admit that charitable societies might establish them under certain circumstances, if they were disposed to devote their time and their money to this object.

The true remedies, or rather the useful palliatives, are to be sought elsewhere. It is above all necessary to modify the spirit of our primary education, and more particularly of the teachers in our public schools ; the school itself should in a far lesser degree stimulate the ambition of the pupil, the desire to put forth the whole strength in the endeavour to succeed in the race of life, and to attain a high standard of material well-being. The scholastic aim ought to be rather directed to the inculcation in the minds of the pupils, if not of contentment with their lot, at least of more modest ideas, and of resignation to manual labour. The primary school of the present day, by shortsightedness of the teachers, the folly of the scholastic programme, and the wild ideas that appear to have taken possession of those who have control of our educational system, is rapidly leading to a general *déclassement*, to universal ambition—and ambition is certainly opposed to the contraction of marriages, and the voluntary acceptance of the burdens of a family.

It is above all necessary to curtail the time that children are kept at school, to adapt it to rural or industrial occupations in such a manner that families may derive some advantages from the labours of their younger members. Formerly, both in the urban and rural districts, children as young as 7 or 8, or at least 10 or 11, performed certain allotted tasks. We admit that this is rather an early age for a child to commence work, but in any case attendance at school should not be obligatory after the child has reached the twelfth year; in no case should the factories and workshops in those countries which have experienced the need of an increased population, be closed to the child who is over 12 years of age—and this is what our neighbours the English, philanthropists certainly, but infinitely more practical than ourselves, have thoroughly realised. In the same way laws prohibiting married women, and those who are *enceinte*, or have recently been confined, from working, are instrumental in diminishing the population. To return, however, to the scholastic system, there is no doubt that discipline should certainly be relaxed in the rural districts, and more especially at the harvest time, and that classes composed of children of a certain age should be allowed to absent themselves in summer.

A kind of ridiculous pedantry would seem for some years past to have found its way into everything. It is useful to know how to read and to write, and to have some knowledge of history and geography, but to acquire these rudiments it surely is not necessary to devote long years of study and application; and, moreover, it is infinitely more useful that men should acquire at an early age a taste for those things which are to occupy them all their lives, that families should increase, and that the population should not be enfeebled. The regulations respecting apprenticeship, by reason of the introduction of too much idealism, are also becoming inept. It is desired that the apprentice should not render any personal service to the master, but then apprenticeship becomes too burdensome, and there is an end of the system.

Again, it may be asked if all the young girls who have adopted liberal or semi-liberal careers are not more or less condemned to celibacy? It would be curious to have a census enumeration of public school-mistresses, married and single, and of females holding government appointments. We are of opinion that the proportion of unmarried women occupying these positions is much greater than in the generality of females, the reason being that the majority of young girls who are appointed to these posts frequently look down upon the simple workman or peasant, and moreover as they are frequently being moved from place to place, they have not the same opportunities of contracting matrimonial alliances as others.

We need hardly point out that it is far from our intention to condemn either education in general, or that of women in particular, but rather is it our desire to point out simply what appears to be necessary to improve and to modify its tendencies. Every age is characterised by its particular craze. The present craze is for education, unlimited and injudicious, and for philanthropy equally unlimited and injudicious, both absolutely superficial. By their aid we have succeeded in producing a mental condition and in creating certain social circumstances which are most unfavourable to the growth of the population.

In conclusion, we may observe that the most efficacious remedy is, for a country like France, which has many attractions for foreigners, to obtain the naturalisation of from 50,000 to 100,000 aliens annually. By this means the number of inhabitants would be increased, and the reproductive power of the country would, at the same time, be largely augmented.

INDEX

2 C

Printed in the United States
137849LV00003B/13/A